WORDSWORTH CLASSICS
OF WORLD LITERATURE

General Editor: Tom Griffith MA, MPhil

THE ODES

Horace
The Odes

IN ENGLISH VERSE

Translations selected and introduced by
Antony Lentin

WORDSWORTH CLASSICS
OF WORLD LITERATURE

This edition published 1997 by Wordsworth Editions Limited
Cumberland House, Crib Street, Ware, Hertfordshire SG12 9ET

ISBN 1 85326 477 6

Typeset by Antony Gray
Printed and bound in Great Britain by
Mackays of Chatham plc, Chatham, Kent

Contents

BOOK TWO

BOOK FOUR

INTRODUCTION

For nearly two millennia the Odes of Horace have been among the lasting and living items from the legacy of classical antiquity. From the Renaissance to the twentieth century they were one of the most cherished of Europe's literary possessions, one of the best-loved of all books of verse. No author from the ancient world has inspired so many translators and imitators. Horace himself predicted that the Odes would last as long as Latin was spoken, in 'distant realms and climes unknown'; but they far outlived his prediction, from end to end of the former Roman empire: in Flemish and Rumanian, in Portuguese, Hungarian and Maltese, in Catalan, Turkish and Hebrew; and well beyond the imperial bounds, from Finnish to Ruthenian, from Arabic to Chinese (in which language he is known as 'Ho-la-tz'u'), not to mention Platt-Deutsch and the dialects of Burgundy, Bavaria and Sicily. Within the British Isles the Odes have appeared in Erse and in Welsh, in Scots (translated by Allan Ramsay in the eighteenth century) and in Devonshire patois (by Rudyard Kipling in the nineteenth). The urge to translate them has been a constant and a characteristic of European civilisation since the Renaissance. As Lord Dunsany (whose own versions appear here) writes, 'perhaps all such translations are as leaves that last only a season or so and need continual renewal, while Horace himself is like an oak that has weathered the ages, as he knew and said that he would.' The purpose of this collection is to introduce or reintroduce the Odes to the present generation of readers in a variety of translations reflecting a continuum of appeal through the tastes of four centuries.

Much of what we know of Horace's life derives from what he

himself tells us. He was born Quintus Horatius Flaccus on 8
December 65 BC in or near Venusia (now Venosa) in central south-
east Italy on the confines of Apulia and Lucania. He was lowborn, a
southerner and an outsider to the governing class. He was sneered at
for these humble origins, something which he never forgot, priding
himself as a small-town provincial made good. His father was a
freedman, an ex-slave who prospered in business as an auctioneer,
bought a local land-holding and took his son to Rome for the best
available education. Horace studied philosophy at Athens, the
university of the ancient world; but while not yet twenty he was
sucked into the supreme political crisis of a collapsed republic. In the
civil war that followed the assassination of Julius Caesar in 44 BC, he
enlisted under the republican leader, Marcus Brutus, as a military
tribune, one of six officers in temporary charge of a legion, a rank
normally reserved for young men of family. The following year he
shared the total defeat of the republican cause at Philippi by the forces
of Caesar Octavianus (the future Augustus).

He returned to Italy under an amnesty, but his father was dead and
his property was confiscated. His prospects were disappointing. He
earned his living as a treasury clerk (*scriba quaestorius*), took to writing
verse and became something of an 'angry young man', known in
literary circles for his *Epodes* and *Satires* (*Sermones*), often wild and
bitter. The new political regime began to consolidate itself. Early in
the 30s BC his fellow-poets Virgil and Varius introduced him to
Gaius Maecenas, Augustus' close political adviser and a wealthy
patron of literature, concerned to encourage acceptance of the
regime by men of letters. This was the crucial breakthrough in his
life. Maecenas not only extended his patronage to Horace, but
became a close, life-long friend, and gave him a small farm in the
Sabine hills north-east of Tibur (Tivoli) some twenty miles from
Rome. Thanks to this act of far-sighted, though not wholly
disinterested generosity, Horace enjoyed the precious leisure to
devote himself exclusively to his poetic craft.

By the time Augustus gained sole ascendancy over the Roman
world in 31 BC with his victory at Actium over Mark Antony and
Cleopatra, Horace had already begun work on the Odes. He never in
fact called them 'odes': that title was given to them in the
Renaissance. For Horace, they were *carmina*, literally 'songs' (though
they were not intended to be sung) or, as we would call them, lyric

poems.[1] They are not a young man's works like the *Epodes,* which were violent and outspoken, but the mellower fruits of his artistic maturity. The first three books, containing eighty-eight poems, appeared in 23 BC when he was forty-two; the fourth and last book of fifteen poems ten years later. His final works, also in verse, were his moral *Epistles* and the *Art of Poetry,* a distillation of his literary creed which was to have a lasting influence on European aesthetics. Commissioned to write a centennial hymn (*Carmen Saeculare*) for the celebratory games held by Augustus in 17 BC, he in effect succeeded Virgil as poet-laureate. According to the historian Suetonius, he began book four of the odes at Augustus' request that he celebrate the recent military triumphs of his step-sons, Drusus and Tiberius; but he declined the emperor's offer to make him his private secretary. Maecenas, in his will, asked Augustus to be mindful of Horace; but Horace outlived his friend by only eight weeks, and died on 27 November 8 BC, a few days short of his fifty-seventh birthday. He was buried on the Esquiline Hill in Rome, next to Maecenas' tomb. Horace was short and, by the time he wrote the odes, a plump and sometimes peppery little man − Augustus called him 'pot-bellied' − and something of a hypochondriac. By his own account he was 'short of stature, prematurely grey, fond of the sun, hot-tempered but easily pacified'. While the Odes were not well received at first, Horace boldly claimed that with them he had created 'a monument more lasting than bronze' (*monumentum aere perennius*) and that he would 'grow ever renewed in the praise of posterity' (III, xxx).

THE APPEAL OF THE ODES

Many have looked back to Horace as one of their own. Petrarch and Erasmus, Du Bellay, Ronsard and Montaigne, Molière and La Fontaine, Diderot and Voltaire, Chénier, Hugo, de Musset and Lamartine; Carducci and Leopardi; Lessing, Wieland, Herder and Hölderlin; in Spain Garcilaso de la Vega, Luis de León and Gongara; Derzhavin, Pushkin, Fet, Blok and Brodsky in Russia; in Britain Burton and Hooker, Thackeray and Stevenson, Kipling and Housman; and in America Emily Dickinson and, in another *genre,* Ira Gershwin.

---

1 The word 'ode', derived from the Greek, also originally meant 'song'. During the Renaissance, several composers in Germany set many of the Odes of Horace to music for four voices.

These names are representatives of countless readers down the ages who in many different countries have looked on Horace as contemporary, compatriot and soulmate. The eighteenth-century German poet Friedrich von Hagedorn hailed him as

> *Horaz, mein Freund, mein Lehrer, mein Begleiter*

> (Horace, my friend, my teacher, my companion)

In successive ages, at particular moments, Horace's lines, familiar from schooldays, have sprung aptly and almost unbidden to mind. For all his 'small Latin', Shakespeare remembered from his schooldays the well-known couplet which begins (Odes I, xxii)

> *integer vitae scelerisque purus*
> *non eget Mauris iaculis neque arcu*

> (the man of pure untainted life
> needs no Moorish javelins or bow.)

He quoted it in *Titus Andronicus,* adding

> O, 'tis a verse in Horace; I know it well:
> I read it in the grammar long ago.

These and other lines from the Odes came aptly to mind to those seeking encouragement or solace. Odes III, iii, from the six so-called 'Roman' odes which begin Book III, has proved a universal favourite in trying times with its stunning evocation of the 'just and resolute man' (*iustum et tenacem propositi virum*):

> *si fractus illabatur orbis*
> *impavidum ferient ruinae*

> (if the whole world should break asunder, the ruins,
> crashing down on him, will find him fearless)

Even in Addison's more elaborate version, the image retains the poise, detachment, simplicity and stoic grandeur of the original:

> Should the whole frame of Nature round him break,
>   In ruin and confusion hurled,
> He, unconcerned, would hear the mighty crack,
>   And stand secure amidst a falling world.

The Horatian scholar Eduard Fraenkel described Horace's couplet as 'a vision of Michelangelesque force'. Beethoven's *Eroica* symphony is another majestic standard of comparison. Many have been stirred by the sublimity of the lines. A Russian prince, Mikhail Shcherbatov, recommended them to the young nobles of the age of Catherine the Great as models of courage and resolution; the Dutch statesman Cornelius de Witt repeated them when facing the lynch-mob that killed him, and the *philosophe* Condorcet as he awaited the guillotine. The novelist Jules Romain put them on the lips of an officer in the trenches before Verdun. Others less courageous have called them to mind in a bucking aircraft or in the dentist's chair.

The Odes, then, have been found a very present help in time of trouble, a summons to rise above adversity. Many lines have a timeless, proverbial quality; and while the suggestion that Horace was of Jewish descent, because some odes recall parts of The Old Testament, is unconvincing, J. W. Mackail aptly called the Odes 'a secular psalter, for daily and yearly and age-long use'. Many a traveller has packed them in his bag or rambled with them ready to hand. 'On every march,' Edward Gibbon recalled of his training with the Hampshire militia during the Seven Years' War, 'in every journey, Horace was always in my pocket and often in my hand.' During the War of American Independence, Boswell recalled hearing Dr Johnson repeat 'over and over again' the lines from Odes I, ii in which Horace threatens war with the Persians. In 1908 there appeared *The Horace Pocket Book,* a sort of vademecum or pagan equivalent of the Gideon Bible. Sometimes, indeed, Horace's reputation has suffered from over-familiarity. His sentiments have been dismissed as commonplaces, all too quotable. Common experience, however, confirms their haunting memorability. Time and again they have struck a responsive chord.

This is one side of the attraction of the Odes. There are others. There is their artistic, thematic and pictorial variety. (In his *Art of Poetry* Horace stressed the similarity between poetry and painting.) From eight to eighty lines in length, they touch on different themes, political and personal, serious and light-hearted, often in the same poem. They range from love, friendship and wine, to virtue and heroism. Then there is the natural background. Horace frequently recalls the southern Italy of his boyhood and the cherished Sabine farm of his maturity. He had long dreamed (he recalled in *Satires* II,

vi) of 'a modest farm, with a few acres of garden, a nearby spring and woodlands. The gods granted this and more.' There are frequent memorable touches of nature in the odes: the Italian landscape in the heat of midsummer, the echoing cascade of Albunea, near Tivoli, the chattering waters of a secluded spring, the Bandusian spring, which Gilbert Highet describes as 'one of the ideal spots in the imagination of thousands of readers' (including Ronsard, who wrote his own ode in imitation, *A la fontaine Bellerie,* and Wordsworth, when he wrote of the river Duddon); the intertwined branches of pine and white poplar, the rustle of briars in a thicket; or the mountain woods in winter, groaning under their weight of snow, the rivers frozen over; ever and anon the sea in its changing moods; such images of nature and the passing seasons often parallelling symbolically the mutations and vicissitudes of human life.

Of the Sabine farm, situated in a 'secluded valley', with its neighbouring hills, groves and streams, Horace wrote:

> *ille terrarum mihi praeter omnis*
> *angulus ridet*
>
> (that corner of the world above all others
> smiles on me)   (II, vi)

Its landscape not only forms the background to many odes but also symbolises a way of life and a philosophy of material and spiritual independence to which Horace had long aspired. His second epode (*Beatus ille*) begins with one of the best known and most frequently imitated invocations of pastoral innocence in western literature

> Happy the man, whose wish and care
>   A few paternal acres bound,
> Content to breathe his native air
>   In his own ground.
>
>   (tr. Alexander Pope)

The philosophy of the odes is at once epicurean, implying escape from the world and personal freedom from care, and at the same time has overtones of the self-sufficient stoic, who masters his desires and limits his ambitions, aiming at Aristotle's 'golden mean', the virtue which lies midway between two extremes. The Sabine farm became the prototype for many rural retreats in Europe's poetic imagination, including Ben Jonson's Penshurst and Voltaire's Ferney. Hölderlin recalled this image of Horace, pastoral, poetic and philosophical, in his poem 'The God of Youth':

> Wie unter Tiburs Bäumen,
>   Wenn da der Dichter saß,
> Und unter Götterträumen
>   Der Jahre Flucht vergaß,
> Wenn ihn die Ulme kühlte,
>   Und wenn sie stolz und froh
> Um Silberblüten spielte,
>   Die Flut des Anio.

> (As when the poet sat under the trees of Tibur, and,
> dreaming of the gods, forgot the passing years; when
> the elm tree shaded him, and when, proud and
> merry, the waves of Anio played among silver
> blossoms.)

In 'The Horatians', Auden, perhaps slightly mockingly, brings up to date this townsman's poetic tendency to associate 'some particular place' with the conventions of the rural idyll:

> In our world all of you share
> a love for some particular
> place and stretch of country, a farm near Tivoli
> or a Radnorshire village.

HORACE'S POETIC ART

In his *Art of Poetry,* Horace insisted that poetry depended as much on craftsmanship as on genius. He considered a long literary apprenticeship and the study and imitation of Greek models to be indispensable in an artist:

> Ye, who seek finished models, never cease,
> By day and night, to read the works of Greece
>
> (tr. Byron)

His models were the lyric poets of the sixth and fifth centuries BC, Alcaeus, Sappho, Anacreon (and other, later poets of the Hellenistic period in the third century BC). Indeed it was the recreation or creative imitation from Greek models which he claimed as his unique achievement and his guarantee of immortality. Discerning contemporaries applauded his versatility in refashioning his prototypes: the poet Ovid called him 'skilled in metre and harmony' (*numerosus*); but his ingenuity has not always endeared him to the romantic temperament, which finds him lame, artificial and uninspired, forgetting that the more 'romantic' Catullus was also known to his contemporaries as 'learned' (*doctus*) and had indeed pioneered the adaptation of Greek metres before Horace. Horace's approach in the writing of his odes, then, was highly self-conscious and sophisticated, too sophisticated, it seems, for his first readers. The odes are not 'profuse strains of unpremeditated art'. 'The first wild onslaught', in Sir Maurice Bowra's words, 'yields to something more meditated and more complex.' The odes were long and carefully fashioned, 'returned to the anvil', in Horace's words, again and again, subjected with meticulous conscientiousness to the discipline which he imposed on himself in compressing the hard Latin language within the steel framework of Greek metres.

Traditional English prosody is usually straightforward. Take the first two lines of Byron's 'She walks in beauty':

> She walks in beauty, like the night
> Of cloudless climes and starry skies.

Each line takes the form of an iambic tetrameter, that is, of four 'feet', or measures, in an alternating rhythm of unstressed and stressed syllables: ⌣ – ⌣ – ⌣ – ⌣ – , and so on. Gray's 'Elegy in a Country Churchyard' is set in five 'feet' rather than four (pentameters instead of tetrameters); but otherwise the rhythm is the same iambic, ⌣ – ⌣ – ⌣ – ⌣ – , more or less throughout the poem:

> The curfew tolls the knell of parting day,
> The lowing herd winds slowly o'er the lea,
> The ploughman homeward plods his weary way,
> And leaves the world to darkness and to me.

The Greek metres taken over by Horace were far more complex. For a modern comparison, one might instance the syncopated lyrics of Ira Gershwin or Cole Porter, except that classical metres were based not on natural stress, as in English, but on syllabic quantities. Horace's commonest metre, the Alcaic (after Alcaeus), is used in one of his best-known odes (I, ix), the ode 'to Thaliarchus' (the opening stanza of which itself derives from a poem by Alcaeus):

ᵕ‒ ᵕ‒‒ ‒ ᵕᵕ ‒ᵕ ‒
vides ut alta stet nive candidum

The same pattern is repeated in the next line:

ᵕ‒ᵕ ‒ ‒ ‒ᵕᵕ‒ ‒ᵕ ‒
Soracte, nec iam sustineant onus

while in the third line the accentuation is quite different:

‒‒ ᵕ‒‒‒ ᵕ‒ᵕ
silvae laborantes, geluque

and in the concluding fourth line of the stanza, the pattern changes again:

‒ ᵕᵕ ‒ ᵕᵕ‒ ᵕ‒‒
flumina constiterint acuto

> (you see how Mount Soracte stands out white,
> covered with deep snow, and the straining woods
> bend beneath their burden, and the rivers have
> stuck, frozen solid.)

The same intricate metrical pattern is repeated in each four-line stanza of the six stanzas of the ode. It is a pattern extremely difficult to reproduce in English. Some translators have attempted it, such as Clough, Lord Lytton and J. B. Leishman, not always wholly successfully. But Dryden, in his version of the ode, sticks to the traditional iambic tetrameter form, with six lines to a stanza for Horace's four, and a rhyming scheme a–b–a–b–c–c:

> Behold yon mountain's hoary height
>   Made higher with new mounts of snow:
> Again behold the winter's weight
>   Oppress the labouring woods below;
> And streams with icy fetters bound
>   Benumbed and cramped to solid ground.

The ode to Thaliarchus is a nature poem, with an informal, breezy tone and an epicurean message. The poet invites Thaliarchus (the name means 'master of the feast') to pile logs on the fire against the winter cold, to open a jar of wine and make merry while he is young. But Horace also uses the same Alcaic metre in his grandest and most uplifting odes, including the 'Roman' odes, from one of which (III, iii) we quoted earlier:

> — — ◡ — —   — ◡◡ — ◡ —
> *iustum et tenacem propositi virum*
> — —◡   — —   —◡   ◡ — ◡ —
> *non civium ardor prava iubentium*
> — — ◡   — — —   ◡ — —
> *non vultus instantis tyranni*
> —◡   ◡ —   ◡◡ —   ◡   — —
> *mente quatit solida neque Auster*

> (the just man, resolute in his purpose, neither the
> clamour of citizens for what is wrong nor the
> tyrant's brutal menaces can shake in his resolve, nor
> the South Wind . . .)

with the resounding final couplet of the next stanza:

> — —   ◡ — —◡   — —
> *si fractus illabatur orbis*
> — ◡◡ —   ◡◡ —   ◡ — —
> *impavidum ferient ruinae.*

> (if the whole world should break asunder, the ruins,
> crashing down on him, will find him fearless.)

The metre next most frequently used in the odes is the Sapphic (after Sappho). This goes as follows in the ode (I, xxii) quoted above by Shakespeare:

> — ◡ —   — —   ◡◡ — ◡   — —
> *integer vitae scelerisque purus*

This accentuation is repeated in the second and third lines:

> — ◡ —   — ◡◡ —   ◡   — —
> *non eget Mauris iaculis neque arcu*
> — ◡ — —   ◡◡ — ◡   — —
> *nec venenatis gravida sagittis*

and in the last line of the stanza, it runs as follows:

> — ◡   ◡ — —
> *Fusce, pharetra*

> (The man of pure untainted life needs no Moorish javelins
> or bow nor, Fuscus, a quiverful of poisoned arrows.)

Attempts at sapphics are rare in English verse. The hymn writer Isaac Watts wrote 'The Day of Judgment' in sapphics; but Samuel

Johnson's version of the Horace ode adheres to the simple iambic tetrameter, with a rhyming scheme a–b–a–b:

> The man, my friend, whose conscious heart
>   With virtue's sacred ardour glows,
> Nor taints with death th'envenomed dart,
>   Nor needs the guard of Moorish bows.

The high moral tone with which the ode begins is sustained in the next stanza, in which Horace tells us that the virtuous man is protected by his rectitude, whatsoever remote spot in the world he may venture to. In the third stanza the mood suddenly changes, with a joke at the reader's expense and Horace's own, as he humorously purports to validate the lofty moralising of the first stanza by instancing his own narrow escape from danger in the shape of a wolf which stole up on him unawares in a wood while he was composing an ode to Lalage! The closing stanzas, half-mocking, half-poignant, are a far cry from what came before. Wherever he may be, in whatever grim locality he may find himself, Horace concludes, in a semi-parody of his second stanza, he will be true to his Lalage:

> — ◡ — — — ◡ ◡ — ◡ — —
> *pone sub curru nimium propinqui*
> — ◡ — — — ◡ ◡ — — —
> *solis in terra domibus negata:*
> — ◡ — — — ◡ ◡ — ◡ — —
> *dulce ridentem Lalagen amabo*
> — ◡ ◡ — —
> *dulce loquentem.*

> (Place me beneath the tropic sun in some
> uninhabitable land: sweetly laughing Lalage I shall
> love, sweetly speaking)

The sentiment here is that of John Gay's 'Were I laid on Greenland's coast':

> Were I sold on Indian soil,
> Soon as the burning day was closed,
> I could mock the sultry toil
> When on my charmer's breast reposed

In both alcaics and sapphics, then, Horace shows incredible versatility, encompassing themes serious and light, philosophical reflection, high moral sentiment, invitations to drink and expressions of amorous affection, often in the same poem.

The third metre most often used by Horace is the Asclepiad (named after the Greek poet Asclepiades). A well-known example is the ode to the Bandusian spring (III, xiii). Take the last stanza of the ode. As with the alcaics and sapphics, the metrical pattern of the first line is repeated in the second:

fies nobilium tu quoque fontium

me dicente cavis impositam ilicem

The third and fourth lines follow a shortened metrical version of the first and second.

saxis, unde loquaces

lymphae desiliunt tuae

> (you too will become famous among springs when I
> sing of the holm-oak overhanging the hollow rocks,
> whence your chattering waters come leaping down)

What is remarkable here is the combined effect of syntax, words, images and sounds set in a metre not hitherto natural to Latin verse. The visual and onomatopoeic effects of the last two lines in that metre most powerfully evoke the sight and sound of water falling from rocks. Clough attempted to emulate these effects by forcing his English translation of the ode into the same metre; but his effort, though ingenious, is laboured by comparison, clumsy and even unclear. It is almost impossible to play with English word-order as Horace did without becoming incoherent. Ronsard, however, in *A la fontaine Bellerie*, sticks fairly close to Horace in syntax, sound, image and metre, and succeeds in conveying much of his sense and spirit:

> *Io! tu seras sans cesse*
> *Des fontaines la princesse,*
> *Moi célébrant le conduit*
> *Du rocher percé, qui darde*
> *Avec un enroué bruit*
> *L'eau de ta source jasarde*
> *Qui trépillante se suit.*

> (Rejoice! You will forever be the queen of
> fountains, when I celebrate the flow gushing from
> the hollow rock, the chattering water of your spring
> ceaselessly dancing down.)

No less remarkable than Horace's metrical dexterity is his exploitation of the potential of word-order. In the ode to the Bandusian spring, 'holm-oak' is placed between 'hollow' and 'rocks', to emphasise the pictorial image of an overarching tree. In the first lines of the ode to Thaliarchus, 'deep' and 'snow' are separated by 'stands out', and 'snow' is followed by 'white Soracte', emphasising the mountain's snow covered peak. It is true that even in English there are a surprisingly large number of ways in which the third line of Gray's Elegy (quoted above) can be rearranged without becoming nonsense, e.g.

> Homeward the ploughman plods his weary way
> His weary way the ploughman homeward plods
> Homeward his weary way the ploughman plods

But this is only possible because both metre and syntax are extremely straightforward. It would be impossible to change the word order in the Dryden or Johnson translations quoted above, and still retain both rhythm and sense. If we rearrange Johnson, we get nonsense, e.g.

> The conscious friend, whose sacred heart,
> My man, with envenomed ardour glows . . .

We could vary Gray's line still further, e.g.

> The weary ploughman plods his homeward way
> Weary, the ploughman plods his homeward way
> The ploughman, weary, plods his homeward way
> The ploughman plods, weary, his homeward way
> His homeward way the weary ploughman plods
> Homeward, his weary way the ploughman plods.

and so on; but, except in the last example, only at the cost of altering Gray's syntax. Gray intended the adjective 'weary' to go with the noun 'way', not with 'the ploughman'; so that changing the word order also changes the sense. In Latin, an inflected language, we can tell from the word-endings exactly which adjective goes with which noun; not so in English. Roman poets thus had far greater scope to consider variation in word-patterns, and only Latin permits the kind of brilliant experimentation in word-order which Horace achieves. What at first may seem a perverse jumble of words produces in fact a mosaic-like pattern. Each word has been selected and arranged with Flaubertian care, belying the immediate impression of easy inevitability. This combination of inspiration and technical elaboration produced what the Roman poet, novelist and critic Petronius called 'Horace's painstaking happy touches' (*curiosa felicitas Horatii*). Nietzsche (of all people) put his finger on this characteristic of the aesthetic experience of the Odes and explains why it can rarely be fully conveyed in translation:

> To this day I have got from no poet the same artistic delight as a Horatian ode gave me from the very first. In certain languages what is achieved here cannot even be hoped for. The mosaic of words in which every word, by sound, by position and by meaning, diffuses its influence to right and left and over the whole, that *minimum* in the compass, that *maximum* thus realised in their energy . . .

THE 'PYRRHA' ODE: A CLASSIC

Take the opening lines of the ode to Pyrrha (I, v), set in the asclepiad metre. This is one of the best known and best loved of all the odes. It is also one of the most finely wrought of Horace's artistic achievement. Its theme loosely suggests the song 'I wonder who's kissing her now'; but instead of wistful regret, Horace, once duped by Pyrrha, predicts misery for her latest youthful victim and professes his own relief at being out of her clutches. Highet calls it an 'anti-love poem'. It begins with an extended question, which runs on into the next stanza:

> *Quis multa gracilis te puer in rosa*
> *perfusus liquidis urget odoribus*
> *grato, Pyrrha, sub antro?*
> *cui flavam religas comam,*
>
> *simplex munditiis? heu . . .*

Literally translated, this reads: 'what slim youth, drenched with liquid odours, presses you, Pyrrha, amid many a rose within a pleasant grotto? For whom do you tie back your yellow hair, plain in your neatness? Alas . . . ' The Latin word-order, however, presents an intricate pattern of detached but interconnecting words, like the stones in the mosaic. The lines are set out again below, the corresponding English expression underneath each Latin word, with numerals to indicate the connections of the parts of speech and in particular which adjective goes with which noun:

> *Quis*[1] *multa*[2] / *gracilis*[1] / *te*[3] / *puer*[1] / *in rosa*[2]
> What / many / slim /you / boy / in rose
> *perfusus*[1] / *liquidis*[4] / *urget*[1] / *odoribus*[4]
> Drenched / with liquid / presses/ odours
>   *grato,*[5] / *Pyrrha,*[3] / *sub antro?*[5]
>   pleasant, / Pyrrha, / within grotto
>   *cui*[1] / *flavam*[5] / *religas*[3] / *comam*[5]
>   to whom / yellow / you tie back / hair

> *simplex munditiis?*[3] *heu* . . .
> plain in neatness? Alas . . .

In the first line, 'boy' not merely meets girl ('you', the girl addressed in the poem), but enlaces her, 'you' having 'slim' on one side and 'boy' on the other, while both 'boy' and 'you' are surrounded by 'many' and 'rose', in a highly atmospheric introductory setting. Not until the second line, however, do we learn that he is indeed embracing her (and the embrace is surrounded by 'liquid' and 'odours'); and only in the third are we told her name and where they are, 'Pyrrha' again being positioned between 'pleasant' and 'grotto'. A charming vignette of an amorous tryst, to which the reader finds himself an onlooker or eavesdropper. Although we know who she is, we do not know who he is: 'Who?' or 'what boy?' or 'which boy?' is the question emphatically put in the first line of the stanza.

The sensuous fragrance of the scene is enhanced by the combination of labials, the r's and l's and sibilants (s's) of *'quis . . . gracilis . . . puer . . . rosa . . . perfusus liquidis urget odoribus grato, Pyrrha, sub antro.'* There are powerful evocations of colour: the roses, Pyrrha's blond hair, the very name Pyrrha (deriving from the Greek word for 'fire'); and even of scent, from the profusion of roses (conveyed in La Fontaine's *dans cet antre secret tout parfumé de roses*) and the perfumes with which the boy is sprayed; and an atmosphere of languor, suggested by the long drawn-out syllables of *multa . . . perfusus liquidis urget . . . flavam*, and the image of Pyrrha tying back her hair. The mood, then, is charged with voluptuous sounds, images, atmosphere and even fragrance. We linger in the present tense. Suddenly we are brought up short by the next word: *heu* – 'alas!' or even 'Oh dear!' The tense now changes to the future. We discover that it does not much matter who the boy is: appearances notwithstanding, Pyrrha, not the boy, is in command of the situation, as he will sooner or later find to his cost. He will live to regret it, like all the other 'poor wretches' (*miseri*) who have fallen for Pyrrha, whom, in an extended metaphor, Horace likens to the sea for her faithless inconstancy, and whose victims include, as it turns out, Horace himself. For unexpectedly but emphatically Horace introduces himself in the last stanza of the poem: the plaque on the temple wall which he has dedicated in gratitude to Neptune (a custom among mariners who survived shipwreck) shows that he too was once a victim of Pyrrha, a rueful survivor of the experience.

The overall mood of the poem is not necessarily in harmony with the formal beauty of expression, and the first stanza may mislead by its stateliness. Or it may not. Is the poet serious or not? He is both. He is ambiguous and ironic. He pokes fun at the boy's innocent credulity, predicting how he will rail at fate. Yet there is also compassion for a fellow-sufferer; and ironic detachment is tinged with envy and regret, a note of *si jeunesse savait, si vieillesse pouvait*. Is Horace's final attitude to Pyrrha just – good riddance? The renunciation seems final enough, but nostalgia as well as humour underlies the poem. David Mulroy writes of 'carefully cultivated ambiguity of tone'; Chris Emlyn Jones contrasts 'structural formality' with 'a lively and colloquial tone'; Kenneth Quinn writes of 'a terse complexity of statement, enlivened by what I can only call a subdued flippancy of tone'. Yet, as Peter Connor observes, 'all this is tempered by a haunting sadness.' Apparently a love-poem, at the same time apparently not. To give the poem a title, such as 'the vamp', as some editors do, is to foreclose on it, to seize on one thematic strand among several and to insist on one particular interpretation. It is Horace's openness to a variety of experiences which engages the reader's attention, arouses his curiosity and by eliciting a variety of conflicting reactions, encourages him to be open-minded about the poem's meaning or meanings.

The Pyrrha ode is an example of what successive generations have recognised as a 'classic', a conscious work of art which speaks to the human condition across the ages. How can all this complexity of word-structure, wit, sophistication, irony, compression and beauty of form and musicality and sensuousness of language, set in a subtle metrical frame, the whole serving to project a dramatic vignette and a particular mood or combination of moods, be conveyed in English? It can't, of course, though plenty have tried. In compiling his multilingual collection of versions of the Pyrrha ode, Sir Ronald Storrs found 451, 181 in English. The problems of vocabulary alone are daunting, partly because the words, ostensibly simple and clear, turn out to depend heavily on their place in the mosaic for their precise shade of meaning. *Gracilis* means slim or slender; but in the contrasting juxtaposition of the boy with Pyrrha, it may suggest 'slight', with undertones of his fragility and vulnerability in the unequal struggle. *Perfusus* can mean either sprinkled, sprayed, or, on the contrary (and more probably) drenched. *Urget*, literally 'is pressing' (hence the English 'urge' (noun and verb) and 'urgent'), is suggestive in every sense. No one is wholly sure of the exact meaning of the adjective *flavus*, which can mean, variously, golden, yellow, auburn and flaxen. And, as Horace asks, 'for whom?' (or as we might say, 'for whose benefit?') is Pyrrha tying back (or, just conceivably, untying) her hair? Is it to please the boy, or to please herself? Does it show her engagement or her disengagement, like doing her nails? And what about the compendious description of Pyrrha's appearance: *simplex munditiis?* One version, 'casually chic', conveys the idea but not the dignity. It is hard too to emulate in English the concision of an inflected language like Latin (which also manages without the definite and indefinite article – 'the' and 'a'. The laconic two-word warning found at Pompeii *cave canem* – 'beware of the dog' – requires four words in English).

Consider Milton's attempt at an equivalent of Horace's opening lines, in a version 'rendered,' as he claimed, 'almost word for word . . . according to the Latin measure, as near as the language will permit':

> What slender youth bedew'd with liquid odours
> Courts thee on roses in some pleasant cave,
> Pyrrha, for whom bind'st thou
> In wreaths thy golden hair,
> Plain in thy neatness?

Twenty-eight words as opposed to Horace's twenty-one, longer by a third. (All four stanzas of this compact ode amount to only 65 words). Milton does convey the sensuousness of the original; but the stanza is heavy on its feet compared with Horace's perfection of the light touch: an elephant dancing a gavotte. An ingenious American version brings Horace up to date (or at least adapts the ode to the 1920s), and brings out his pace, energy and humour; but sacrifices dignity to slang:

> Who's the sleek kid, Pyrrha, with perfume there,
> Rushing you at the rose-grown rendezvous,
> For whom you've bobbed up your peroxide hair
> To play the ingénue?

Another American tries to bring Pyrrha even more up to date in the last two lines; but, again, liveliness and sophistication are purchased at the cost of ephemerality and triviality:

> For whom do you
> Slip into something simple by, say, Gucci?

POETRY AND PERSONALITY IN THE ODES

Not the least attraction of the odes is the personality, the voice and presence which runs through them and in which so many across the centuries suppose they have found a kindred spirit. Yet Horace's personality is not so easy to pin down or so readily to be taken on trust as was once assumed from the revelations he chooses to make or the masks he chooses to assume in the odes. For many the charm lies in an apparently equable, happy temperament. He attained, or so it would appear, the imperturbability (*ataraxia*) of the Epicureans:

> *Aequam memento rebus in arduis*
> *servare mentem, non secus in bonis*
> *   ab insolenti temperatam*
> *   laetitia, moriture Delli.*

> Be sure, when times are out of joint,
>   To keep a level head, and try
> To keep a cool one, when things point
>   To triumph, Tom. You too must die.
>
>   (II, iii, tr. L. E. Gielgud)

But the giving of this advice, echoed by Kipling:

> If you can meet with Triumph and Disaster
> And treat those two impostors just the same

does not necessarily mean that Horace succeeded in taking it.

Nor, as Dr Johnson pointed out, can it be assumed from the frequent celebration of wine and good cheer that Horace had a naturally sanguine temperament. The evidence could equally suggest a melancholy observer of life's brevity, seeking to banish dull care (*atra cura*) with drink and oppressed (like Johnson himself) by mortality.

> *pallida Mors aequo pulsat pede pauperum tabernas*
> *regumque turris. o beate Sesti,*
> *vitae summa brevis spem nos vetat incohare longam.*
> *iam te premet nox fabulaeque Manes*

> Yes, but pallid Death at your
> Palace gates at last will beat
> With the same imperious feet
> As at any cottage door.
> Blest are you – but life is brief.
> Plans mature – but planners fade.
> Death shall take you like a thief.
> You shall join the Shades, a Shade.

> (I, iv, tr. L. E Gielgud)

Horace preached the good sense and sanity of the man of total integrity and composure. If he achieved this himself, it was a triumph of hard work in self-knowledge and self-mastery. The Sabine farm symbolised the Garden of Epicurus; it was a townsman's ideal of rural innocence, calm pleasures, self-sufficiency and peace of mind, rather than an actuality. We know that Horace was sometimes bored and hankered for Rome. Still less was permanent happiness guaranteed, since, whatever his philosophical detachment, happiness depended on contingencies outside the poet's control. In his prayer to Apollo (I, xxxi) he asked:

> *frui paratis et valido mihi,*
> *Latoe, dones, at precor, integra*
> *cum mente, nec turpem senectam*
> *degere nec cithara carentem.*

> Grant, God of song, this humble lot:
> But to enjoy what I have got,
> And, I beseech thee, keep my mind entire
> In age without disgust, and with the cheerful lyre.

> (tr. Christopher Smart)

A heartfelt plea for mental and physical wellbeing (with which Montaigne, plagued by kidney-stones, identified and with which he concluded his *Essays*).

Nature is portrayed by Horace as beautiful and welcoming:

> *quo pinus ingens albaque populus*
> *umbram hospitalem consociare amant*
> *ramis? quid obliquo laborat*
> *lympha fugax trepidare rivo?*

> (Why do the giant pine and white poplar love to
> proffer friendly shade, intertwining their branches? Why
> does the stream go coursing down its tortuous channel?)

> (II, iii)

Yet Nature can also be savage and terrifying, 'romantic' even, as in the mountainous wilds of the Balkans, evoked in his ode to Bacchus (III, xxv).

> *non secus in iugis*
> *exsomnis stupet Euhias*
> *Hebrum prospiciens et nive candidam*
> *Thracen ac pede barbaro*
> *lustratam Rhodopen, ut mihi devio*
> *ripas et vacuum nemus*
> *mirari libet.*

> So on the hills doth a
> Sleepless Bacchanal stand at the
> Sight of Hebrus amazed, sight of the snowy-white
> Thrace, and where the barbarians
> Range o'er Rhodope hill: as in my wilderment
> Bank and forest and solitude
> I with wonder behold.

> (tr. Clough)

The security of the Sabine farm is fragile and circumscribed. Horace is well aware that the pathetic fallacy *is* a fallacy: he was once almost killed by lightning, and a falling tree nearly did for him, as he more than once reminds us. In the Lalage ode he recounts the dangerous encounter with the wolf. And in how many odes does he insist *pulvis et umbra sumus* – we are dust and shadow. Lawrence Durrell, in 'On first looking into Loeb's Horace', wrote of 'the sad heart of Horace',

> Who studiously developed his sense of death
> Till it was all around him.

But is this true, or wholly true, of Horace? As another critic points out, far from indulging in romantic agonising, Horace's is 'not an unpleasant melancholy. There is no fretting or fuming. There is no morbidity.'

Nor do we find a consistent pattern to his philosophical, religious or political convictions. An Epicurean in the ode to Thaliarchus, a Stoic in the 'Roman' odes; both at different times or even in the same poem (as in the Lalage ode). As Highet points out, 'in fact Horace's odes teach at least two different and incompatible lessons.' His attitude to the gods oscillates between literary allusion, playful irony, respect for the piety of country rituals, reverence for traditional Roman values and an apparent belief in destiny. In II, vii, after admitting to having abandoned his shield in his flight from the battle of Philippi (an allusion to the same ironic expression in Alcaeus, Anacreon and Archilochus), he refers to his being wafted safely from the battlefield by the god Mercury:

> *sed me per hostis Mercurius celer*
> *denso paventem sustulit aere*

> But nimble Hermes hid me safe
>   In thickest mist, and bore me far
> From fears and foes

> (II, vii, tr. W. S. Marris)

The allusion here is to Hermes' similar rescue of Hector in the *Iliad*. Horace's tone is clearly ironic. As Fraenkel rather ponderously explains: 'it must be firmly stated that Horace, the son of an ageing civilisation, the pupil of refined and sceptical philosophers, did not write for people who would credit him with the belief that in the autumn of the year 42 BC an Olympian god went to the trouble of producing, on the battlefield of Philippi, a special cloud or mist to wrap around an unknown young man and so remove him out of harm's way.' Quite so. Likewise, Horace is unlikely to have believed that Julius Caesar was a god in heaven, still less that Augustus, who treated him on terms of teasing familiarity, was a living god, however much he might be revered by provincials or superstitious orientals.

> quos inter Augustus recumbens
> purpureo bibit ore nectar

> Where now Augustus, mixed with heroes, lies,
> And to his lips the nectar bowl applies:
> His ruddy lips the purple tincture show,
> And with immortal stains divinely glow

> (III, iii, tr. Addison)

When Horace wrote that, he was closer to the humour of Ovid's *Metamorphoses* than to Virgil's grave intimations of Rome's god-given destiny. 'What inspired him,' Fraenkel suggests, 'was not a personal religion of his own, nor, for that matter, a religion of any of his contemporaries, but beliefs of a remote past, ennobled and perpetuated in works of poetry.' We can agree with Fraenkel at any rate to this extent, that Horace was open and aesthetically responsive to Greek mythology and Roman religion, without being himself a believer, or for that matter, necessarily a non-believer.

In the seventh satire of his second book of *Satires*, addressing the stoic paradox that the only truly free man is the wise man, the man of integrity, self-mastery and composure, Horace describes this ideal in memorable terms: 'Who, then, is free? The wise man, who is lord over himself, whom neither poverty, nor death, nor bonds affright, who bravely defies his passions and scorns ambition, who in himself is whole, smooth and rounded (*totus, teres atque rotundus*), against whose polished exterior no external force can prevail and whom Fortune always batters herself in vain.' This reminds us of Shakespeare's Horatio, 'more of an antique Roman than a Dane' (and is the name 'Horatio' significant?), in Hamlet's description:

> A man that fortune's buffets and rewards
> Hath ta'en with equal thanks: and blest are those

Whose blood and judgment are so well commingled
That they are not a pipe for fortune's finger
To sound what stop she please. Give me that man
That is not passion's slave, and I will wear him
In my heart's core, ay, in my heart of heart,
As I do thee.

In the six 'Roman' odes at the beginning of Book III, Horace celebrates the stoic virtues. In III, v, he paints a striking portrait of a stoic hero, Regulus, a Roman commander captured by the Carthaginians and sent by them to Rome in 250 BC with peace terms, on condition that he return to Carthage if the terms were declined. According to tradition, Regulus himself advised the Senate to reject them, and brushing aside the senators' remonstrances, returned with sublime imperturbability to captivity and death:

atqui sciebat quae sibi barbarus
tortor pararet; non aliter tamen
dimovit obstantis propinquos
et populum reditus morantem

quam si clientum longa negotia
diiudicata lite relinqueret,
tendens Venafranos in agros
aut Lacedaemonium Tarentum.

He knew the torture that awaited him,
  The thing that Carthage would prepare,
Yet put aside his kinsmen staying him,
  The anxious townsfolk, with as light a care

As though, his client's long-drawn business done,
  And judgment given, he set out that day
For green Venafrum in its olive groves,
  Seaward Tarentum, for a holiday.

(tr. Helen Waddell)

Was Horace a turncoat who betrayed the republican cause by becoming a lickspittle to Augustus in return for a comfortable life? He never denied his republican past or his republican comrades-in-arms. He made a point of admitting his inglorious flight from Philippi and he dedicated odes to republicans who carried on the struggle afterwards. He referred admiringly to the 'noble death' of Cato. If he also came to accept and to welcome the peace of Augustus, he had cause. He had personal experience of the bitter decades of bloodshed, proscriptions, anarchy and uncertainty, living half his life against that background and the rest with those memories. He could not know whether the civil wars which dragged down the republic in bloodshed were truly over. Yet he sometimes felt uncomfortable with the laureate's mantle and the public approval of the regime which he was expected to provide. Augustus himself put his finger on Horace's misgivings when he asked if he feared that 'posterity will think the worse of you for appearing to be a friend of mine?' He wrote the 'political' odes, but urbanely evaded other similar commissions, claiming that he could not emulate Homer or Pindar. He prized and he could claim to have maintained his independence and integrity. Ode I, xxxvii, which celebrates Augustus' victory at Actium, also pays startling tribute to the heroism of the vanquished Cleopatra. 'One cannot help feeling,' as Chris Emlyn-Jones puts it, 'that this was not exactly the victory ode Augustus would himself have chosen.'

The moralist was also most certainly a hedonist, with his frequent summons to enjoy the present hour with drink and merriment. In I, viii he complains, or appears to complain, that Sybaris (the allusion to 'Sybarite' is plain) has given up outdoor sports and spends his time with a girl. In the very next ode, to Thaliarchus, he urges Thaliarchus to do likewise. The champion of military virtue, patriotic heroism, respect for the gods, civic duty and 'family values' was a bachelor, who admitted to casual affairs with members of both sexes and advised his dedicatees to ignore politics for the sake of pleasure and the escapism that gave peace of mind at least for the day. The poet who claimed immortality through his verse warns constantly of mortality:

> *sapias, vina liques, et spatio brevi*
> *spem longam reseces. dum loquimur, fugerit invida*
> *aetas: carpe diem, quam minimum credula postero.*

> Be wise! drink free, and in so short a space
> Do not protracted hopes of life embrace.
> Whilst we are talking, envious Time doth slide:
> This day's thine own; the next may be denied.

> (I, xi, tr. Sir Thomas Hawkins)

The personality behind the verse, then, is complex, layered and nuanced; the odes project an allusive, reflective artist, steeped in literary tradition; they convey a range of emotions and invite a variety of responses in the reader: humour, tinged with sadness, high seriousness, set off and saved from pomposity by the almost all-pervading irony and self-mockery. In the final analysis, neither biography nor politics are strictly relevant to our enjoyment of the Odes. As was well said, *ce n'est pas avec des idées que l'on fait des vers: c'est avec des mots*. If, whether as stoic or epicurean, he genuinely achieved the ability to rise above or sublimate passion – and the answer to this can never be known – he yet understood and mediated it in his verse with tenderness and poignancy. Another Latin poet, Persius, summed up a common reaction in stating that Horace 'plays about the heartstrings' (*circum praecordia ludit*). If Pyrrha never existed, or if it turned out that the Odes were written by a Vestal virgin, it should make no difference to our pleasure in them.

HORACE'S ENGLISH READERS

The first printed edition of Horace appeared in Italy in about 1470. A French edition was published in Paris in 1498 and another twenty by 1500. Britain came late to Horace. The first British edition was published in London in 1574. The first French translation of the Odes in 1579 predated the earliest English versions by nearly half a century; but the odes were already taught in English grammar-schools, as we know from Shakespeare.

> Nor marble, nor the gilded monuments
> Of princes, shall outlive this powerful rhyme

is another Shakespearean echo of Horace, from his *exegi monumentum* (III, xxx), and English literature is full of such echoes and allusions even from before the Elizabethan age. Sir Thomas Wyatt, Henry Howard, Earl of Surrey, Drayton, Dyer, Sidney, Raleigh, Campion and other Renaissance translators were fired by enthusiasm for Horace and a passion to give him new life. Sir Thomas Hawkins, one of the first to translate substantial selections from the Odes in 1625, called him 'the best of lyric poets, containing much morality and sweetness', and described his own efforts as but a pale 'reflection from that brighter body of his odes'. To Hawkins and his contemporaries, the Odes had something memorable to say: 'Behold in them morality touched, and virtue heightened, with clearness of spirit and accurateness of judgment.'

The lyric poets of the seventeenth century were particularly well attuned to Horace's delicacy and spirit, and reproduced both his public and private side to great effect. The ode came into its own as a distinct genre in English verse. Ben Jonson, dubbed 'the Horace of our time', Herrick, Shirley, Marvell and Cowley all played a part in establishing Horace's reputation in England, by imitation as much as translation. Herrick's 'Gather ye rosebuds while ye may', is characteristically Horatian, as is his convivial ode to Sir Clipseby Crew:

> Then cause we Horace to be read,
>   Which sung, or said,
>   A goblet to the brim
> Of lyric wine, both swelled and crowned
>   Around
>   We quaff to him.

In his 'Horatian ode upon Cromwell's return from Ireland', Marvell recalls the 'Regulus' ode in his cameo of the Lord Protector:

> Who, from his private gardens, where
>   He lived reservèd and austere
>   (As if his highest plot
>   To plant the bergamot).

Milton, we have seen, translated the Pyrrha ode, though his ponderousness sits ill with Horace's gracefulness. But he remembered the sensuous imagery of the ode's first stanza, and elaborated it when he came to describe Adam and Eve in *Paradise Lost:*

> These, lulled by nightingales, embracing slept,
> And on their naked limbs the flowery roof
> Showered roses.

The cavalier poets who fought in the Civil War and went into exile appreciated Horace's bitter-sweet nostalgia, while Restoration libertines seized with gusto on his praise of drink and his ironic love lyrics. Indeed seventeenth-century England, with its political vicissitudes and uncertainty, experience of personal changes of fortune, and a consequent passion and cynicism, perhaps comes closest to the spirit of the Odes and to what Alexander Brome, in his collection of translations first published in 1666, hailed as 'the wit and truth of his excellent sayings'. Significantly Brome also stressed Horace's role as a model for the aristocratic courtiers of Charles II and 'the *haut goût* which the wit and truth of his sayings gave', describing him as 'much a *gentleman* in his nature and demeanour'. The Earl of Roscommon also asserted the Restoration's identification with Horace and his assimilation into British culture, social and philosophical as well as literary:

> Rome was not better by her Horace taught
> Than we are here, to comprehend his thought.

Horace was famously taken up in the ordered and polite age of Queen Anne, when Addison, Steele, Prior and Pope held him up as the arbiter of literary taste through his *Art of Poetry*, and acclaimed his sedate 'Augustan' public utterances. Indeed his poetic reputation in our own day has probably suffered from his lasting association with notions of 'correctness', 'decorum' and the more prosaic qualities of the Age of Reason. The eighteenth century not only confirmed him as a permanent 'classic' in Europe's literary canon, but in effect naturalised and domesticated him, turning him into a bourgeois gentleman of the type held out in the *Spectator*, a respectable and hackneyed source of unexceptionable tags of worldly wisdom and good breeding, a gift to the essayist or statesman. Already by 1733 Swift sardonically advised up-and-coming poets to

> Get scraps of Horace from your friends
> And have them at your fingers' ends.

Pope, author of *Imitations of Horace*, probably had the *Epistles* in mind rather than the Odes when he wrote his well-known lines, but they sum up the eighteenth-century view of Horace as man of the world and easy-going moraliser:

> Horace still charms with graceful negligence,
> And without method talks us into sense;
> Will, like a friend, familiarly convey
> The truest notions in the easiest way.

In the eighteenth century, when, as Dr Johnson said, classical quotation became 'the *parole* of literary men', the Odes reached their widest readership in Britain, with over 260 published editions. All the main novelists quoted them: Richardson, Sterne, Smollett and especially Fielding; so did Lord Chesterfield in his letters, Gibbon in his *History of the Decline and Fall of the Roman Empire*, and the statesmen Burke, Pitt, Fox and Sheridan in their parliamentary orations. Collins imitated them in his own odes, and so, to a lesser extent, did Gray. The line from Gray's Elegy discussed earlier

> The ploughman homeward plods his weary way

comes from Odes III, vi, by way of Roscommon's translation

> Home with their weary team they took their way

Yet the Romantics, even Shelley, also took to him. The opening lines of Keats' 'Ode to a Nightingale' come straight from one of the *Epodes*, and its closing lines echo Odes III, iv, where Horace refers to the strains of the muse:

> *auditis an me ludit amabilis*
> *insania? audire et videor pios*
> *errare per lucos, amoenae*
> *quos et aquae subeunt et aurae.*

> (Do you hear it? Or does some delightful madness
> delude me? I seem to hear it and to be wandering
> through sacred groves where pleasant streams flow
> and breezes blow.)

Keats applies the image to the song of the nightingale:

> Past the near meadows, over the still stream,
>   Up the hill-side, and now 'tis buried deep
>   In the next valley-glade:
> Was it a vision, or a waking dream?
>   Fled is that music – do I wake or sleep?

Wordsworth too, responding to Horace's feel for nature, acknowledged him as 'my great favourite'. So did Leigh Hunt. Browning knew the Odes well, Tennyson reputedly by heart. 'Read Horace every day of your life,' he advised Austin Dobson. So many Victorians made the pilgrimage to the site of the Sabine farm that neighbouring peasants supposed that Horace was an Englishman. The

Regulus ode inspired Macaulay in his *History of England* to paint a similar image of his hero, William of Orange, taking leave of the States-General of Holland before setting out for England: 'he stood among his weeping friends calm and austere, as if he had been about to leave them only for a short visit to his hunting-grounds at Loo'. Thackeray and Trollope quoted Horace almost as much as did the novelists of the eighteenth century. To do so continued to mark social status: it was a characteristic of the gentleman. In *The Newcomes*, Thackeray wrote of the need to give young Clive Newcome enough Latin 'to enable him to quote Horace respectably through life'. 'Fat, beery, beefy Horace', complained one who disliked the mid-Victorian anglicised stereotype of cheerful clubmanship and convivial *vers de société* (of which both Thackeray and Tennyson produced some fine examples). By the time such eminent Victorians as John Conington, Professor of Latin at Oxford, Sir Theodore Martin, biographer of the Prince Consort, and Gladstone himself had each published versions of the complete Odes, translating them had become a conventional gentlemanly pastime, a forerunner of the crossword puzzle. An anthologist of English versions, writing in 1880, described this as 'a time when each succeeding year witnesses the advent of at least one new Horatian translator'. The clerisy continued to find the Odes a handy reach-me-down. Horace's tags were, in Tennyson's words,

> jewels five words long
> That on the stretched forefinger of all time
> Sparkle for ever.

In Edwardian Britain, when a classical education was still the norm, the Odes remained a central part of the cultural baggage of the educated. In 'Regulus' (1908), one of Kipling's short stories of public school life, the Latin master, Mr King, tries to bring the ode to life to a bored class of fifth-formers: 'Regulus was not thinking about his own life. He was telling Rome the truth. He was playing for his side.' The sporting metaphor had powerful resonances of duty and convention in British upper-class society. For some disenchanted subalterns of World War I, Horace became a hated 'establishment' figure, representative of the terrible old clubmen who cheered them on to the front. From the horror of the trenches, Wilfred Owen notoriously spurned as 'the old lie' the celebrated line from III, ii, *dulce et decorum est pro patria mori* ('it is sweet and becoming to die for your country'). Owen was reacting against what he saw as the unthinking nationalism of schoolmasters and poets who harnessed Horace in the service of the British empire, and the by now philistine concept of the gentleman, connected, as Cyril Connolly noted at Eton, with concepts of 'character' and team-spirit. Eighty years after his brother's death on the Somme, Lord Denning recalled with regret how he used to end all his letters to him with the *dulce et decorum* tag. 'That was an awful thing to write . . . It was the way we thought then but it was wrong.' Ezra Pound had denounced Europe at the time as 'a botched civilisation', for which, in the bloodbath of the war:

> Died some, pro patria,
> non 'dulce' non 'et decor'

In 1930 Pound launched the most vehement attack of the postwar reaction against Horace – 'bald-headed, pot-bellied, underbred, sycophantic, less poetic than any other great master of literature . . . a liar of no mean pomposity . . . a humbug.'

And yet . . . the attraction survived the Somme and the schoolmasters and the debunking of the 1920s. Even Pound eventually came back to him. In *A Time of Gifts* (1977) Patrick Leigh Fermor writes of how in 1934, after leaving the King's School, Canterbury, at eighteen, he trekked across Europe from the Rhine to Constantinople, with Horace's *Odes* in his knapsack like so many before him. He also recalls a Horatian episode from his wartime experiences a few years later near Mount Ida in Crete. As dawn broke over the mountain crest, a captured German general in the British camp murmured the first lines of the ode to Thaliarchus (I, ix):

> *Vides ut alta stet nive candidum*
> *Soracte. . .*

> (you see how Mount Soracte stands out white,
> covered with deep snow)

'It was one of the ones I knew!' the author records. 'I continued from where he had broken off . . . and when I'd finished, after a long silence, he said: 'Ach so, Herr Major!' It was very strange. As though, for a long moment, the war had ceased to exist. We had both drunk at the same fountains long before; and things were different between us for the rest of our time together.'

As we have seen, it was not always so. In the Middle Ages, while Virgil was almost an honorary Christian, Horace's cheerful paganism made the Odes less acceptable; in the nineteenth century Matthew Arnold made the not wholly dissimilar complaint that 'Horace wants seriousness.' What of today's generation? In 1970, the American journal *Arion* published replies to a questionnaire about the extent of interest in Horace which it had circulated to a variety of literary figures. The replies were ambivalent. Respect for his craftsmanship and chiselled perfection was qualified by an underlying dissatisfaction that stems at heart from the romantic tradition. Pushkin had put this well in the nineteenth century: 'There are people who do not acknowledge any poetry that is not passionate or exalted; there are people who consider even Horace to be prosaic (is it because he is calm, intelligent, rational?).' Even Goethe, who took much from Horace, had complained that he lacked 'any genuine poetic quality'; and Landor's admiration for the beauty of some dozen odes was also tempered by the frequent complaint that Horace lacked spontaneous feeling: 'no true passion here.' Increasing scholarly knowledge of his Greek sources may have served to confirm the suspicion that Horace was derivative, witnessing experience at second hand. 'My admiration for him is cold,' the novelist Brigid Brophy admitted, 'I never catch myself reading him spontaneously.' Other Latin poets who caught modern attention with their 'romantic' qualities, Lucretius, Catullus, Propertius, Tibullus and Ovid, made Horace seem old-fashioned, complacent and dull.

It does not need the rise of feminism or the orthodoxy of 'political correctness' to explain his overall lack of appeal to women. While his male friendships – with Septimius, Varus, Virgil, Maecenas and others – are deeply felt, the Lydias, Lyces, Lalages, Chloes, Pyrrhas and Cynaras of the odes are often treated light-heartedly, even flippantly; and his treatment of older women is positively Gilbertian. This did not, however, deter imitations of the Pyrrha ode in the eighteenth century by Aphra Behn, Lady Mary Wortley Montagu and Anna Seward, the 'Swan of Lichfield'; and in 1994 a monograph appeared (*Time and the Erotic in Horace's Odes* by R. Ancona, Duke University Press), which discussed Horace sympathetically from a feminist perspective. Other disincentives include loss of empire, the cult of egalitarianism, the marginalisation of public verse, a generation uncomfortable with a poet who had little regard for 'the mob', and celebrated the regime of Augustus. The historian Ronald Syme was thinking of contemporary dictatorships in Europe when he published his classic study of Augustus' consolidation of power, *The Roman Revolution*, in 1939. In Syme's view, now more open to question, Horace 'appeared to surrender to . . . a fervent sympathy with martial and imperial ideals.' By contrast Eduard Fraenkel, a refugee from Hitler, thought Horace at his best in the political odes. Poems like the ode to the spring of Bandusia, describing sacrificial victims, will doubtless displease devotees of 'animal rights'.

Among those who have not taken to Horace were successive generations of schoolboys into whom he was dinned ever since becoming, as he wryly complained, a set book in his own lifetime (though Creech, Johnson, Chatterton and Patrick Brontë made translations from the odes in their teens or twenties).

> Then farewell, Horace, whom I hated so,
> Not for thy faults, but mine: it is a curse
> To understand, not feel thy lyric flow,
> To comprehend, but never love thy verse

Byron wrote in *Childe Harold* (though he later produced a racy version of the *Art of Poetry*). While Catullus appeals instantly to the romantic instincts of the adolescent, Horace and Horatians are generally suspect to the young. As Auden puts it:

> Enthusiastic
> youth writes you off as cold, who cannot be found on
> barricades, and never shoot
> either yourselves or your lovers.

Like Byron, like Pound, one comes back to Horace. John Henry Newman wrote that 'passages which to a boy are but rhetorical commonplaces . . . at length come back to him when long years have passed . . . and pierce him, as if he had never known them before.' Kipling wrote that this common school experience 'taught me to loathe Horace for two years, to forget him for twenty, and then to love him for the rest of my days and through many sleepless nights.' Kipling co-authored a *Fifth Book of Horace*, a series of parodies that could have been written only from affection by someone steeped in the original.

Meanwhile, Latin has all but disappeared from the curriculum of secondary education not only in Britain but across Europe, so that at a time when political integration is being preached by the great and the good in the name of European unity, the language which lies at the heart of our common civilisation is probably known to fewer people than at any time since the Dark Ages.[2] Even for the well-read, Horace, writing in a 'dead' language, is scarcely more than a name. Gilbert Highet could confidently define the *Odes* as 'one of the few absolutely central and unchallengeable classics in Latin and in the whole of western literature'. That was in 1957. How true is this forty years on? For professional classicists, admittedly, never before have there been so many excellent editions of the Odes, with lively and imaginative commentaries. Reinterpretation flourishes among the dons. A monograph appearing in 1992 was devoted to the study of a single ode, the ode to Thaliarchus, and cited no less than seventy other examples of recent writing on that ode. Books and articles on Horace cascaded from the scholarly presses on the bimillennium of his death in 1992/93. But for 'the common reader' or for creative writers and poets, can it really be claimed that Horace still retains his former standing? On the other hand it may be salutary to recall that even in his own day, as he complained, the *Odes* were 'caviare to the general'. And that, at the time of writing, there are calls at least in Italy for the reintroduction of the teaching of Latin as the birthright of every educated Italian. In Britain, the Classics Department of the Open University, which already teaches Greek, hopes to offer a course for those wishing to learn Latin. Signs of a desire to reclaim our classical heritage could signal a rebirth of interest in one of its most perfect productions.

HORACE'S ENGLISH TRANSLATORS AND THIS EDITION

Everyone who has tried knows that Horace is dauntingly hard to translate. 'The lyrical part of Horace,' as Dr Johnson wrote, 'never can be properly translated. So much of the excellence is in the numbers [i.e. use of metres] and the expression'; and Philip Francis, the most popular eighteenth-century translator of Horace, stated that Horace was 'perhaps the most difficult author in the Latin tongue'. This has not deterred innumerable imitators: from Sidney, Raleigh, Campion,

---

2 In 1996 Latin attracted fewer than 12,000 entries even at GCSE. 1625 took A-level Latin, half as many as in 1975.

Marvell, Cowley, Swift and Pope to Louis Macneice; and Horace has
influenced still more. Some of the imitations are superlatively good,
classics in their own right, notably Campion's imitation of I, xxii,
'The man upright of life', Sir Henry Wotton's 'The Character of a
Happy Life'; Marvell's 'Horatian Ode upon Cromwell's return from
Ireland' and, perhaps the greatest of all, Dryden's version of III, xxix,
of which he wrote: 'I have endeavoured to make it my masterpiece in
English.' Unfortunately it is too free to rank as translation in its
entirety. Yet parts of it are beyond praise:

> Happy the man, and happy he alone,
> He, who can call today his own;
> He who, secure within, can say:
> Tomorrow do thy worst, for I have lived today!
> Be fair or foul, or rain or shine,
> The joys I have possess'd, in spite of fate, are mine.
> Nor Heaven itself upon the past has power,
> But what has been, has been, and I have had my hour.

This is a magnificent rendering of two Horatian stanzas, and a
reincarnation of his idea. 'I prefer almost any Horatian ode by almost
any English poet to almost any ode actually by Horace,' declared
Brigid Brophy. With brilliant gems like this, no wonder.

Although so many have tried their hand at translation (since the
mid-seventeenth century the temptation has been addictive, and
Horace has found more translators than any other classical poet), on
the whole the translations proper do not rise to the same level of
excellence with a life of their own. There are good translations of
many odes; there are some very good versions of some odes; and here
the anthologist is killed for choice, since in this edition, only one
translation is given for each poem. Not every ode has found a good
translator. But then not all 103 of the odes maintain the same level of
excellence. If even Homer, as Horace admitted, 'sometimes nods off
to sleep', then so does Horace. The Roman critic Quintilian implied
this, when he commented that Horace 'sometimes rises to heights of
eloquence', and Landor quite rightly argued that he could not sustain
them for long. Horace himself was the first to admit that this was so,
that he lacked Pindar's power to soar, having more of the bee than
the eagle. But while every reader will have his or her likes and

dislikes, there is general agreement about the twenty or so all-time favourites. These have attracted numerous translators, sometimes, as with the Pyrrha ode, over a hundred apiece. Even so, as was suggested earlier with the example of the Pyrrha ode, the difficulties of translating Horace are legion, and at best, the reader glimpses the original through a glass darkly.

In approaching the translations, my principles of selection have been simple, subjective and aesthetic: to include them on their merits as I perceived them through the pleasure they gave me. I have sought for versions that pass muster as poems in their own right, often a tall order. This being so, I have occasionally blurred the distinction between translation and imitation. While many versions have stood the test of time, I readily accept that no one editor's taste can be more than provisional. Having made a final selection of some forty translators, I find that each century since the seventeenth is represented, the seventeenth particularly so. With regret I have omitted Ben Jonson's otherwise magnificent version of IV, i because of one line. 'If a fit liver thou dost seek to toast' seems disconcertingly suggestive of breakfast in an Edwardian country-house rather than lovesickness. At the other end of the timescale, I have felt able to include only six translators since 1940; and even Sir Edward Marsh's fine version of the Cleopatra ode (I, xxxvii) – and it is not the only one – comes close to bathos in a line almost ruined by the current connotation of the word 'gay'. As for 'modernism' generally, no doubt my attitude is that of the man whom Horace mocked as 'he who praises the good old days when he was a boy'. Most of the later versions I have read seem to me uninspired. Either they are the kind of doggerel usually composed for greetings-cards, or else they subscribe to the 'modernist' heresy aptly and amusingly guyed by C. E. Montague. Montague takes the Burns quatrain

> We twae hae paidlet i' the burn,
> Fra' morning sun till dine;
> But seas between us braid hae roar'd
> Sin' auld lang syne.

A 'modern' rendering, Montague suggests, might go something like this:

Both of us
Once
Lived
   on
      the
Doon.

He is
   now
     in
The States.

A reputable American scholar-poet attempts to put over the conci-
sion of the Pyrrha ode; but the result seems to me too close to
Montague's parody for comfort:

> O Pyrrha who
> Is holding you
> Now, roses above you, under you – who,
> All perfumed, loves your yellow hair

Many scholars think highly of the translations of Ezra Pound. I can
only say that tastes differ. I would gladly have included Scottish
versions were I qualified to judge them. I like the sound of Alan
Ramsay's rendering of stanza 2 of the Thaliarchus ode:

> Then fling on coals, and ripe the ribs,
> And beek the house baith butt and ben,
> That mutchken stoup it hads but dribs,
> Then let's get in the tappit hen.

but can only guess at the exact meaning of this rousing quatrain,
whose vocabulary, to a Sassenach, suggests Edward Lear.

I would equally gladly have included more translations by women
had I found any that were good enough: the eighteenth century, as
was mentioned earlier, saw several versions by women. To include
them merely because they are by women would be to betray the
purpose of this selection, which is to aim at such renderings as give
the original the kiss of life and speak to us afresh across the centuries,
so that, as Horace predicted in III, xxx:

non omnis moriar, multaque pars mei
vitabit Libitinam: usque ego postera
crescam laude recens

(not all of me will die: much of me will survive the
grave: I shall be forever contemporary through the
praise of posterity)

Or, in the brave mid-seventeenth-century version by Barten Holyday:

I will not wholly die; my better part
Shall 'scape the sullen hearse: bright fame shall raise
My memory renewed, with future praise.

ANTONY LENTIN
The Open University

Horace himself almost certainly arranged the odes in the order in which they have come down to us. The addressees of the odes are identified in the list of contents. But introductory subtitles, supplied by later scholiasts, commentators or editors, are given only where provided by the individual translator. To do otherwise would be to impose or prescribe an editorial reading of the poem not expressly authorised by Horace, and to deprive the reader of the right and pleasure of interpreting Horace for himself or herself. Each English version is followed by the name of the translator and the date, sometimes approximate, of composition or publication. Brief explanatory notes at the end of the book are intended to provide the minimum information necessary. Readers who seek more are recommended to the scholarly editions of the odes and works of interpretation listed below.

Each ode is printed in Latin on the left hand page, opposite the English version. The juxtaposition should please those who retain their Latin or may be tempted to brush it up, or even to learn the language, and it is essential for anyone who wants to compare Horace with his translators and to judge the success of the metamorphoses. The Latin text is from *The Works of Horace*, edited by E. C. Wickham, Volume I, *The Odes, Carmen Saeculare, and Epodes*, Clarendon Press, Oxford, 1874. A number of emendations proposed by Sir Edward Marsh have been adopted.

FURTHER READING

Horace and his influence
(Items particularly recommended are marked with an asterisk)

Mary R. Thayer, *The Influence of Horace on the Chief English Poets of the Nineteenth Century*, New Haven 1916

Caroline Goad, *Horace in the English Literature of the Eighteenth Century*, New Haven 1918

Orazio nella letteratura mondiale, Istituto di studi romani, Rome 1936

*L. P. Wilkinson, *Horace and his Lyric Poetry*, Cambridge University Press, 1945; paperback edition, Bristol Classical Press, 1994

Alfred Noyes, *Portrait of Horace*, Sheed and Ward, London 1947

*Gilbert Highet, *The Classical Tradition. Greek and Roman Influences on Western Literature*, Oxford University Press, 1949; revised paperback edition 1967

*Gilbert Highet, 'Horace', in *Poets in a Landscape*, Hamish Hamilton, London 1957, pp. 114–60

Eduard Fraenkel, *Horace*, Clarendon Press, Oxford 1957; Oxford Paperbacks, 1966

*Ronald Storrs, *Ad Pyrrham*, Oxford University Press, 1959

Carol Maddison, *Apollo and the Nine. A History of the Ode*, Routledge and Kegan Paul, London 1960

Steele Commager, *The Odes of Horace. A Critical Study*, Yale University Press, 1962

Grant Showerman, *Horace and his influence*, Cooper Square Publishers, New York 1963

M. Owen Lee, *Word, Sound and Image in the Odes of Horace*, University of Michigan Press, Ann Arbor 1969

Wolfgang Busch, *Horaz in Russland*, Eidos Verlag, Munich 1964

Kenneth Quinn, 'Horace as a love poet. A reading of *Odes* I.5', in Niall Rudd (ed.) *Essays on Classical Literature*, Cambridge, 1972, pp. 103–21

Chris Emlyn-Jones, 'Augustan Poetry', units 6–8 of *Rome: The Augustan Age*, The Open University Press, Milton Keynes 1982, reprinted 1992

Niall Rudd, 'Horace', in E. J. Kenney (ed.) *The Cambridge History of Classical Literature. II. Latin Literature*, Cambridge University Press, 1982, pp. 370–404

Daniel M. Hooley, *The Classics in Paraphrase. Ezra Pound and Modern Translators of Latin Poetry*, Susquehanna University Press, Selinsgrove 1988

M. P. Citti, 'Riche et pauvre Horace. La présence d'Horace au XIX siècle en France', in R. Chavallier (ed.) *Présence d'Horace*, publications de l'Université de Tours, 1988, pp. 75–86

G. Maillat, 'Hölderlin et Horace', in *Présence d'Horace* (see above), pp. 147–59

David Armstrong, *Horace*, Yale, 1989

M. C. J. Putnam, 'Horace *Carm.* 2.9: Augustus and the Ambiguity of Encomium', in K. A. Raaflaub and Mark Toher (eds), *Between Republic and Empire. Interpretations of Augustus and his Principate*, University of California Press, Berkeley 1990, pp. 212–38

*Lowell Edmunds, *From a Sabine Jar. Reading Horace Odes I. 9*, University of North Carolina Press, 1992

C. Martindale and D. Hopkins, *Horace Made New. Horatian Influences on British Writing from the Renaissance to the Twentieth Century*, Cambridge University Press, 1993

Niall Rudd (ed.), *Horace 2000: a celebration: essays for the bimillennium*, Duckworth, London 1993

Thomas Poiss, 'Orazio e la Germania', in *Atti del Convegno di Licenza*, Comitato nazionale per le celebrazioni del bimillennario della morte di Q. Orazio Flacco, Edizioni Osanna, Venosa 1994, pp. 247–62

S. J. Harrison (ed.), *Homage to Horace. A Bimillennary Celebration*, Clarendon Press, Oxford 1995

R. Lyne, *Horace. Behind the Public Poetry*, Yale, 1995

Editions and translations of the Odes

Recent editions of the Odes include those of Kenneth Quinn (Macmillan, Bristol Classical Press 1980) and David West, *Horace Odes I. Carpe Diem* (Clarendon Press, Oxford 1995).

There are prose translation of the Odes by Christopher Smart (ed. Robert Anderson 1832), E. C. Wickham (Clarendon Press, Oxford 1903) and by E. C. Bennett with a facing Latin text in the Loeb Classical Library series (Heinemann 1918, frequently reprinted).

The best complete modern verse translations in English to my mind are those of Sir Edward Marsh (Macmillan, 1941) and Lord Dunsany (Heinemann, 1947). There are more recent translations by James Michie (Penguin, 1967), W. G. Shepherd (Penguin, 1983), David Mulroy (University of Michigan Press, 1994) and Stuart Lyons (Staffordshire University Press, 1996). *Horace in English*, edited by D. S. Carne-Ross and Kenneth Haynes (Penguin, 1996) contains a variety of English translations of many odes.

NOTES ON THE TRANSLATORS

Joseph Addison (1672–1719), poet, essayist and playwright. As a traveller in Italy, had works of Horace with him. Contributed to Richard Steele's *The Tatler* and co-edited *The Spectator* with him. His neo-classical tragedy *Cato* (1713) much admired in its day. **3**, 3.

Francis Atterbury (1662–1732), high church Bishop of Rochester under the Tories. His Jacobite convictions landed him in the Tower of London in 1722, and in exile abroad. He died in Paris, but was buried in Westminster Abbey. **4**, 3.

Sir John Beaumont (*c.*1583–1627), poet, elder brother of playwright Francis Beaumont. Ennobled by Charles I. A recusant Catholic. His best known poem is *Bosworth Field*. **3**, 29.

Patrick Branwell Brontë (1817–1848), brother of Anne, Charlotte and Emily Brontë. At first considered the genius of the family, but overshadowed by his sisters. Addicted to drink and drugs, died of consumption. His translation of *Odes*, Book I, probably written in his early twenties, but not published until 1938, is an astonishing *tour de force* in the romantic idiom. His versions of odes to the gods suggest the influence of Haworth parsonage. **1**, 10; 11; 24; 26; 27; 28; 29; 35; 36.

William Cartwright (1611–1643), poet, playwright and preacher, zealous royalist. His play *The Royal Slave* was acted before Charles I. An expert linguist in Latin, Greek, French and Italian. **4**, 13.

Thomas Chatterton (1752–1770), poet, precocious author of remarkable verses, notably poems which he passed off as those of a monk of the fifteenth century. Committed suicide after his forgery was exposed. Brilliantly imitative. **1**, 19.

Arthur Hugh Clough (1819–1861), poet, pupil of Dr Arnold at Rugby, Fellow of Oriel College, Oxford, but lost his faith and resigned his fellowship. Professor of English, University College, London. In his translations attempts to follow Horace's metres. **3**, 13; 23; 25.

William Cowper (1731–1800), reclusive but versatile poet, author of *The Task* (1785), the ballad 'John Gilpin' and many of the *Olney Hymns*. Translated Homer. Combined a classical clarity with a pre-romantic sensibility. **1**, 38.

Richard Crashaw (*c.*1613–1649), poet, fellow of Peterhouse, Cambridge, but went into exile in France and Italy on becoming a Roman Catholic. Wrote religious poems. **2**, 13.

Thomas Creech (1659–1700), headmaster of Sherborne School, he translated Lucretius (1682), for which he was elected fellow of Wadham College, Oxford, where he spent most of his life. Also translated Theocritus and Manilius. His *Horace* (1684) was an extraordinary achievement, completed before he was twenty-five. It ran to six editions by 1737, after which it was superseded by the translation by Philip Francis. Disappointed in love and finances, Creech committed suicide. **1**, 15; 16; 17.

Wentworth Dillon, fourth Earl of Roscommon (*c.*1633–1685), poet, nephew of the Earl of Strafford, born in Ireland, educated and travelled in France and Italy. Came to England only after the Restoration. Became Irish MP. Enjoyed literary reputation as author of verse *Essay upon Translated Verse* and translator of Horace's *Art of Poetry* (1684). According to Dr Johnson, as a translator 'he is elegant, but not great'. **3**, 6.

Austin Dobson (1840–1921), poet, studied in Strasbourg. Earned his living at the Board of Trade, but devoted most of his energy to his writings. A prolific versifier, mostly in artificial French forms. **3**, 26.

John Dryden (1631–1700), poet, playwright, satirist and critic. Celebrated in verse successive changes of political regime: Cromwell and Charles II, who appointed him Poet Laureate (1668). Wrote satire *Absalom and Achitophel* in support of future James II, on whose accession he became Roman Catholic. Deprived of laureateship under William III. Translated Lucretius, Juvenal and Persius and in 1697 produced his celebrated version of Virgil's *Aeneid*. His translations from Horace among the finest in English. **1**, 3; 9.

John Evelyn (1655–1699), translator, son of John Evelyn the diarist. **1**, 8.

Sir Richard Fanshawe (1608–1664), diplomat, translator and poet. Royalist during civil war, sent as envoy to Spain by Charles I, who knighted him. Latin secretary in Holland to future Charles II. After the Restoration, became MP for Cambridge University, ambassador to Portugal and then Spain. Translated from Italian, Spanish and Portuguese (Camoen's *Lusiads*). His *Selected Parts of Horace, Prince of Lyricks* (1652) among the earliest substantial translations from the odes. Consciously modelled his conduct on the principles of Horace, whom he called 'of all the Latin poets the fullest fraught with excellent morality'. **1**, 2; 18; 34; **2**, 1; 4; 17; **4**, 2; 8.

David Ferry (born 1924), poet, professor of English at Wellesley College. Author of a study of Wordsworth, three books of verse and a translation of *Gilgamesh* (1992). His translations from Horace are clear, simple and informal. **1**, 1.

Thomas Flatman (1637–1688), lawyer, poet and miniature painter. Fellow of the Royal Society 1668. His *Poems and Songs* (1674) were republished four times in his lifetime. **2**, 19; **3**, 8; 12; 15; 21; **4**, 1; 11.

Philip Francis (c.1708–1773), born in Ireland. Schoolmaster, rector of Barrow, Suffolk, chaplain to Chelsea Hospital. His translation of the works of Horace (1743–47) went through many editions in the eighteenth and early nineteenth century. Dr Johnson said of it: 'Francis has done it the best. I'll take his, five out of six, against them all.' **2**, 14; **4**, 5.

Lewis Evelyn Gielgud (1894–1953), lieutenant-colonel, soldier, humanitarian, man of letters. Wounded in World War I, worked for International Red Cross between the wars and after World War II and also for UNESCO. Wrote novels, plays, a travel book and translations from French, Latin and Polish. His translations from Horace neat and compact. **1**, 4; 32; **2**, 3; 10; **3**, 1; 2.

Sir Thomas Hawkins (?–1640), Catholic recusant, translator from Latin and French. His *Horace* (1625) one of the earliest English translations of the odes. Ran to four editions by 1638. Called Horace 'the best of lyric poets, containing much morality and sweetness'. **1**, 11; **2**, 11; 18; **3**, 7; 11; 14; 16; 18; **4**, 12.

Barten Holyday (1593–1661), divine and translator, chaplain to Charles I, archdeacon of Oxford, translated *Horace. The Best of Lyrick Poets* (1652), Persius and Juvenal. **3**, 20; 30.

Thomas Hood (1799–1845), poet and comic writer. Edited literary periodicals, but his career beset by considerable poverty. His romantic sensibility and feel for Horace's rich sonority tempered by sense of humour in his version of the much-translated 'Pyrrha' ode. **1**, 5.

Alfred Edward Housman (1859–1936), poet and classical scholar. Author of *A Shropshire Lad* (1896), Professor of Latin at London and Cambridge. Translated *Odes* IV, vii, which he thought 'the most beautiful poem in ancient literature'. Ian Scott Kilvert observes that his 'idiom and diction, conspicuously Saxon though they are, seem perfectly matched to the original.' 4, 7.

Samuel Johnson (1709–1784), poet, essayist, critic, lexicographer. Wrote *London* (1738) and *The Vanity of Human Wishes* (1749) in imitation of Juvenal. Edited *The Rambler.* His *English Dictionary* (1755) made him famous. Wrote *Journey to the Western Isles of Scotland* (1775) and *Lives of the Poets* (1779–81). Translated several odes while still at school. 1, 22; 2, 9; 20.

Ben Jonson (1573–1637), poet and playwright. Served in the Low Countries against the Spaniards. Turned to the stage, but killed an actor in a brawl. Temporarily became Roman Catholic. Wrote *Every Man in his Humour* (1598) and many other plays. Known as 'the English Horace'. His translation of the *Art of Poetry* was published in 1640. 3, 9.

James Blair Leishman (1902–1963), lecturer in English literature at Oxford. Published *The Metaphysical Poets* (1934), a study of Donne (1962) and many volumes of translation from Rilke and Hölderlin. Published metrical translations from the odes in *Translating Horace* (1956). 2, 5; 3, 28.

Henry Thomas Liddell, first Earl of Ravensworth (1797–1878), Northumberland politician. Tory MP for Durham (1837–47) and Liverpool (1853–55) before succeeding his father as Baron Ravensworth in 1855. Created Earl of Ravensworth 1874. Translated Horace's Odes (1858). 3, 17; 4, 14.

Edward George Earle Bulwer-Lytton, first Baron Lytton (1803–1873), novelist and politician. Prolific author of influential historical novels, notably *The Last Days of Pompeii* (1834) and *Rienzi* (1835). His metrical translations of Horace's *Odes* (1869) are ingenious, but sometimes incoherent. 1, 30.

Sir William Sinclair Marris (1873–1945), classical scholar, civil servant in India, Governor of Assam, and then of the United Provinces in the 1920s; member of the Council of India. Vice-Chancellor of Durham University 1932–34. His translation of the *Odes* (1912) competent and compact. Also translated Homer and Catullus. 2, 6; 7; 15; 3, 22; 27; 4, 4.

Sir Edward Marsh (1872–1953), scholar and patron of the arts. Gained first-class honours in classics at Oxford and won the

Chancellor's medal. A civil servant in Colonial Office, and private secretary to Winston Churchill before and after World War I, and then to several other statesmen. Published *Georgian Poetry 1912–1921*, wrote a biography of Rupert Brooke (1918), and translated the Fables of La Fontaine. His complete *Odes of Horace* (1941) is perhaps the best twentieth-century translation. **1**, 6; 7; 14; 20; 23; 27; **2**, 12; **3**, 19; **4**, 6.

Richard Newcourt (?–1716), notary public and proctor-general of the Court of Arches. Contributed to Alexander Brome's multi-authored *The Poems of Horace*. **1**, 33; **3**, 10.

Thomas Otway (*c*.1652–1685), Restoration playwright, author of *Venice Preserved* (1682). **2**, 16.

Christopher Pitt (1699–1748), fellow of New College, Oxford, rector of Pimperne in Dorset, poet and translator of Virgil and Horace. **1**, 12.

Edward John Moreton Drax Plunkett, eighteenth Baron Dunsany (1878–1957), Irish peer, novelist, dramatist and poet. Fought in South African War and both World Wars. Wounded in 1916. Published *The Odes of Horace* (1947). **2**, 2; **3**, 14; **4**, 15.

Sir Charles Sedley (*c*.1639–1701), Restoration playwright and poet and wit at the court of Charles II. Prospered under James II, but transferred his allegiance to William III. His translation of the ode 'to Barine' is perhaps the most brilliant re-creation in English of any of the odes. **2**, 8.

Sir Edward Sherburne (1616–1702), fought on royalist side in the Civil War. Translated two of Seneca's plays and other works from Latin and Greek. **4**, 10.

Christopher Smart (1722–1771), poet, resigned his fellowship of Pembroke College, Cambridge, to live by his pen in London. Unbalanced, but produced a remarkable poem, the *Song to David*. Translated Horace in prose (1765) and in verse (1767). Eventually went mad, lived in asylum and died in debtors' gaol. **1**, 31.

George Stepney (1663–1707), diplomat and poet, envoy to German states. **4**, 9.

Sir William Temple (1628–1699), diplomat, statesman and essayist. Employed on various missions abroad. Much consulted by Charles II, but disapproving his policies, retired into private life. Took no part in the Revolution of 1688, and mindful of Horace's example, refused the secretaryship of state. **1**, 13.

Helen Waddell (1889–1965), lectured in medieval literature at Oxford. Author of highly successful and influential *The Wandering Scholars* (1927), *Medieval Latin Lyrics* (1929) and a novel, *Peter Abelard* (1933). **3**, 5.

John Wilmot, second Earl of Rochester (1647–1680), notorious Restoration profligate, wit and poet. Author of satires and love lyrics. **3**, 4.

Young Gentlemen of Mr Rule's Academy at Islington. An anonymous student or students published a spirited translation in the Academy's *Poetical Blossoms* in 1766. **1**, 25.

SOURCES OF TRANSLATIONS IN THIS EDITION

Sir Thomas Hawkins, *Odes of Horace, the best of lyrick poets*, 1625

Sir Richard Fanshawe, *Selected Parts of Horace, Prince of Lyricks*, 1652

Barten Holyday, *All Horace. His Lyricks or his Four Books of Odes*, 1652

Alexander Brome, *The Poems of Horace,* rendered into English verse by several persons, 1666, 2nd edition 1671, 3rd edition 1680

Thomas Flatman, *Poems and Songs*, 1683

Thomas Creech, *The Odes, Satyrs, and Epistles of Horace*, 1684

Christopher Pitt, *Poems and Translations*, 1727

Poetical Blossoms by the Young Gentlemen of Mr Rule's Academy, 1766

The Works of Horace, translated into verse by Christopher Smart, Volume I, 1767

Horace, translated by Philip Francis, DD. With an appendix, containing translations of various odes by Ben Jonson, Cowley, Milton, Dryden, Pope, Addison, Swift, Bentley, Chatterton, G. Wakefield, Porson, Byron, etc. Volume II, A. J. Valpy, 1831

Lord Ravensworth, *Odes of Horace*, Upham and Beet, 1858

Lord Lytton, *Odes and Epodes of Horace*, Blackwood, 1869

Sir John Beaumont, *The Poems*, edited by A. B. Grosart, 1869

Horace's Odes. Established and imitated by various hands, selected and arranged by Charles W. S. Cooper, George Bell & Sons, 1880

Horace: the Odes. Translated by the most eminent English scholars and poets (Frederick Warne, 1889)

The Odes of Horace, Translated into English Verse by W. S. Marris, Oxford University Press 1912

Austin Dobson, *Collected Poems*, Kegan Paul, 1913

Sir Charles Sedley, *Poetical and Dramatic Works*, edited by V. de Sola Pinto, Constable, 1928

The Odes of Horace in English Verse. Latin text with translations by various hands chosen by H. E. Butler, G. Bell, 1929

Thomas Otway, *Works*, edited by J. C. Ghosh, Clarendon Press, Oxford 1932

The Miscellaneous and Unpublished Writings of Charlotte and Patrick Branwell Brontë, Volume I, Basil Blackwell, Oxford 1938

The Odes of Horace. Translated into English Verse by Edward Marsh, Macmillan, 1941

The Odes of Horace. Translated by Lord Dunsany, Heinemann, 1947

Horace in Modern Dress. A Selection from the Odes of Horace rendered into English verse by L. E. Gielgud, Imp. Union, Paris 1951

J. B. Leishman, *Translating Horace*. Thirty Odes translated into the original metres with the Latin text and an introductory and critical essay, Bruno Cassirer, Oxford 1956

John Dryden, *The Poems*, edited by James Hinsley, Vol. I, Clarendon Press, Oxford 1958

Sir Edward Sherburne, *Poems and Translations*, edited by F. J. Beeck, Van Gorcum, 1961

Ben Jonson, *The Complete Poetry*, edited by William B. Hunter, jr, New York University Press 1963

William Cowper, *Poetical Works*, edited by H. S. Milford, 4th edition, Oxford University Press 1967

Thomas Chatterton, *The Complete Works*, edited by Donald S. Taylor, Vol. I, Clarendon Press, Oxford 1971

Richard Crashaw, *The Complete Poetry*, edited by George Walton Williams, New York University Press, 1972

Arthur Hugh Clough, *The Poems*, 2nd edition, edited by F. L. Mulhauser, Clarendon Press, Oxford 1974

Samuel Johnson, *The Poems*, edited by David Nichol Smith and Edward L. McAdams, Clarendon Press, Oxford 1974

A. E. Housman, *The Collected Poems*, Jonathan Cape, 1986

More Latin Lyrics. From Virgil to Milton. Translated by Helen Waddell, Gollancz, 1980

Horace in English, edited by D. S. Carne-Ross, Penguin, 1996

BOOK ONE

I

Maecenas atavis edite regibus,
o et praesidium et dulce decus meum,
sunt quos curriculo pulverem Olympicum
collegisse iuvat, metaque fervidis
evitata rotis palmaque nobilis   5
terrarum dominos evehit ad deos;
hunc, si mobilium turba Quiritium
certat tergeminis tollere honoribus;
illum, si proprio condidit horreo
quidquid de Libycis verritur areis.   10
gaudentem patrios findere sarculo
agros Attalicis condicionibus
numquam dimoveas ut trabe Cypria
Myrtoum pavidus nauta secet mare.
luctantem Icariis fluctibus Africum   15
mercator metuens otium et oppidi
laudat rura sui; mox reficit ratis
quassas, indocilis pauperiem pati.
est qui nec veteris pocula Massici
nec partem solido demere de die   20
spernit, nunc viridi membra sub arbuto
stratus, nunc ad aquae lene caput sacrae.
multos castra iuvant et lituo tubae
permixtus sonitus bellaque matribus
detestata. manet sub Iove frigido   25
venator tenerae coniugis immemor,
seu visa est catulis cerva fidelibus,
seu rupit teretes Marsus aper plagas.
me doctarum hederae praemia frontium

1

Maecenas, you, descended from many kings,
O you who are my stay and my delight,
There is the man whose glory it is to be
So famous even the gods have heard the story

Of how his chariot raised Olympic dust,
The dazzling wheel making the smoking turn;
And there is he whose bliss it is to be carried
Up to the honours of office on the shifting

Shoulders of the crowd; and he whose pride
Is that his barns hold everything that can
Be gathered from the Libyan fields of grain.
And there's the man who with his little hoe

Breaks the hard soil of his poor father's farm,
But all the money there is could never persuade
That man to cross the sea, a quaking sailor.
And the fearful merchant in his wallowing vessel,

As the storm comes on longs for his native village
And longs for the quiet fields surrounding it –
And then of course next year refits his ship,
Unable to forgo the profit of it.

And there's the man who likes his cup of wine,
Taking his ease in the busiest time of the day,
Under the shady boughs of the green arbutus
Or near the secret source of some murmuring brook.

There are those who love encampments, and love the
        confused
Music of trumpet and clarion sounding together
And are in love with the wars their mothers hate.
And all the night long, out in the bitter cold,

dis miscent superis, me gelidum nemus   30
nympharumque leves cum Satyris chori
secernunt populo, si neque tibias
Euterpe cohibet nec Polyhymnia
Lesboum refugit tendere barbiton.
quodsi me lyricis vatibus inseres,   35
sublimi feriam sidera vertice.

II

Iam satis terris nivis atque dirae
grandinis misit Pater et rubente
dextera sacras iaculatus arces
     terruit urbem,

terruit gentis, grave ne rediret   5
saeculum Pyrrhae nova monstra questae,
omne cum Proteus pecus egit altos
     visere montis,

piscium et summa genus haesit ulmo
nota quae sedes fuerat columbis,   10
et superiecto pavidae natarunt
     aequore dammae.

vidimus flavum Tiberim retortis
litore Etrusco violenter undis
ire deiectum monumenta regis   15
     templaque Vestae,

If his faithful dogs have startled up a deer
Or if a wild boar has broken through the snare,
The hunter waits, forgetful of his bride;
All night the bride at home waits for the hunter.

What links *me* to the gods is that I study
To wear the ivy wreath that poets wear;
The cool sequestered grove, in which I play
For nymphs and satyrs dancing to my music,

Is where I am set apart from other men —
Unless the muse Euterpe takes back the flute
Or Polyhymnia untunes the lyre.
But if you say I am truly among the poets,

Then my exalted head will knock against the stars.

David Ferry (1996)

2

Enough of hail and cruel snow
Hath Jove now show'red on us below,
Enough with thund'ring steeples down
    Frighted the town,

Frighted the world, lest Pyrrha's reign,
Which of new monsters did complain,
Should come again, when Proteus' flocks
    Did climb the rocks,

And fish in tops of elm-trees hung,
Where birds wont build their nests, and sung,
And the all-covering sea did bear
    The trembling deer.

We yellow Tiber did behold
Back from the Tyrrhene ocean rolled,
Against the fane of Vesta pour
    And Numa's tower;

Iliae dum se nimium querenti
iactat ultorem, vagus et sinistra
labitur ripa Iove non probante u–
    xorius amnis.   20

audiet civis acuisse ferrum
quo graves Persae melius perirent,
audiet pugnas vitio parentum
    rara iuventus.

quem vocet divum populus ruentis   25
imperi rebus? prece qua fatigent
virgines sanctae minus audientem
    carmina Vestam?

cui dabit partis scelus expiandi
Iuppiter? tandem venias precamur   30
nube candentis umeros amictus,
    augur Apollo;

sive tu mavis, Erycina ridens,
quam Iocus circum volat et Cupido;
sive neglectum genus et nepotes   35
    respicis auctor,

heu nimis longo satiate ludo,
quem iuvat clamor galeaeque leves
acer et Mauri peditis cruentum
    vultus in hostem;   40

sive mutata iuvenem figura
ales in terris imitaris almae
filius Maiae patiens vocari
    Caesaris ultor:

serus in caelum redeas diuque   45
laetus intersis populo Quirini,
neve te nostris vitiis iniquum
    ocior aula

Whilst the uxorious river swears
He'll be revenged for Ilia's tears,
And over both his banks doth rove,
   Unbid of Jove.

Our children, through our faults but few,
Shall hear that we, their fathers, slew
Our countrymen; who might as well
   The Persians quell.

What god shall we invoke to stay
The falling empire? With what lay
Shall holy nuns tire Vesta's prayer-
   resisting ear?

To whom will Jove the charge commend
Of purging us? At length descend,
Prophetic Phoebus, whose white neck
   A cloud doth deck;

Or Venus, in whose smiling rays
Youth with a thousand cupids plays;
Or Mars, if thou at length canst pity
   Thy long-plagued city.

Alas, we long have sported thee,
To whom 'tis sport bright casks to see,
And grim aspects of Moorish foot
   With blood and soot;

Or wingèd Hermes, if 'tis you
Whom in Augustus' form we view,
With this revenging th'other flood
   Of Julius' blood:

Return to heaven late, we pray,
And long with us the Romans stay,
Nor let disdain of that offence
   Snatch thee from hence.

tollat; hic magnos potius triumphos,
hic ames dici pater atque princeps,   50
neu sinas Medos equitare inultos
    te duce, Caesar.

III

    Sic te diva potens Cypri,
sic fratres Helenae, lucida sidera,
    ventorumque regat pater
obstrictis aliis praeter Iapyga,
    navis, quae tibi creditum   5
debes Vergilium, finibus Atticis
    reddas incolumem precor,
et serves animae dimidium meae.
    illi robur et aes triplex
circa pectus erat, qui fragilem truci   10
    commisit pelago ratem
primus, nec timuit praecipitem Africum
    decertantem Aquilonibus
nec tristis Hyadas nec rabiem Noti,
    quo non arbiter Hadriae   15
maior, tollere seu ponere vult freta.
    quem mortis timuit gradum,
qui siccis oculis monstra natantia,
    qui vidit mare turbidum et
infamis scopulos Acroceraunia?   20
    nequiquam deus abscidit
prudens Oceano dissociabili
    terras, si tamen impiae
non tangenda rates transiliunt vada.
    audax omnia perpeti   25
gens humana ruit per vetitum nefas.
    audax Iapeti genus
ignem fraude mala gentibus intulit.

Love here victorious triumphs rather,
Love here the name of Prince and Father,
Nor let the Medes unpunished ride,
   Thou being our guide.

Sir Richard Fanshawe (1652)

3

So may the auspicious queen of love,
And the twin stars (the seed of Jove),
And he who rules the raging wind,
To thee, O sacred ship, be kind,
And gentle breezes fill thy sails,
supplying soft Etesian gales,
As thou, to whom the muse commends
The best of poets and of friends,
Dost thy committed pledge restore,
And land him safely on the shore;
And save the better part of me
From perishing with him at sea.
Sure he, who first the passage tried,
In hardened oak his heart did hide,
And ribs of iron armed his side!
Or his at least, in hollow wood
Who tempted first the briny flood;
Nor feared the winds' contending roar,
Nor billows beating on the shore ;
Nor Hyades portending rain ;
Nor all the tyrants of the main.
What form of death could him affright
Who, unconcerned, with steadfast sight,
Could view the surges mounting steep,
And monsters rolling in the deep?
Could through the ranks of ruin go,
With storms above, and rocks below?
In vain did Nature's wise command

post ignem aetheria domo
subductum macies et nova febrium   30
    terris incubuit cohors,
semotique prius tarda necessitas
    leti corripuit gradum.
expertus vacuum Daedalus aëra
    pennis non homini datis: 35
perrupit Acheronta Herculeus labor.
    nil mortalibus ardui est:
caelum ipsum petimus stultitia neque
    per nostrum patimur scelus
iracunda Iovem ponere fulmina.   40

Divide the waters from the land,
If daring ships, and men profane,
Invade the inviolable main;
The eternal fences overleap,
And pass at will the boundless deep.
No toil, no hardship can restrain
Ambitious man inured to pain;
The more confined, the more he tries,
And at forbidden quarry flies.
Thus bold Prometheus did aspire,
And stole from heaven the reed of fire:
A train of ills, a ghastly crew,
The robber's blazing track pursue;
Fierce Famine, with her meagre face,
And fevers of the fiery race,
In swarms the offending wretch surround,
All brooding on the blasted ground;
And limping Death, lashed on by Fate,
Comes up to shorten half our date.
This made not Daedalus beware,
With borrowed wings to sail in air:
To Hell Alcides forced his way,
Plunged through the lake, and snatched the prey.
Nay, scarce the gods, or heavenly climes
Are safe from our audacious crimes:
We reach at Jove's imperial crown,
And pull the unwilling thunder down.

John Dryden (1685)

IV

Solvitur acris hiems grata vice veris et Favoni,
　　　trahuntque siccas machinae carinas,
ac neque iam stabulis gaudet pecus aut arator igni,
　　　nec prata canis albicant pruinis.
iam Cytherea choros ducit Venus imminente Luna,　　　　5
　　　iunctaeque Nymphis Gratiae decentes
alterno terram quatiunt pede, dum gravis Cyclopum
　　　Vulcanus ardens urit officinas.
nunc decet aut viridi nitidum caput impedire myrto
　　　aut flore terrae quem ferunt solutae;　　　　10
nunc et in umbrosis Fauno decet immolare lucis,
　　　seu poscat agna sive malit haedo.
pallida Mors aequo pulsat pede pauperum tabernas
　　　regumque turris. o beate Sesti,
vitae summa brevis spem nos vetat incohare longam.　　　　15
　　　iam te premet nox fabulaeque Manes
et domus exilis Plutonia: quo simul mearis,
　　　nec regna vini sortiere talis,
nec tenerum Lycidan mirabere, quo calet iuventus
　　　nunc omnis et mox virgines tepebunt.　　　　20

4

Bitter Winter melts away.
  Spring's delicious breezes blow.
  Little ships on rollers go
Down the beaches to the bay.
Now the ox disdains the stall,
  Now the ploughman leaves the fire,
Now the frosts that whitened all
  From the meadowlands retire.

Venus now the dances leads,
  While the Moon in Heaven stands.
  Nymphs and Graces, taking hands,
Step their measures on the meads;
And the lame Olympian Smith
  Feeds and fans the awful fires
In the Thunderer's Forges, with
  Giants serving him for squires.

Through the thawing ground appear
  Crocuses and myrtle sprigs,
  Meet to sport with masks and wigs
Now that Carnival is near;
And the Master of the Glade,
  Pan, prescribes a roast of lamb
Now for picnics in the shade,
  Or a kid with marjoram.

Yes, but pallid Death at your
  Palace gates at last will beat
  With the same imperious feet
As at any cottage door.
Blest are you — but life is brief.
  Plans mature — but planners fade.
Death shall take you like a thief.
  You shall join the Shades, a Shade.

V

Quis multa gracilis te puer in rosa
perfusus liquidis urget odoribus
    grato, Pyrrha, sub antro ?
      cui flavam religas comam,

simplex munditiis? heu quotiens fidem   5
mutatosque deos flebit et aspera
    nigris aequora ventis
      emirabitur insolens,

qui nunc te fruitur credulus aurea,
qui semper vacuam, semper amabilem   10
    sperat, nescius aurae
      fallacis! miseri, quibus

intemptata nites. me tabula sacer
votiva paries indicat uvida
    suspendisse potenti   15
      vestimenta maris deo.

Yes, and in the Shadow Land,
   Never, never shall the dice
   Roll for you, nor waiters ice
Dry Moselle at your demand.
Death will be the end of joy,
   End of all that here began —
Will, your little wonder boy,
   Soon will be a ladies' man.

Lewis Evelyn Gielgud (1951)

5

Ah, Pyrrha, tell me, whose the happy lot
To woo thee on a couch of lavish roses,
Who, bathed in odorous dews, in his fond arms encloses
   Thee, in some happy grot?

For whom those nets of golden-gloried hair
Dost thou entwine in cunning carelessnesses?
Alas, poor boy! who thee, in fond belief, caresses,
   Deeming thee wholly fair!

How oft shall he thy fickleness bemoan,
When fair to foul shall change; and he unskilful
In pilotage, beholds, with tempest wildly wilful,
   The happy calm o'erthrown!

He who now hopes that thou wilt ever prove
All void of care, and full of fond endearing,
Knows not that varies more than zephyrs ever veering,
   The fickle breath of love.

Ah, hapless he to whom, like seas untried,
Thou seemest fair! That my sea-going's ended
My votive tablet proves, to those dark gods suspended,
   Who o'er the waves preside.

Thomas Hood (1860)

VI

Scriberis Vario fortis et hostium
victor Maeonii carminis alite,
quam rem cumque ferox navibus aut equis
    miles te duce gesserit:

nos, Agrippa, neque haec dicere nec gravem   5
Pelidae stomachum cedere nescii
nec cursus duplicis per mare Ulixei
    nec saevam Pelopis domum

conamur, tenues grandia, dum pudor
imbellisque lyrae Musa potens vetat   10
laudes egregii Caesaris et tuas
    culpa deterere ingeni.

quis Martem tunica tectum adamantina
digne scripserit aut pulvere Troico
nigrum Merionen aut ope Palladis   15
    Tydiden superis parem?

nos convivia, nos proelia virginum
sectis in iuvenes unguibus acrium
cantamus vacuis, sive quid urimur
    non praeter solitum leves.   20

6

Let Varius chant your praises: he is heir
    To Homer's wing, and the victorious feats
    In which you lead your armies and your fleets
Can with befitting state declare.

Not mine, Agrippa, those high acts to sing,
    Nor yet Achilles sulking by the brine,
    Or horrid chronicle of Pelops' line,
Or sly Ulysses' sea-faring.

Small wits, small themes! I know my humble place,
    Nor would the Muse of my unwarlike lyre
    Suffer my verse with ineffectual fire
Your fame or Caesar's to disgrace.

Some worthier scribe retail the hard alloy
    Of Mars his tunic ; or the fearful odds
    When Diomed armed by Pallas fought with Gods,
Or Merion, black with dust of Troy.

To feast and dance I frame an idle song,
    And broil of sharp-nail'd girls their swains defying:
    Even should some warmer fancy set me flying,
You must not bid me soar too long.

                                        Sir Edward Marsh (1941)

VII

Laudabunt alii claram Rhodon aut Mytilenen
    aut Epheson bimarisve Corinthi
moenia vel Baccho Thebas vel Apolline Delphos
    insignis aut Thessala Tempe:
sunt quibus unum opus est intactae Palladis urbem   5
    carmine perpetuo celebrare et
undique decerptam fronti praeponere olivam:
    plurimus in Iunonis honorem
aptum dicet equis Argos ditisque Mycenas:
    me nec tam patiens Lacedaemon   10
nec tam Larisae percussit campus opimae,
    quam domus Albuneae resonantis
et praeceps Anio ac Tiburni lucus et uda
    mobilibus pomaria rivis.
albus ut obscuro deterget nubila caelo   15
    saepe Notus neque parturit imbris
perpetuo, sic tu sapiens finire memento
    tristitiam vitaeque labores
molli, Plance, mero, seu te fulgentia signis
    castra tenent seu densa tenebit   20
Tiburis umbra tui. Teucer Salamina patremque
    cum fugeret, tamen uda Lyaeo
tempora populea fertur vinxisse corona,
    sic tristis adfatus amicos:
'quo nos cumque feret melior fortuna parente,   25
    ibimus, o socii comitesque.
nil desperandum Teucro duce et auspice Teucro;
    certus enim promisit Apollo
ambiguam tellure nova Salamina futuram.
    O fortes peioraque passi   30
mecum saepe viri, nunc vino pellite curas;
    cras ingens iterabimus aequor.'

7

Let others hymn the glories of Rhodes or Mytilene,
    Ephesus the golden, or Tempe, Thessaly's pride,
Battlemented Corinth on twin seas pillioned,
    Delphi by Apollo, Thebes by Bacchus dignified.
Some never cease inditing of virgin Pallas' city,
    Plucking all its olive-leaves to twine their singing-crowns;
Some to honour Juno vaunt the cavalcades of Argos,
    Some Mycenae, wealthiest of the Grecian towns.
I would never tune a string for hardy Lacedaemon,
    Never turn a stave for Larissa's bounteous loam;
Only let me sweetly sing Albunea's echoing cavern,
    And the rocks where Anio leaps down in sudden foam,
Only praise through all my days the grove of old Tiburnus,
    Where between the apple trees the lightfoot rillets roam.

Plancus, leave the pennon'd camp, come home to woody Tibur,
    And as the white South Wind of Spring at last withholds his rain
And wipes the dusky clouds away, forget your weary labours
    Over a bowl of mellow wine, that routs dull care and pain.
When Teucer put his angered sire and Salamis behind him,
    'Tis told that with a poplar wreath he crowned his beaded brow
Glowing with the heady fumes of sorrow-easing Bacchus,
    And thus bespake his troubled friends, clustered round the prow:

'Whithersoever Fortune lead us, kinder than a father,
    Fellows and companions, together we will sail.
Dream not of despairing, while Teucer guards and guides you,
    Trusting in Apollo, whose promise cannot fail.
To a new land he calls us, to build another Salamis –
    Great-heart comrades, you and I have shared worse ills than these;
Fill with wine your cups and mine, tonight we drown our bodings,
    Then tomorrow forth once more over the vasty seas.'

Sir Edward Marsh (1941)

VIII

Lydia, dic, per omnis
te deos oro, Sybarin cur properes amando
    perdere, cur apricum
oderit campum, patiens pulveris atque solis,
    cur neque militaris   5
inter aequalis equitet, Gallica nec lupatis
    temperet ora frenis?
cur timet flavum Tiberim tangere? cur olivum
    sanguine viperino
cautius vitat neque iam livida gestat armis   10
    bracchia, saepe disco,
saepe trans finem iaculo nobilis expedito?
    quid latet, ut marinae
filium dicunt Thetidis sub lacrimosa Troiae
    funera, ne virilis   15
cultus in caedem et Lycias proriperet catervas?

IX

Vides ut alta stet nive candidum
Soracte, nec iam sustineant onus
    silvae laborantes, geluque
        flumina constiterint acuto.

8

Lydia, I conjure you, say,
Why haste you so to make away
   Poor Sybaris with love?
Why hates he now the open air?
Why heat, and clouds of dust to bear,
   Does he no more approve?

Why leaves he off his martial pride?
Why is he now afraid to ride
   Upon his Gallic steed?
Why swims he not the Tiber o'er?
Or wrestles as he did before?
   Whence do his fears proceed?

Why boasts he not his limbs grown black
With bearing arms, or his strong back
   With which he threw the bar?
Is he like Thetis' son concealed,
And from all manly sports withheld,
   To keep him safe from war?

John Evelyn (c.1670)

9

Behold yon mountain's hoary height
   Made higher with new mounts of snow:
Again behold the winter's weight
   Oppress the labouring woods below;
And streams with icy fetters bound
Benumbed and cramped to solid ground.

dissolve frigus ligna super foco   5
large reponens atque benignius
   deprome quadrimum Sabina,
     o Thaliarche, merum diota:

permitte divis cetera, qui simul
stravere ventos aequore fervido   10
   deproeliantis, nec cupressi
     nec veteres agitantur orni.

quid sit futurum cras fuge quaerere et
quem Fors dierum cumque dabit lucro
   appone, nec dulcis amores   15
     sperne puer neque tu choreas,

donec virenti canities abest
morosa. nunc et campus et areae
   lenesque sub noctem susurri
     composita repetantur hora,   20

nunc et latentis proditor intimo
gratus puellae risus ab angulo
   pignusque dereptum lacertis
     aut digito male pertinaci.

With well-heaped logs dissolve the cold
    And feed the genial hearth with fires;
Produce the wine that makes us bold,
    And sprightly wit and love inspires;
For what hereafter shall betide
God (if 'tis worth His care) provide.

Let Him alone with what He made,
    To toss and turn the world below;
At His command the storms invade,
    The winds by His commission blow,
Till with a nod He bids them cease,
And then the calm returns and all is peace.

Tomorrow and its works defy;
    Lay hold upon the present hour,
And snatch the pleasures passing by
    To put them out of Fortune's power;
Nor love nor love's delights disdain –
Whate'er thou gett'st today, is gain.

Secure those golden early joys
    That youth unsoured with sorrow bears,
Ere with'ring time the taste destroys
    With sickness and unwieldy years.
For active sports, for pleasing rest,
This is the time to be possest;
The best is but in season best.

Th' appointed hour of promised bliss,
    The pleasing whisper in the dark,
The half-unwilling willing kiss,
    The laugh that guides thee to the mark,
When the kind nymph would coyness feign
And hides but to be found again –
These, these are joys the gods for youth ordain.

John Dryden (1685)

X

Mercuri, facunde nepos Atlantis,
qui feros cultus hominum recentum
voce formasti catus et decorae
   more palaestrae,

te canam, magni Iovis et deorum   5
nuntium curvaeque lyrae parentem,
callidum quidquid placuit iocoso
   condere furto.

te, boves olim nisi reddidisses
per dolum amotas, puerum minaci   10
voce dum terret, viduus pharetra
   risit Apollo.

quin et Atridas duce te superbos
Ilio dives Priamus relicto
Thessalosque ignis et iniqua Troiae   15
   castra fefellit.

tu pias laetis animas reponis
sedibus virgaque levem coerces
aurea turbam, superis deorum
   gratus et imis.   20

10

Merry God of Atlas' strain,
Whose eloquence taught mortal men
   In time's remotest age,
To lay their savage wildness by,
And but in friendly rivalry
   Their skill or strength to engage;

Hail, Herald of thy heavenly Sire!
Hail, parent of the crooked lyre!
   To praise thee be my pride;
Thou God endowed, with matchless skill
Whate'er, in wanton jest, at will
   Thy hand may steal – to hide!

For, long ago, when, young and gay
From him whose glory guides the day
   His cattle thou didst wile,
Although the thief he frowned upon,
Yet, when his quiver too was gone
   He could not choose but smile.

"Twas Thou that led rich Priam on
When, to redeem his slaughtered son,
   He left sad Troy behind,
And safe escaped Atrides' ire,
And foemen, round each Argive fire
   Against that Troy combined.

'Tis Thou that guidest good men home;
Our spirits urging to the tomb
   Before thy golden rod;
Grateful alike to him who reigns
O'er Hell's dim, desolate domains,
   And to heaven's highest God.

Patrick Branwell Brontë (1840)

XI

Tu ne quaesieris, scire nefas, quem mihi, quem tibi
finem di dederint, Leuconoë, nec Babylonios
temptaris numeros. ut melius, quidquid erit, pati,
seu pluris hiemes seu tribuit Iuppiter ultimam,
quae nunc oppositis debilitat pumicibus mare   5
Tyrrhenum: sapias, vina liques, et spatio brevi
spem longam reseces. dum loquimur, fugerit invida
aetas: carpe diem, quam minimum credula postero.

XII

Quem virum aut heroa lyra vel acri
tibia sumis celebrare, Clio?
quem deum? cuius recinet iocosa
    nomen imago

aut in umbrosis Heliconis oris   5
aut super Pindo gelidove in Haemo,
unde vocalem temere insecutae
    Orphea silvae

arte materna rapidos morantem
fluminum lapsus celerisque ventos,   10
blandum et auritas fidibus canoris
    ducere quercus?

quid prius dicam solitis parentis
laudibus, qui res hominum ac deorum,
qui mare et terras variisque mundum   15
    temperat horis ?

unde nil maius generatur ipso,
nec viget quicquam simile aut secundum:

11

Strive not, Leuconoë, to know what end
The gods above to me or thee will send;
Nor with astrologers consult at all,
That thou mayst better know what can befall;
Whether thou liv'st more winters, or thy last
Be this, which Tyrrhen waves 'gainst rocks do cast.
Be wise! drink free, and in so short a space
Do not protracted hopes of life embrace.
Whilst we are talking, envious Time doth slide:
This day's thine own; the next may be denied.

Sir Thomas Hawkins (1625)

12

What man, what hero, will you raise,
    By the shrill pipe, or deeper lyre!
What god, O Clio, will you praise,
    And teach the Echoes to admire?

Amidst the shades of Helicon,
    Cold Haemus' top, or Pindus' head,
Whence the glad forests hastened down,
    And danced as tuneful Orpheus played.

Taught by the muse, he stopped the fall
    Of rapid floods, and charmed the wind:
The listening oaks obeyed the call,
    And left their wondering hills behind.

Whom should I first record, but Jove,
    Whose sway extends o'er sea and land,
The king of men and gods above,
    Who holds the seasons in command?

To rival Jove, shall none aspire;
    None shall to equal glory rise;

proximos illi tamen occupavit
  Pallas honores.   20

proeliis audax, neque te silebo,
Liber, et saevis inimica Virgo
beluis, nec te, metuende certa
  Phoebe sagitta.

dicam et Alciden puerosque Ledae,   25
hunc equis, illum superare pugnis
nobilem; quorum simul alba nautis
  stella refulsit,

defluit saxis agitatus umor,
concidunt venti fugiuntque nubes,   30
et minax, quod sic voluere, ponto
  unda recumbit.

Romulum post hos prius an quietum
Pompili regnum memorem an superbos
Tarquini fascis, dubito, an Catonis   35
  nobile letum.

Regulum et Scauros animaeque magnae
prodigum Paulum superante Poeno
gratus insigni referam Camena
  Fabriciumque.   40

hunc et incomptis Curium capillis
utilem bello tulit et Camillum
saeva paupertas et avitus apto
  cum lare fundus.

crescit occulto velut arbor aevo   45
fama Marcelli; micat inter omnis
Iulium sidus velut inter ignis
  luna minores.

gentis humanae pater atque custos,
orte Saturno, tibi cura magni   50
Caesaris fatis data: tu secundo
  Caesare regnes.

But Pallas claims beneath her sire
   The second honours of the skies.

To thee, O Bacchus, great in war,
   To Dian will I strike the string,
Of Phoebus wounding from afar,
   In numbers like his own I'll sing.

The muse Alcides shall resound;
   The twins of Leda shall succeed;
This for the standing fight renowned,
   And that for managing the steed,

Whose star shines innocently still:
   The clouds disperse; the tempests cease;
The waves, obedient to their will,
   Sink down, and hush their rage to peace.

Next shall I Numa's pious reign,
   Or thine, O Romulus, relate;
Or Rome, by Brutus freed again;
   Or haughty Cato's glorious fate?

Or dwell on noble Paulus' fame,
   Too lavish of the patriot's blood?
Or Regulus' immortal name,
   Too obstinately just and good?

These, with Camillus brave and bold,
   And other chiefs of matchless might,
Rome's virtuous poverty of old
   Severely seasoned to the fight.

Like trees, Marcellus' glory grows
   With an insensible advance;
The Julian star, like Cynthia, glows,
   Who leads the planetary dance.

The Fates, o sire of human race,
   Intrust great Caesar to thy care;
Give him to hold thy second place,
   And reign thy sole vicegerent here.

ille seu Parthos Latio imminentis
egerit iusto domitos triumpho,
sive subiectos Orientis orae   55
    Seras et Indos,

te minor laetum reget aequus orbem;
tu gravi curru quaties Olympum,
tu parum castis inimica mittes
    fulmina lucis.   60

XIII

Cum tu, Lydia, Telephi
cervicem roseam, cerea Telephi
    laudas bracchia, vae meum
fervens difficili bile tumet iecur.
    tum nec mens mihi nec color   5
certa sede manent, umor et in genas
    furtim labitur, arguens
quam lentis penitus macerer ignibus.
    uror, seu tibi candidos
turparunt umeros immodicae mero   10
    rixae, sive puer furens
impressit memorem dente labris notam.
    non, si me satis audias,
speres perpetuum dulcia barbare
    laedentem oscula quae Venus   15
quinta parte sui nectaris imbuit.
    felices ter et amplius
quos irrupta tenet copula nec malis
    divulsus querimoniis
suprema citius solvet amor die.   20

And whether India he shall tame,
    Or to his chains the Seres doom;
Or mighty Parthia dreads his name,
    And bows her haughty neck to Rome;

While on our groves thy bolts are hurled,
    And thy loud car shakes heaven above,
He shall with justice awe the world,
    To none inferior but to Jove.

Christopher Pitt (1727)

13

When thou commend'st the lovely eyes
    Of Telephus, that for thee dies,
His arms of wax, his neck, or hair;
Oh! how my heart begins to beat!
My spleen is swell'd with gall and heat,
And all my hopes are turn'd into despair.

Then both my mind and colour change,
My jealous thoughts about me range,
    In twenty shapes, my eyes begin,
The stealing drops, as from a still,
Like winter springs, apace to fill,
Fall down, and tell what fires I feel within.

When his reproaches make thee cry,
And thy fresh cheeks with paleness die,
    I burn to think you will be friends;
When his rough hand thy bosom strips,
Or his fierce kisses tear thy lips,
I die, to see how all such quarrel ends.

Ah! never hope a youth to hold
So haughty, and in love so bold:
    What can him tame in anger keep
Whom all this fondness can't assuage,
    Who even kisses turns to rage,
Which Venus does in her own nectar steep?

XIV

O navis, referent in mare te novi
fluctus! o quid agis? fortiter occupa
 portum! nonne vides ut
  nudum remigio latus,

et malus celeri saucius Africo,   5
antennaeque gemant, ac sine funibus
 vix durare cavernae
  possint imperiosius

aequor? non tibi sunt integra lintea,
non di quos iterum pressa voces malo.   10
 quamvis Pontica pinus,
  silvae filia nobilis,

iactes et genus et nomen inutile,
nil pictis timidus navita puppibus
 fidit. tu, nisi ventis   15
  debes ludibrium, cave.

nuper sollicitum quae mihi taedium,
nunc desiderium curaque non levis,
 interfusa nitentis
  vites aequora Cycladas.   20

Thrice happy they whose gentle hearts,
Till death itself their union parts,
　　An undisturbèd kindness holds,
Without complaints or jealous fears,
Without reproach or spited tears,
Which damps the kindest heats with sudden colds.

Sir William Temple (1668)

14

Hold, hold the port, fair bark, while yet thou mayst,
Ere fresh tides wash thee back to sea! oh haste!
　　Look how thy sides are shorn
　　Of oars, thy canvas torn,

Hark how the yard-arms yell, the shivering mast
Cracks in the onset of the Libyan blast!
　　Oh rope thy ribs, before
　　The surge with greedy roar

Comes foaming down to work its tyrant will.
Thy gods are deaf, though thou beseech them still,
　　And desperately invoke
　　That venerable oak,

Thy Pontic sire, whose pride thou dost inherit.
Think not with thy gay painted poop to inspirit
　　The frantic crew, or brave
　　The mocking of the wave.

Fair bark, so late my care, my hope, my fear,
Now more than ever cherished, go not near
　　The gilded Cyclades
　　That lock the sundering seas.

Sir Edward Marsh (1941)

XV

Pastor cum traheret per freta navibus
Idaeis Helenen perfidus hospitam,
ingrato celeris obruit otio
    ventos, ut caneret fera

Nereus fata: mala ducis avi domum,   5
quam multo repetet Graecia milite,
coniurata tuas rumpere nuptias
    et regnum Priami vetus.

heu heu, quantus equis, quantus adest viris
sudor! quanta moves funera Dardanae   10
genti! iam galeam Pallas et aegida
    currusque et rabiem parat.

nequiquam Veneris praesidio ferox
pectes caesariem grataque feminis
imbelli cithara carmina divides,   15
    nequiquam thalamo gravis

hastas et calami spicula Gnosii
vitabis strepitumque et celerem sequi
Aiacem; tamen heu serus adulteros
    cultus pulvere collines.   20

non Laertiaden, exitium tuae
gentis, non Pylium Nestora respicis?
urgent impavidi te Salaminius
    Teucer, te Sthenelus sciens

pugnae, sive opus est imperitare equis,   25
non auriga piger. Merionen quoque
nosces. ecce furit te reperire atrox
    Tydides melior patre,

15

When faithless Paris stole away,
And carried Helen through the sea,
   Then Nereus stilled the wind:
He quieted the angry seas,
And lulled the billows into ease,
Ease to the lovers' haste unkind.

Whilst thus he sang: Thou carry'st home
Thine own, false youth, and country's doom,
   Whom Greeks shall fetch again,
With all their force; and all combine
To break that wicked match of thine,
And ancient Priam's noble reign.

What labour, ah! what dust and heat!
And how the men and horses sweat!
   Ah, Troy what fates engage!
E'en furious Pallas now prepares
Her helmet and her shield for wars,
Her dreadful chariot, and her rage.

In vain shalt thou thy safety place
In Venus' aid, and paint thy face,
   In vain adorn thy hair;
In vain thy feeble harp shalt move
And sing soft tales of easy love,
To please the wanton and the fair.

In vain shalt thou avoid thy foe,
The wingèd dart and Cretan bow,
   Things grievous to thy joys;
In vain, with grief, shalt fear to view
Stout Ajax eager to pursue,
And strive to fly the hated noise.

quem tu, cervus uti vallis in altera
visum parte lupum graminis immemor,   30
sublimi fugies mollis anhelitu,
        non hoc pollicitus tuae.

iracunda diem proferet Ilio
matronisque Phrygum classis Achillei;
post certas hiemes uret Achaicus   35
        ignis Iliacas domos.

But ah! too late, ah! much too late,
Thou shalt endure the stroke of fate,
    And find the Gods are just;
Too late thou shalt deserv'dly feel
The force of the revenging steel,
And soil th'adulterous locks in dust.

Dost thou not see grave Nestor's age,
And fierce Ulysses' wily rage,
    The ruin of thy state?
Nor Teucer's brave undaunted force,
Nor Stheneleus, that drives his horse
As furious and fast as fate?

Ah! thou shalt see Merione
In Trojan dust severely gay,
    And fierce Tydides rave;
Look how he frowns, and roves about
To find the feeble Paris out,
Tydides, as his father brave.

These, feeble Paris, thou shalt fly,
As trembling does, whose fears espy
    A lion in a grove;
They leave their herbs, with panting breath,
They strive to shun pursuing death;
Was this thy promise to thy love!

Achilles, angry for a wrong,
Shall Troy's approaching fate prolong;
    But, after certain years,
Thessalian flames and Grecian fire
Shall o'er the proudest piles aspire,
And fill the matrons' eyes with tears.

Thomas Creech (1684)

XVI

O matre pulchra filia pulchrior,
quem criminosis cumque voles modum
   pones iambis, sive flamma
     sive mari libet Hadriano.

non Dindymene non adytis quatit   5
mentem sacerdotum incola Pythius,
   non Liber aeque, non acuta
     sic geminant Corybantes aera,

tristes ut irae, quas neque Noricus
deterret ensis nec mare naufragum   10
   nec saevus ignis nec tremendo
     Iuppiter ipse ruens tumultu.

fertur Prometheus addere principi
limo coactus particulam undique
   desectam et insani leonis   15
     vim stomacho apposuisse nostro.

irae Thyesten exitio gravi
stravere et altis urbibus ultimae
   stetere causae cur perirent
     funditus imprimeretque muris   20

hostile aratrum exercitus insolens.
compesce mentem: me quoque pectoris
   temptavit in dulci iuventa
     fervor et in celeris iambos

misit furentem: nunc ego mitibus   25
mutare quaero tristia, dum mihi
   fias recantatis amica
     opprobriis animumque reddas.

16

O daughter fair, of greater charms
Than those with which thy mother warms,
    My guilty verses how you please
Destroy in flames (though scarce so hot
As that fierce rage with which I wrote)
    Or in the angry sea.

Not Cybele such heat inspires,
Ne'er Phoebus with such raging fires
    His prophet's soul possessed;
Not Bacchus' self can raise a man
Half so much as anger can,
    When once it burns the breast.

Nor tears nor kindness can assuage,
Nor force nor danger curb the rage,
    It ventures boldly on;
It scorns to be confined by Jove,
Or all the thund'ring powers above,
    But by its boundless self alone.

When bold Prometheus first began,
As story goes, to make a man,
    From every thing he snatched a part
To furnish out his clay,
And to complete his rude essay,
    He placed a lion's fury in the heart.

'Twas rage that made the brothers hate,
Rage wrought Thyestes' wond'rous fate;
    'Twas rage that killed the child;
That fed the father with the son,
And when it saw the mighty mischief done,
    Stood by, and (what was strange) it smiled.

XVII

Velox amoenum saepe Lucretilem
mutat Lycaeo Faunus et igneam
    defendit aestatem capellis
        usque meis pluviosque ventos.

impune tutum per nemus arbutos   5
quaerunt latentis et thyma deviae
    olentis uxores mariti,
        nec viridis metuunt colubras

'Tis that that raises all our wars,
And brings our dangers and our fears,
   When the insulting foe,
Whilst anger burns and rage prevails,
O'er towns' and cities' ruined walls
   Doth draw the heavy plough.

Then curb thy anger, charming maid,
That once my heedless youth betrayed;
   It raised a deadly flame;
And hurried on my thoughtless muse
In swift iambics to abuse
   And wanton with thy fame.

But now I do repent the wrong,
And now compose a softer song
   To make thee just amends.
Recant the errors of my youth,
And swear those scandals were not truth;
   So you and I be friends.

Thomas Creech (1684)

17

Swift Faunus oft Lyceum leaves behind,
   And to my pleasing farm retreats;
      And from the summer heats
Defends my goats, and from the rainy wind.

O'er vales, o'er craggy rocks, and hills they stray,
   Seek flow'ry thyme, and safely browse
      And wanton in the boughs;
Nor fear an angry serpent in the way.

nec Martialis haediliae lupos,
utcumque dulci, Tyndari, fistula   10
   valles et Usticae cubantis
     levia personuere saxa.

di me tuentur, dis pietas mea
et musa cordi est. hic tibi copia
   manabit ad plenum benigno   15
     ruris honorum opulenta cornu:

hic in reducta valle Caniculae
vitabis aestus et fide Teia
   dices laborantis in uno
     Penelopen vitreamque Circen: 20

hic innocentis pocula Lesbii
duces sub umbra, nec Semeleius
   cum Marte confundet Thyoneus
     proelia, nec metues protervum

suspecta Cyrum, ne male dispari   25
incontinentis iniciat manus
   et scindat haerentem coronam
     crinibus immeritamque vestem.

No lurking venom swells the harmless mould.
   The kids are safe, the tender lambs
      Lie bleating by their dams,
Nor hear the evening wolves grin round the fold.

Soft rural lays through every valley sound;
   By low Ustica's purling spring
      The shepherds pipe and sing,
Whilst from the even rocks the tunes rebound.

Kind heav'n defends my soft abodes,
   I live the gods' peculiar care,
      Secure and free from fear;
My songs and my devotion please the gods.

Here naked truth, love, peace, good nature reign,
   And here to thee shall plenty flow,
      And all her riches show,
To raise the honour of the quiet plain.

Here crooked vales afford a cool retreat;
   Or underneath an arbour's shade,
      For love and pleasure made,
Thou shalt avoid the dog-star's raging heat;

And sweetly sing the harmless wars of love,
   How chaste Penelope's desires
      And wanton Circe's fires
With various heats for one Ulysses strove:

At noon with wine the fiery beams assuage
   Beneath a shade on beds of grass;
      And take a chirping glass,
But drink not on till mirth boils up to rage.

Ne'er fear thy old gallant, he's far away,
   He shall not see, nor seize, nor tear
      Thy chaplet from thy hair;
We shall have leisure, and have room to play.

Thomas Creech (1684)

XVIII

Nullam, Vare, sacra vite prius severis arborem
circa mite solum Tiburis et moenia Catili.
siccis omnia nam dura deus proposuit, neque
mordaces aliter diffugiunt sollicitudines.
quis post vina gravem militiam aut pauperiem crepat?   5
quis non te potius, Bacche pater, teque, decens Venus?
ac ne quis modici transiliat munera Liberi,
Centaurea monet cum Lapithis rixa super mero
debellata, monet Sithoniis non levis Euhius,
cum fas atque nefas exiguo fine libidinum   10
discernunt avidi. non ego te, candide Bassareu,
invitum quatiam, nec variis obsita frondibus
sub divum rapiam. saeva tene cum Berecyntio
cornu tympana, quae subsequitur caecus Amor sui
et tollens vacuum plus nimio Gloria verticem   15
arcanique Fides prodiga, perlucidior vitro.

XIX

Mater saeva Cupidinum
Thebanaeque iubet me Semelae puer
et lasciva Licentia
finitis animum reddere amoribus.
urit me Glycerae nitor   5
splendentis Pario marmore purius:
urit grata protervitas
et vultus nimium lubricus aspici.
in me tota ruens Venus
Cyprum deseruit, nec patitur Scythas   10

18

Of all the trees, plant me the sacred vine
In Tibur's mellow fields, and let it climb
Catilus' walls: for Jove doth cares propound
To sober heads, which in full cups are drown'd.
Of want, or war, who cries out after wine?
Thee, father Bacchus, thee, fair Erycine,
Who doth not sing? but through intemp'rate use,
Lest Liber's gifts you turn into abuse,
Think of the Centaurs' brawl, fought in their cans,
With Lapithes; and to Sithonians
Heavy Evous, when their heated blood
Makes little difference betwixt what's good
And what is not. No, gentle Bassareu,
I will not force thee; nor betray to view
Thy vine-clad parts; suppress thy Thracian hollow
And dismal din, which blind self-love doth follow,
And glory-puffing heads with empty worth,
And a glass bosom, pouring secrets forth.

Sir Richard Fanshawe (1652)

19

Yes! I am caught, my melting soul
To Venus bends without control,
   I pour th'empassioned sigh.
Ye gods! what throbs my bosom move,
Responsive to the glance of Love,
   That beams from Stella's eye.

O how divinely fair that face,
And what a sweet resistless grace
   On every feature dwells;

　　　et versis animosum equis
Parthum dicere nec quae nihil attinent.
　　　hic vivum mihi caespitem, hic
verbenas, pueri, ponite turaque
　　　bimi cum patera meri: 15
mactata veniet lenior hostia.

XX

Vile potabis modicis Sabinum
cantharis, Graeca quod ego ipse testa
conditum levi, datus in theatro
　　　cum tibi plausus,

care Maecenas eques, ut paterni   5
fluminis ripae simul et iocosa
redderet laudes tibi Vaticani
　　　montis imago.

Caecubum et prelo domitam Caleno
tum bibes uvam: mea nec Falernae   10
temperant vites neque Formiani
　　　pocula colles.

And on those features all the while,
The softness of each frequent smile,
   Her sweet good nature tells.

O Love! I'm thine, no more I sing
Heroic deeds – the sounding string
   Forgets its wonted strains;
For ought but Love the lyre's unstrung,
Love melts and trembles on my tongue
   And thrills in every vein.

Invoking the propitious skies,
The green-sod altar let us rise;
   Let holy incense smoke.
And if we pour the sparkling wine,
Sweet gentle peace may still be mine;
   This gentle chain be broke.

Thomas Chatterton (1803)

20

There's Sabine for you, when you come this way,
   In sober country tankards – nothing grand,
   But sealed with my own hand
In a Greek pitcher, on that famous day,

Dear knight Maecenas, when the playhouse rose
   To greet you, and your father Tiber's shore
   Sent back the joyful roar,
While the gay Vatican echo shrilled applause.

Then Caecuban to follow, if you will,
   Or else Calenian; I do not run
   To old Falernian,
Or the rich oozings of the Formian hill.

Sir Edward Marsh (1941)

XXI

Dianam tenerae dicite virgines,
intonsum, pueri, dicite Cynthium
    Latonamque supremo
      dilectam penitus Iovi.

vos laetam fluviis et nemorum coma, 5
quaecumque aut gelido prominet Algido
    nigris aut Erymanthi
      silvis aut viridis Cragi.

vos Tempe totidem tollite laudibus
natalemque, mares, Delon Apollinis, 10
    insignemque pharetra
      fraternaque umerum lyra.

hic bellum lacrimosum, hic miseram famem
pestemque a populo et principe Caesare in
    Persas atque Britannos 15
      vestra motus aget prece.

21

Virgins, sing the Virgin Huntress;
   Youths, the youthful Phoebus, sing;
Sing Latona, she who bore them
   Dearest to the eternal King.

Sing the heavenly maid who roves
   Joyous, through the mountain groves;
She who winding waters loves;
   Let her haunts her praises ring!

Sing the vale of Peneus' river;
   Sing the Delian deity;
The shoulder glorious with its quiver,
   And the lyre of Mercury.

From our country, at our prayer –
   Famine, plague, and tearful war
These, benign, shall drive afar
   To Persia's plains or Britain's sea.

Patrick Branwell Brontë (1840)

XXII

Integer vitae scelerisque purus
non eget Mauris iaculis neque arcu
nec venenatis gravida sagittis,
    Fusce, pharetra,

sive per Syrtis iter aestuosas   5
sive facturus per inhospitalem
Caucasum vel quae loca fabulosus
    lambit Hydaspes.

namque me silva lupus in Sabina,
dum meam canto Lalagen et ultra   10
terminum curis vagor expeditis,
    fugit inermem,

quale portentum neque militaris
Daunias latis alit aesculetis
nec Iubae tellus generat, leonum   15
    arida nutrix.

pone me pigris ubi nulla campis
arbor aestiva recreatur aura,
quod latus mundi nebulae malusque
    Iuppiter urget;   20

pone sub curru nimium propinqui
solis in terra domibus negata:
dulce ridentem Lalagen amabo,
    dulce loquentem.

22

The man, my friend, whose conscious heart
   With virtue's sacred ardour glows,
Nor taints with death th' envenomed dart,
   Nor needs the guard of Moorish bows.

O'er icy Caucasus he treads,
   Or torrid Afric's faithless sands
Or where the famed Hydaspes spreads
   His liquid wealth through barbarous lands.

For while in Sabine forests charmed
   By Lalage, too far I strayed,
Me – singing careless and unarmed –
   A furious wolf approached – and fled.

No beast more dreadful ever stained
   Apulia's spacious wilds with gore,
No beast more fierce Numidia's land
   (The lion's thirsty parent) bore.

Place me where no soft summer gale
   Among the quivering branches sighs,
Where clouds condensed for ever veil
   With horrid gloom the frowning skies.

Place me beneath the burning zone,
   A clime denied to human race,
My flame for Lalage I'll own;
   Her voice, her smiles, my song shall grace.

Samuel Johnson (1743)

XXIII

Vitas inuleo me similis, Chloe,
quaerenti pavidam montibus aviis
    matrem non sine vano
        aurarum et siluae metu.

nam seu mobilibus veris inhorruit   5
adventus foliis seu virides rubum
    dimovere lacertae,
        et corde et genibus tremit.

atqui non ego te tigris ut aspera
Gaetulusve leo frangere persequor: 10
    tandem desine matrem
        tempestiva sequi viro.

XXIV

Quis desiderio sit pudor aut modus
tam cari capitis? praecipe lugubris
cantus, Melpomene, cui liquidam pater
    vocem cum cithara dedit.

ergo Quintilium perpetuus sopor   5
urget! cui Pudor et Iustitiae soror,
incorrupta Fides, nudaque Veritas
    quando ullum inveniet parem?

multis ille bonis flebilis occidit,
nulli flebilior quam tibi, Vergili.   10
tu frustra pius heu non ita creditum
    poscis Quintilium deos.

23

You shun me, Chloe, like a fawn
That on the wild untrodden screes
Seeks her shy mother, startled if a breeze
Rustles among the trees;
For if the first faint shivering dawn
Of earliest spring
Sets the young leaves a-whispering,
Or the green lizards shake
A bramble in the brake,
She stands with knocking heart and trembling knees.

Yet no fierce tiger I, dear child,
No lion from the Libyan wild
In hot pursuit to seize
And crunch you – quit at last your mother's side!
'Tis time you were a bride.

Sir Edward Marsh (1941)

24

Oh! what shall check our sorrowing
    Above the grave of one so dear?
Melpomene! descend, and bring
Thy godgiven lyre, whose solemn string
    Alone, 'tis meet for us to hear.

Why does the eternal sleep of death
    Compose Quintilius in its reign?
And Truth, and modesty, and faith
Unstained by taint of earthly breath –
    When shall they see his like again!

With tears his ashes good men mourn
    And none – my Virgil, more than thee!
Who weariest heaven for their return
From the dread darkness of their urn;
    A joy – alas! Forbidden to be!

quid si Threicio blandius Orpheo
auditam moderere arboribus fidem,
num vanae redeat sanguis imagini,   15
    quam virga semel horrida,

non lenis precibus fata recludere,
nigro compulerit Mercurius gregi?
durum: sed levius fit patientia
    quidquid corrigere est nefas.   20

XXV

Parcius iunctas quatiunt fenestras
iactibus crebris iuvenes protervi,
nec tibi somnos adimunt, amatque
    ianua limen,

quae prius multum facilis movebat   5
cardines; audis minus et minus iam
'me tuo longas pereunte noctes,
    Lydia, dormis?'

invicem moechos anus arrogantis
flebis in solo levis angiportu,   10
Thracio bacchante magis sub inter-
    lunia vento,

cum tibi flagrans amor et libido,
quae solet matres furiare equorum,
saeviet circa iecur ulcerosum,   15
    non sine questu

Though thou couldst move a Thracian wood
  With song more sweet than Orpheus' strain,
Thou couldst not bid the frozen blood
Through the cold veins to pour its flood;
  Or call the buried back again:

For Mercury, in a shadowy train
  Impells them downward – deaf to prayer:
'Tis hard – but know, when we complain –
That, which to strive against were vain,
  Patience will make us bear!

Patrick Branwell Brontë (1840)

25

The bloods and bucks of this lewd town
  No longer shake your windows down
    With knocking:

Your door stands still, no more you hear
  'I die for you, o Lydia dear',
    Love's god your slumber rocking.

Forsaken, in some narrow lane
  You in your turn will loud complain,
    Gallants no more engaging:

Whilst north winds roar, and lust, whose pow'r
  Makes madding mares the meadows scour
    Is in your bosom raging.

You're griev'd, and quite eat up with spleen,
  That ivy and sweet myrtle green
    Young men alone long after;

laeta quod pubes hedera virenti
gaudeat pulla magis atque myrto,
aridas frondis hiemis sodali
    dedicet Hebro.　　　　　　　　　　20

XXVI

Musis amicus tristitiam et metus
tradam protervis in mare Creticum
    portare ventis, quis sub Arcto
      rex gelidae metuatur orae,

quid Tiridaten terreat, unice　　　　　　　5
securus. o quae fontibus integris
    gaudes, apricos necte flores,
      necte meo Lamiae coronam,

Piplei dulcis! nil sine te mei
prosunt honores: hunc fidibus novis,　　　10
    hunc Lesbio sacrare plectro
      teque tuasque decet sorores.

And that away they dried leaves throw,
   And let them down the river go
      With laughter.

The Young Gentlemen of Mr Rule's Academy at Islington
(1766)

26

To the wave and the wind, while the muses are kind,
   My cares and my sorrows I'll fling;
Nor e'er with the question will trouble my mind
   Of the snow-covered north, who is king:
Or what is the dread, o'er the Parthian's head –
   That the shades of misfortune may bring.

O, Goddess divine, the first of the Nine,
   Who lovest the fountain clear,
A garland of spring's sweetest offerings twine
   For the brows of my Lamia dear,
Since oh! without Thee honour to me
   Nor pleasure nor profit can bear!

Thou and thy sisters, his praises to sing,
Once more awaken the Lesbian string!

Patrick Branwell Brontë (1840)

XXVII

Natis in usum laetitiae scyphis
pugnare Thracum est: tollite barbarum
   morem, verecundumque Bacchum
     sanguineis prohibete rixis.

vino et lucernis Medus acinaces   5
immane quantum discrepat: impium
   lenite clamorem, sodales,
     et cubito remanete presso.

vultis severi me quoque sumere
partem Falerni? dicat Opuntiae   10
   frater Megillae, quo beatus
     vulnere, qua pereat sagitta.

cessat voluntas? non alia bibam
mercede. quae te cumque domat Venus,
   non erubescendis adurit   15
     ignibus, ingenuoque semper

amore peccas. quidquid habes, age
depone tutis auribus. a! miser,
   quanta laborabas Charybdi,
     digne puer meliore flamma.   20

quae saga, quis te solvere Thessalis
magus venenis, quis poterit deus?
   vix illigatum te triformi
     Pegasus expediet Chimaera.

27

My friends, across the joyous bowl
  'Tis barbarous to fight;
Expel such customs from the soul,
  Nor shame with such a sight
Of mutual brawling blows and blood,
The presence of the modest god.

The dashing cup and lighted hall
  With arms but ill agree;
So cease at once that impious brawl,
  And sit content with me.
Say – would you have me drain tonight
The heady cup that shines so bright?

And let Megilla's brother tell
  From whence the arrow flew,
And struck by whose bright eyes he fell,
  Come, let him tell me true:
Does he from such confession shrink? –
Nay – on no other terms I'll drink.

Whatever heart thine own inspire, –
  Thou needst not blush to me –
I know thou ownst a noble fire,
  And lovest generously:
So what thou feelest – hopes, or fears,
Disclose them all to faithful ears.

Ah! hapless youth! I feel thy state;
  If there thy passions rove;
Ah, worthy of a happier fate –
  A more requited love!
In what a wild Charybdis tossed
Blindly loving! early lost!

XXVIII

Te maris et terrae numeroque carentis harenae
　　mensorem cohibent, Archyta,
pulveris exigui prope litus parva Matinum
　　munera, nec quicquam tibi prodest
aerias temptasse domos animoque rotundum　　　　　5
　　percurrisse polum morituro.
occidit et Pelopis genitor, conviva deorum,
　　Tithonusque remotus in auras,
et Iovis arcanis Minos admissus, habentque
　　Tartara Panthoiden iterum Orco　　　　　　　10
demissum, quamvis clipeo Troiana refixo
　　tempora testatus nihil ultra
nervos atque cutem morti concesserat atrae,
　　iudice te non sordidus auctor
naturae verique. sed omnis una manet nox　　　　15
　　et calcanda semel via leti.
dant alios Furiae torvo spectacula Marti;
　　exitio est avidum mare nautis;
mixta senum ac iuvenum densentur funera; nullum
　　saeva caput Proserpina fugit.　　　　　　　20
me quoque devexi rapidus comes Orionis
　　Illyricis Notus obruit undis.
at tu, nauta, vagae ne parce malignus harenae
　　ossibus et capiti inhumato
particulam dare: sic, quodcumque minabitur Eurus　　25
　　fluctibus Hesperiis, Venusinae

What skilful witch can free thine heart
   From deadlier witchery?
What wizard with Thessalian art –
   What god can rescue thee?
For thee scarce Pegasus could bear
From such a dire Chimera's snare.

                      Patrick Branwell Brontë (1840)

28

Archytas, thou, whose spirit, Sea and Land
   With unbeclouded gaze hast wandered o'er,
Liest, mouldering 'neath a scanty heap of sand
   In unknown burial, on Apulia's shore.

Nor aught avails if now that thou couldst trace
   With master mind the mansions of the sky;
Nor that thy thoughts explored all nature's face,
   Since – fashioned mortal – thou wert doomed to die.

So fell the man who shared the feasts of heaven;
   So passed Tithonus from our world below;
So perished Minos, unto whom 'twas given
   The secret counsels of heaven's king to know;

So deeps of Tartarus Euphorbus hold,
   Though teaching nought but body bows to death
By the famed shield, that Trojan warfare told,
   Yet he himself twice o'er resigned his breath:

No mean explorer – he, of moral lore,
   Nor lightly learnèd in the ways of God:
But – one dread midnight looms our sight before;
   One path of death must once by all be trod.

Some shed their life blood on the battle plain;
   Some sleep, unwaking, 'neath the ocean swell;
Thickens, of old and young, the funeral train;
   No head can scape the cruel queen of hell.

plectantur silvae te sospite, multaque merces
    unde potest tibi defluat aequo
ab Iove Neptunoque sacri custode Tarenti.
    neglegis immeritis nocituram   30
postmodo te natis fraudem committere? fors et
    debita iura vicesque superbae
te maneant ipsum: precibus non linquar inultis,
    teque piacula nulla resolvent.
quamquam festinas, non est mora longa: licebit   35
    iniecto ter pulvere curras.

XXIX

Icci, beatis nunc Arabum invides
gazis, et acrem militiam paras
    non ante devictis Sabaeae
        regibus, horribilique Medo

nectis catenas? quae tibi virginum   5
sponso necato barbara serviet?
    puer quis ex aula capillis
        ad cyathum statuetur unctis,

doctus sagittas tendere Sericas
arcu paterno? quis neget arduis   10
    pronos relabi posse rivos
        montibus et Tiberim reverti,

cum tu coemptos undique nobilis
libros Panaeti Socraticam et domum
    mutare loricis Hiberis,   15
        pollicitus meliora, tendis?

Me, too, tempestuous winds that oversweep
 Illyria's waters, whelmed beneath the main;
So, sailor, stop! a little sand to heap
 O'er my poor relics, beat by wind and rain:

That so may heaven, whenever storms o'erblow
 Venusia's forests, or Hesperia's sea,
Preserve, and bid unbounded riches flow
 By Jove, and guardian Neptune showered on thee.

But if, neglectingly, thou'lt pass me by,
 Thy guiltless children for thy guilt shall pay,
Nor all the pomp of future piety
 Avail to wash their fathers' fault away:
 I would not stay thee – I would only pray
That thrice, a little sand thou'dst scatter o'er my clay.

Patrick Branwell Brontë (1840)

29

Iccius, shall Arabian treasures
 Tempt thee with their charms?
Wilt thou fly from peaceful pleasures,
 And arouse to arms?
Chains and slavery wilt thou bring
To the East's unconquered King;
Or the Mede whom, combating,
 Danger only warms?

Who's the Maid thou'lt snatch, lamenting
 O'er her lover gone;
Soft relenting – soon consenting
 To be thine alone?
Who shall be the bright-haired boy
Waiting with thy cup of joy,
And, like his father, skilled to employ
 The arms to China known?

XXX

O Venus, regina Cnidi Paphique,
sperne dilectam Cypron et vocantis
ture te multo Glycerae decoram
 transfer in aedem.

fervidus tecum puer et solutis   5
Gratiae zonis properentque Nymphae
et parum comis sine te Iuventas
 Mercuriusque.

Who'll deny that torrents, rushing,
   To their fountains flow;
Tiber's waters upward gushing
   From the plains below,
When – designed for nobler pride –
Thou thy learning layest aside,
Books exchanging, to provide
   War's untutored show?

Patrick Branwell Brontë (1840)

30

Venus, o queen of Cnidos and of Paphos,
Spurn thy loved Cyprus – here transfer thy presence:
Decked is the fane to which, with incense lavish,
   Glycera calls thee.

Bring with thee, glowing rosy red, the Boy-god,
Nymphs and loose-girdled Graces, and if wanting
Thee, wanting charm – bring Youth, nor let persuasive
   Mercury fail us.

Edward Bulwer-Lytton, Lord Lytton (1869)

XXXI

Quid dedicatum poscit Apollinem
vates? quid orat de patera novum
   fundens liquorem? non opimae
     Sardiniae segetes feraces,

non aestuosae grata Calabriae   5
armenta, non aurum aut ebur Indicum,
   non rura quae Liris quieta
     mordet aqua taciturnus amnis.

premant Calenam falce quibus dedit
fortuna vitem, dives et aureis   10
   mercator exsiccet culullis
     vina Syra reparata merce,

dis carus ipsis, quippe ter et quater
anno revisens aequor Atlanticum
   impune. me pascunt olivae,   15
     me cichorea levesque malvae.

frui paratis et valido mihi,
Latoe, dones, at precor, integra
   cum mente, nec turpem senectam
     degere nec cithara carentem.   20

31

What shall the pious poet pray
Upon the dedication day;
What vow prefer to this Phoebean shrine,
While from the bowl he pours the first-fruits of his wine?

Not the rich crop Sardinia yields,
Nor of Calabria's sunny fields
The herds I ask, nor elephants nor gold,
Nor grounds of which still Liris leaves the tale untold.

Let the Calenian grape be press'd
By those whom fortune has possess'd;
Let the rich merchant in gold cups exhaust
The wine which to replace his Syrian venture cost:

Dear to the Gods, since thrice or more
In one year he can travel o'er
Th'Atlantic sea undamaged, while with me
Sweet olives, mallows light, and chicory agree.

Grant, God of song, this humble lot:
But to enjoy what I have got.
And, I beseech thee, keep my mind entire
In age without disgust, and with the cheerful lyre.

Christopher Smart (1767)

XXXII

Poscimur. si quid vacui sub umbra
lusimus tecum, quod et hunc in annum
vivat et pluris, age dic Latinum,
    barbite, carmen,

Lesbio primum modulate civi,   5
qui ferox bello, tamen inter arma
sive iactatam religarat udo
    litore navim,

Liberum et Musas Veneremque et illi
semper haerentem puerum canebat   10
et Lycum nigris oculis nigroque
    crine decorum.

o decus Phoebi et dapibus supremi
grata testudo Iovis, o laborum
dulce lenimen, mihi cumque salve   15
    rite vocanti.

XXXIII

Albi, ne doleas plus nimio memor
immitis Glycerae neu miserabilis
decantes elegos, cur tibi iunior
    laesa praeniteat fide,

insignem tenui fronte Lycorida   5
Cyri torret amor, Cyrus in asperam
declinat Pholoen; sed prius Apulis
    iungentur capreae lupis,

32

Lute, from my idle meditation
   If you can mould a measure fit
To live but half a generation,
   Speak, lute, and make a song of it.

The lute delighted Troubadours,
   In battle bold, between their tourneys,
And Captains wrecked on rocky shores,
   Refitting ship for further journeys.

They sang the praise of Song and Wine
   And Love, and Love's impatient Boy.
'Black eyes,' they sang, 'How bright they shine,'
   And 'Raven locks engender Joy.'

Apollo loved the lute, and Jove
   To grace his feasts ordained the lute
That lightens labour. Lute, reprove
   My idle moods, and be not mute.

Lewis Evelyn Gielgud (1951)

33

Away, away fond fool, what, dost thou sigh
   Because thy mistress thee forsakes,
   And in thy room another takes?
Is this the cause of all thy whining poetry?

Pox on't, forbear, for it is ten to one
   That he, whom now she loves, will be
   Slighted ere long as much as thee,
and 'tis no more than what a thousand else have done.

quam turpi Pholoe peccet adultero.
sic visum Veneri, cui placet imparis   10
formas atque animos sub iuga aenea
    saevo mittere cum ioco.

ipsum me melior cum peteret Venus,
grata detinuit compede Myrtale
libertina, fretis acrior Hadriae   15
    curvantis Calabros sinus.

XXXIV

Parcus deorum cultor et infrequens
insanientis dum sapientiae
    consultus erro, nunc retrorsum
        vela dare atque iterare cursus

cogor relictos: namque Diespiter,   5
igni corusco nubila dividens
    plerumque, per purum tonantis
        egit equos volucremque currum,

quo bruta tellus et vaga flumina,
quo Styx et invisi horrida Taenari   10
    sedes Atlanteusque finis
        concutitur. valet ima summis

mutare et insignem attenuat deus,
obscura promens; hinc apicem rapax
    fortuna cum stridore acuto   15
        sustulit, hic posuisse gaudet.

Were it my case, I swear: the wolf and lamb
   Should sooner down together lie,
   Than e'er it should be said that I
Once courted her again; let her go and be damn'd.

Love is a witch, 'tis true, which oft times doth
   Persons of different humours tie
   Together most unequally,
To the great discontent and slavery of both.

But yet I'll have the lass that's fair and free,
   'Twixt whose embracing arms I may
   Wanton as doth the rivers play
Between their banks: 'tis such a one is fit for me.

Richard Newcourt (1680)

34

I that have seldom worshipped Heav'n,
As to a mad sect too much giv'n,
My former ways am forced to balk,
And after the old Light to walk.

For cloud-dividing, lightning-Jove
Through a clear firmament late drove
His thund'ring horses and swift wheels,
With which supporting Atlas reels;

With which earth, seas, the Stygian lake
And Hell with all her Furies, quake.
It shook me too. God pulls the proud
From his high seat, and from their cloud

Draws the obscure; levels the hills,
And with their earth the valleys fills.
'Tis all He does, He does it all:
Yet this blind mortals fortune call.

Sir Richard Fanshawe (1652)

XXXV

O diva, gratum quae regis Antium,
praesens vel imo tollere de gradu
   mortale corpus vel superbos
      vertere funeribus triumphos,

te pauper ambit sollicita prece   5
ruris colonus, te dominam aequoris
   quicumque Bithyna lacessit
      Carpathium pelagus carina.

te Dacus asper, te profugi Scythae,
urbesque gentesque et Latium ferox   10
   regumque matres barbarorum et
      purpurei metuunt tyranni,

iniurioso ne pede proruas
stantem columnam, neu populus frequens
   ad arma cessantis, ad arma   15
      concitet imperiumque frangat.

te semper anteit serva Necessitas,
clavos trabalis et cuneos manu
   gestans aena, nec severus
      uncus abest liquidumque plumbum.   20

te Spes et albo rara Fides colit
velata panno, nec comitem abnegat,
   utcumque mutata potentis
      veste domos inimica linquis.

at vulgus infidum et meretrix retro   25
periura cedit, diffugiunt cadis
   cum faece siccatis amici
      ferre iugum pariter dolosi.

35

Goddess of Antium, mighty to raise
The lowly aloft, or the high to abase;
Mighty the pomp of a Triumph to turn
To the darkness and dust of the funeral urn;

Mighty to govern the land or the sea;
Alike the poor husbandman prays unto thee,
And the sailor, whose vessel afar from home,
Drives through the dangers of ocean's foam:

The Dacian and Scythian, the city and plain,
Rome the victorious, and Monarchs who reign
O'er hordes of barbarians – and Tyrants of pride,
To thee would do reverence – with thee would abide!

The column still standing – Oh! do not o'erwhelm;
Nor waken to war with a weary realm
The nations, whose swords are scarce cold in their sheath,
Lest they threaten our Empire with danger and death.

Before thee stalks Fate to obey thy command,
With the engines of death in her brazen hand –
Wedges and hooks for torments dread,
And the iron spike, and the molten lead.

Hope and faith, rarely seen, clothed in white, hover near
    thee
And cheerfully follow, and steadfast revere thee,
When, altered in aspect, thou hastest away
From the Halls of the great, to the haunts of decay:

But the perjured wanton, and faithless crowd
Fly from the friendship they recently vowed;
And the friends, when the gold and the goblet are gone,
Leave the dregs to their host, from his poverty flown.

serves iturum Caesarem in ultimos
orbis Britannos et iuvenum recens   30
   examen Eois timendum
      partibus Oceanoque rubro.

eheu, cicatricum et sceleris pudet
fratrumque. quid nos dura refugimus
   aetas? quid intactum nefasti   35
      liquimus? unde manum iuventus

metu deorum continuit? quibus
pepercit aris? o utinam nova
   incude diffingas retusum in
      Massagetas Arabasque ferrum!   40

XXXVI

   Et ture et fidibus iuvat
placare et vituli sanguine debito
      custodes Numidae deos,
qui nunc Hesperia sospes ab ultima
      caris multa sodalibus,   5
nulli plura tamen dividit oscula
      quam dulci Lamiae, memor
actae non alio rege puertiae
      mutataeque simul togae.
Cressa ne careat pulchra dies nota,   10
      neu promptae modus amphorae,
neu morem in Salium sit requies pedum,
      neu multi Damalis meri
Bassum Threicia vincat amystide,
      neu desint epulis rosae   15
neu vivax apium neu breve lilium.
      omnes in Damalin putris
deponent oculos, nec Damalis novo
      divelletur adultero
lascivis hederis ambitiosior.   20

Fortune! be watchful in Britain, afar,
Over Caesar, departed again to war;
And shine on our soldiers, a terrible band
To the far off east, and the Red sea strand.

Alas how disgraceful! when brother 'gainst brother
Deals blows that his arm should have dealt on another!
What crimes have we shunned in this iron time?
Forborne from what sacrilege? fled from what crime?

From what blood, for what god did our people refrain?
Or shrink from polluting what altar or fane?
Great Goddess! our blunted swords sharpen once more
Not in *our own* but our *Foemen's* gore!

Patrick Branwell Brontë (1840)

36

Incense hither bring,
And tune the joyful string,
And with offerings please the powers who Numida defend,
For his safe return again
From western wilds of Spain,
To greet and to be greeted by each long dissevered friend.

And he'll none more gladly see
Than, dearest Lamia, thee!
Whose life with his – together taught – from infancy did twine:
So mark this day with white;
And whirl in dances light;
Nor a brimming glass forget to pass of soul-awakening wine!

Nor let jovial Bassus yield
To Damalis the field,
Though seasoned well and skilled the Thracian cup to drain;
Nor let the lily fair,
Or the rose, be wanting there;
With long lived parsley blooming above the festal train:

XXXVII

Nunc est bibendum, nunc pede libero
pulsanda tellus, nunc Saliaribus
   ornare pulvinar deorum
      tempus erat dapibus, sodales.

antehac nefas depromere Caecubum   5
cellis avitis, dum Capitolio
   regina dementis ruinas
      funus et imperio parabat

contaminato cum grege turpium
morbo virorum, quidlibet impotens   10
   sperare fortunaque dulci
      ebria. sed minuit furorem

vix una sospes navis ab ignibus,
mentemque lymphatam Mareotico
   redegit in veros timores   15
      Caesar ab ltalia volantem

remis adurgens, accipiter velut
mollis columbas aut leporem citus
   venator in campis nivalis
      Haemoniae, daret ut catenis   20

fatale monstrum; quae generosius
perire quaerens nec muliebriter
   expavit ensem nec latentis
      classe cita reparavit oras;

While wanders every eye
    In hot idolatry
On Damalis, all else in beauty conquering,
    But whom nothing can remove
    From her new awakened love;
Fixed faster than the ivy boughs that round the oak trees cling.

Patrick Branwell Brontë (1840)

37

Now, comrades, to drink deep,
Now with free foot to beat the ground,
Now with rich feasts and goblets crowned
The tables of the Gods to heap!
Before this hour, it had been sin
To broach our Formian from the long-stored bin,
While with her lewd and leprous crew the Queen,
Drunk with fair fortune, setting never a bound
To vast insensate hope, sat plotting ruin
To Rome's high Capitol, and the undoing
Of Rome's proud empery. But that rage was quenched
When scarce one galleon scaped the flames; and now
Her wits, with Mareotic dazed and drenched,
Cleared, and she knew the truth; for with fast prow
And oars onrushing Caesar drove her back
From the Italian coast, as when a hawk
Drives helpless doves, or on the Haemonian plain
The hunter drives a hare – bent all to chain
The baleful Pest. She, resolute to die
Royally, with no womanish fears
Or craven tears
Blenched from the sword, nor sought to fly
With her swift fleet to any sheltering land,
But viewed with steady eye
Her palace rased; then with unfaltering hand
Grasped the fell snake, as 'twere a festal cup,

ausa et iacentem visere regiam   25
vultu sereno, fortis et asperas
   tractare serpentis, ut atrum
     corpore combiberet venenum,

deliberata morte ferocior,
saevis Liburnis scilicet invidens   30
   privata deduci superbo
     non humilis mulier triumpho.

XXXVIII

Persicos odi, puer, apparatus,
displicent nexae philyra coronae;
mitte sectari, rosa quo locorum
   sera moretur.

simplici myrto nihil allabores   5
sedulus curo: neque te ministrum
dedecet myrtus neque me sub arta
   vite bibentem.

And with her body drank its venom up,
In calm deliberate death too proud
To freight Liburnian galleys, and be shown
In triumph, fallen from her throne,
The mockery of a Roman crowd.

Sir Edward Marsh (1941)

38

Boy, I hate their empty shows,
    Persian garlands I detest,
Bring not me the late-blown rose,
    Lingering after all the rest.

Plainer myrtle pleases me,
    Thus outstretched beneath my vine;
Myrtle more becoming thee,
    Waiting with thy master's wine.

William Cowper (1815)

NOTES TO BOOK ONE

1

Euterpe; **Polyhymnia**: the muses of music and lyric poetry.

2

Pyrrha: and her husband, Deucalion, survived the mythical flood sent by Jupiter to punish mankind.

Proteus' flocks: Proteus was a sea-god, similar to the 'old man of the sea'. His flocks were seals.

Fane (temple) **of Vesta** and **Numa's tower**: prominent buildings in Rome. The priestesses of Vesta, goddess of the hearth, were known as the vestal virgins.

uxorious river: the Tiber was wedded to Ilia, once a vestal virgin, who drowned in the river.

the Persians: Parthians.

casks: helmets.

foot: infantry.

Prince and Father: Augustus took the title *Princeps* in 23 BC and later that of *Father of his Country*.

3

the twin stars: Gemini (Castor and Pollux).

Etesian gales: trade winds.

Hyades: constellation thought to portend rain.

Prometheus: one of the Titans, the son of Iapetus. Stole fire from the gods, and gave it to mankind. See also 1.16.

Daedalus: made wings of wax to enable himself and his son, Icarus, to fly.

Alcides: Hercules, who stole Cerberus, the hound of hell, from the underworld.

4

Olympian Smith: Vulcan.

the Thunderer: Jupiter.

5

votive tablet: sailors surviving shipwreck would set up a temple plaque in thanksgiving to the sea-god, Neptune.

6

Varius: contemporary epic poet.

Agrippa: military commander and close associate of Augustus.

Achilles sulking: the wrath of Achilles is a theme of Homer's *Iliad*.

horrid chronicle of Pelops' line: the catastrophes of the house of Pelops were subjects of classical tragedy.

Caesar: Augustus.

Diomed: Diomedes, bravest, after Achilles, of the Greeks at Troy.

Merion: Meriones, a Greek warrior.

7

Pallas' city: Athens.

Albunea: nymph of a spring and grotto at Tibur.

Anio: tributary of the Tiber, forming a spectacular waterfall near Tibur.

Teucer: Greek warrior from Salamis, from where he was exiled by his father. He founded a new Salamis in Cyprus.

8

Sybaris: from a town of the same name in southern Italy, associated with luxurious living.

Thetis' son: Thetis, mother of Achilles, disguised him in girl's clothing, hoping to prevent his fighting in the Trojan war.

9

Thaliarchus (see Table of Contents): *the name means leader of the feast, master of ceremonies.*

yon mountain: Soracte.

10

God of Atlas' strain: Mercury was the grandson of Atlas.

heavenly Sire: Jupiter.

his cattle thou didst wile: Mercury stole the cattle of the gods from Apollo.

Priam: king of Troy, guided by Mercury, made his way unseen through the Greek camp to recover the body of his son, Hector.

Atrides: the sons of Atreus, Agamemnon and Menelaus, who led the Greek army.

Argive: Greek.

12

Clio: the muse of history.

Helicon: mountain in central Greece sacred to Apollo and the Muses.

Haemus; Pindus: Haemus means Thrace, Pindus was a mountain range in northern Greece.

Alcides: Hercules.

the twins of Leda: Castor and Pollux.

Numa: second king of Rome.

Romulus: legendary founder of Rome.

Brutus: expelled Rome's last king, Tarquin.

Cato: ally of Pompey in the civil war against Julius Caesar. His suicide, after their defeat at the battle of Thapsus (46 BC), was regarded as a noble death in the stoic tradition.

Paulus: consul during Hannibal's invasion of Italy, he died in the catastrophic Roman defeat at Cannae (216 BC).

Regulus: Roman general during the first Punic War. Celebrated in *Odes* 3, 5.

Camillus: defeated the Gauls in 390 BC.

Marcellus: Augustus' nephew and intended successor. He died in 23 BC.

the Julian star: the descendants of Julius Caesar, notably Augustus.

Cynthia: the moon.

Caesar: Augustus.

Seres: the Chinese.

14

thy Pontic sire: timber from the Black Sea coast (Pontus).

Cyclades: a circle of Aegean islands.

15

Nereus: a sea-god.

Ajax, Nestor, Ulysses, Teucer, Stheneleus, Meriones: Greeks prominent in the Trojan war.

Tydides: Diomedes, son of Tydeus.

16

iambics: abusive verse was often written in the iambic metre.

Cybele: an eastern goddess, worshipped with orgiastic rites.

Prometheus: one of the Titans, the son of Iapetus. He created mankind from clay, and then later gave them fire stolen from the gods.

Thyestes: Atreus and his brother Thyestes committed many terrible crimes against each other and took mutual revenge, culminating in Atreus' tricking Thyestes into eating the flesh of his own sons.

17

Faunus: Roman god of forests and the countryside; often identified with the Greek god Pan.

Lyceum: or rather Lycaeus, mountain in Arcadia, the abode of Faunus.

Ustica: a valley near Horace's Sabine farm.

Penelope; Circe: Penelope was Ulysses' faithful wife, Circe the witch who detained him on her island on his return from Troy.

18

Catilus: legendary founder of Tibur.

Erycine: Venus.

Liber, Evous, Bassareus: other names of Bacchus, god of wine.

Lapithes: mythological Thracian tribe.

Sithonians: Thracians, notorious for wild intemperance.

20

Vatican: the Vatican hill.

applause: on Maecenas' recovery from illness.

21

virgin huntress: the goddess Diana.

vale of Peneus' river: the vale of Tempe, in Thessaly.

Delian deity: Apollo.

22

Hydaspes: tributary of the Indus.

Numidia: North Africa.

24

Melpomene: the muse of tragedy.

26

the Parthian: Tiridates.

27

the modest God: Bacchus.

Charybdis: a legendary whirlpool.

Pegasus . . . Chimera: Pegasus was the winged horse from whose back Bellerophon slew the mythical Chimera.

28

Archytas: astronomer and geometrician.

the man who shared the feasts of heaven: Tantalus, who was punished for his presumption by relegation to the underworld, just out of reach of food and drink.

Tithonus: was granted the gift of immortality, but not of agelessness: eventually he withered away.

Minos: was punished by being made a judge in the underworld.

Euphorbus: a Trojan warrior. The philosopher Pythagoras (sixth century BC), who believed in reincarnation, claimed, as proof that he had been Euphorbus in a previous existence, to have recognised Euphorbus' shield. Horace's point is that even Pythagoras was mortal.

Venusia: Horace's birthplace.

Hesperia's sea: Hesperia means 'the western land', and is used both of Italy and Spain. Here probably Spain. 'Hesperia's sea' is the western Mediterranean.

a little sand: until the body was buried, the soul was condemned to wander in limbo and could not be received in the underworld. The scattering of three handfuls of earth constituted formal burial.

31

the dedication day: Augustus dedicated a new temple to Apollo in 28 BC.

Liris: the river dividing Latium from Campania.

35

goddess of Antium: at Antium there was a temple in honour of the goddess Fortuna.

Caesar: Augustus.

37

Mareotic: an Egyptian wine.

Haemonian plain: Thessaly, in northern Greece.

Liburnian galleys: light, rapid galleys, with which Augustus defeated Antony and Cleopatra at Actium (31 BC). They were modelled on the pirate vessels of the Liburni, a tribe in Illyria.

BOOK TWO

I

Motum ex Metello consule civicum
bellique causas et vitia et modos
   ludumque Fortunae gravisque
     principum amicitias et arma

nondum expiatis uncta cruoribus,   5
periculosae plenum opus aleae,
   tractas, et incedis per ignis
     suppositos cineri doloso.

paulum severae Musa tragoediae
desit theatris: mox ubi publicas   10
   res ordinaris, grande munus
     Cecropio repetes cothurno,

insigne maestis praesidium reis
et consulenti, Pollio, curiae,
   cui laurus aeternos honores   15
     Delmatico peperit triumpho.

iam nunc minaci murmure cornuum
perstringis auris, iam litui strepunt,
   iam fulgor armorum fugaces
     terret equos equitumque vultus.   20

audire magnos iam videor duces
non indecoro pulvere sordidos,
   et cuncta terrarum subacta
     praeter atrocem animum Catonis.

Iuno et deorum quisquis amicior   25
Afris inulta cesserat impotens
   tellure victorum nepotes
     rettulit inferias Iugurthae.

1

The civil war from the first seeds,
The causes of it, vices, tides
    Of various chance, and our prime
    Fatal alliance, and the swords

Sheathed, but not yet hung up and oiled,
The quarrels fully reconciled,
    Thou writ'st a work of hazard great,
    And walk'st on embers in deceit-

ful ashes raked. Let thy severe
Tragical muse a while forbear
    The stage: this public task then done,
    Thy buskins high again put on,

Afflicted clients' grand support,
And light to the consulting court;
    Whom thy Dalmatic triumph crowned
    With deathless bays. Hark how the sound

Of thy braced drums awakes old fears,
Thy trumpets tingle in our ears;
    How clattering arms make the horse shog,
    And from the horseman's face the blood.

Now, now amidst the common herd
See the great generals fight, besmeared
    With glorious dust: and quelled, the whole
    World, but unconquered Cato's soul!

Juno and whatever gods
To Africk, friends, yielded to th' odds
    Of Rome; the victors' grandsons made
    A sacrifice to Jugurth's shade.

quis non Latino sanguine pinguior
campus sepulcris impia proelia   30
   testatur auditumque Medis
     Hesperiae sonitum ruinae?

qui gurges aut quae flumina lugubris
ignara belli? quod mare Dauniae
   non decoloravere caedes?   35
     quae caret ora cruore nostro?

sed ne relictis, Musa procax, iocis
Ceae retractes munera neniae,
   mecum Dionaeo sub antro
     quaere modos leviore plectro.   40

What field, manured with Daunian blood,
Shows not in graves our impious feud,
   And the loud crack of Latium's fall,
   Heard to the Babylonian wall?

What lake, what river's ignorant
Of the sad war? What sea with paint
   Of Latin slaughter, is not red?
   What land's not peopled with our dead?

But, wanton Muse, lest leaving toys,
Thou should'st turn odes to elegies,
   Let us in Dioneïan cell
   Seek matter for a lighter quill.

Sir Richard Fanshawe (1652)

II

Nullus argento color est avaris
abdito terris, inimice lamnae
Crispe Sallusti, nisi temperato
    splendeat usu.

vivet extento Proculeius aevo,   5
notus in fratres animi paterni;
illum aget penna metuente solvi
    Fama superstes.

latius regnes avidum domando
spiritum, quam si Libyam remotis   10
Gadibus iungas et uterque Poenus
    serviat uni.

crescit indulgens sibi dirus hydrops,
nec sitim pellit, nisi causa morbi
fugerit venis et aquosus albo   15
    corpore languor.

redditum Cyri solio Phraaten
dissidens plebi numero beatorum
eximit Virtus, populumque falsis
    dedocet uti   20

vocibus, regnum et diadema tutum
deferens uni propriamque laurum,
quisquis ingentis oculo irretorto
    spectat acervos.

2

Crispus Sallustius, no colour shines
    In treasure until put to temperate use.
You are against ore hidden in the mines
    That grudge to let it loose.

Lives Proculeius to a distant day,
    Kind to his brothers, even as a sire:
Fame on her wings will carry him away,
    Which will not ever tire.

By curbing natural greed more wide you'll reign
    Than if you should join Libya to Cadiz
And both the Carthages should appertain
    To your dependencies.

The dreadful dropsy by indulgence grows.
    One cannot drive out thirst until the cause
Of the disease from the pale body goes
    And lethargy withdraws.

Virtue, dissenting from the populace,
    Excludes Phraates from the fortunate,
Though seated on the throne whose glories trace
    From Cyrus; no false prate

She teaches, and she gives the diadem,
    The sceptre and the laurel, to the man
Who can see heaped-up treasuries, and them
    With unmoved vision scan.

Lord Dunsany (1947)

III

Aequam memento rebus in arduis
servare mentem, non secus in bonis
   ab insolenti temperatam
     laetitia, moriture Delli,

seu maestus omni tempore vixeris, 5
seu te in remoto gramine per dies
   festos reclinatum bearis
     interiore nota Falerni.

quo pinus ingens albaque populus
umbram hospitem consociare amant 10
   ramis? quid obliquo laborat
     lympha fugax trepidare rivo?

huc vina et unguenta et nimium brevis
flores amoenae ferre iube rosae,
   dum res et aetas et sororum 15
     fila trium patiuntur atra.

cedes coemptis saltibus et domo
villaque flavus quam Tiberis lavit;
   cedes, et exstructis in altum
     divitiis potietur heres. 20

divesne prisco natus ab Inacho
nil interest an pauper et infima
   de gente sub divo moreris,
     victima nil miserantis Orci.

omnes eodem cogimur, omnium 25
versatur urna serius ocius
   sors exitura et nos in aeternum
     exsilium impositura cumbae.

3

Be sure, when times are out of joint,
  To keep a level head, and try
To keep a cool one, when things point
  To triumph, Tom. You too must die.

Death waits for all – for men that fret
  Day in, day out, and men that dine
At festal boards in arbours set,
  And drink their toasts in vintage wine.

Here, cedars tall and poplars grey
  Touch branches, mingling shade with shade,
And streams essay to wash away
  The banks their busy currents made,

So let refreshments here be brought
  And lovely, evanescent roses –
For health is nothing, wealth is nought,
  When unrelenting Fate forecloses.

Your towered halls and broad estate
  Will still be there, when you are dead.
The river place you could not wait
  To buy, will be inherited.

The hand of Death no more will spare
  A gentleman of high degree
Than any beggar, poor and bare
  And basely born as base can be.

One end awaits us all. Our fate
  Is fixed. The ferry-boat is sent
To carry all men, soon or late,
  To their perpetual banishment.

Lewis Evelyn Gielgud (1951)

IV

Ne sit ancillae tibi amor pudori,
Xanthia Phoceu, prius insolentem
serva Briseis niveo colore
   movit Achillem;

movit Aiacem Telamone natum   5
forma captivae dominum Tecmessae;
arsit Atrides medio in triumpho
   virgine rapta,

barbarae postquam cecidere turmae
Thessalo victore et ademptus Hector   10
tradidit fessis leviora tolli
   Pergama Grais.

nescias an te generum beati
Phyllidis flavae decorent parentes:
regium certe genus et penatis   15
   maeret iniquos.

crede non illam tibi de scelesta
plebe delectam, neque sic fidelem,
sic lucro aversam potuisse nasci
   matre pudenda.   20

bracchia et vultum teretesque suras
integer laudo; fuge suspicari
cuius octavum trepidavit aetas
   claudere lustrum.

4

To love a serving-maid's no shame:
The white Briseïs did enflame
Her lord, Achilles, and yet none
　　Was prouder known.

Stout Telamonian Ajax proved
His captive's slave; Atrides loved
In midst of all his victories
　　A girl, his prize,

When the barbarian side went down,
And Hector's death rendered the town
Of Troy more easy to be carried,
　　By Grecians wearied.

Knowst thou from whom fair Phyllis springs?
Thou may'st be son-in-law to kings;
She mourns, as one deposed by fate,
　　From regal state.

Believe 't, she was not poorly born:
Phoceus, such faith, so brave a scorn
Of tempting riches, could not come
　　From a base womb.

Her face, round arms and ev'ry limb
I praise unsmit. Suspect not him
On whom love's wild-fire age doth throw
　　Its cooling snow.

Sir Richard Fanshawe (1652)

V

Nondum subacta ferre iugum valet
cervice, nondum munia comparis
 aequare nec tauri ruentis
  in venerem tolerare pondus.

circa virentis est animus tuae   5
campos iuvencae, nunc fluviis gravem
 solantis aestum, nunc in udo
  ludere cum vitulis salicto

praegestientis. tolle cupidinem
immitis uvae: iam tibi lividos   10
 distinguet Autumnus racemos
  purpureo varius colore.

iam te sequetur: currit enim ferox
aetas et illi quos tibi dempserit
 apponet annos: iam proterva   15
  fronte petit Lalage maritum,

dilecta quantum non Pholoe fugax,
non Chloris albo sic umero nitens
 ut pura nocturno renidet
  luna mari, Cnidiusve Gyges,   20

quem si puellarum insereres choro,
mire sagaces falleret hospites
 discrimen obscurum solutis
  crinibus ambiguoque vultu.

5

She cannot yet, with bending submissiveness,
support the yoke, match labouring fellowship,
    or tolerate some bull's torrential
rise and descent in the rites of Venus.

Among the verdant meadows your heifer's mind
finds full contentment: now in the cooling stream
    assuaging heat, now all-intent on
innocent sport with her calf-companions

among the river-sallows. Restrain the lust
for grapes unmellowed. Colourful Autumn soon
    will deck for you those now already
darkening clusters in deepest purple.

She'll soon pursue you (Time, irrestrainably
careering, adds those years he deprives you of
    to hers), and soon with wanton boldness
Lalage also will seek a consort:

she more belov'd than fugitive Pholoë,
than Chloris even, gleaming with shoulders white
    as cloudless moon in still nocturnal
ocean reflected, or Cnidian Gyges,

whose gender, should you place him among the girls,
would baffle guests of sharpest sagacity,
    obscured so well by loosely flowing
locks and a face that were fit for either.

James Blair Leishman (1956)

VI

Septimi, Gadis aditure mecum et
Cantabrum indoctum iuga ferre nostra et
barbaras Syrtis, ubi Maura semper
   aestuat unda,

Tibur Argeo positum colono   5
sit meae sedes utinam senectae,
sit modus lasso maris et viarum
   militiaeque!

unde si Parcae prohibent iniquae,
dulce pellitis ovibus Galaesi   10
flumen et regnata petam Laconi
   rura Phalantho.

ille terrarum mihi praeter omnis
angulus ridet, ubi non Hymetto
mella decedunt viridique certat   15
   baca Venafro,

ver ubi longum tepidasque praebet
Iuppiter brumas, et amicus Aulon
fertili Baccho minimum Falernis
   invidet uvis.   20

ille te mecum loccus et beatae
postulant arces: ibi tu calentem
debita sparges lacrima favillam
   vatis amici.

6

Friend that art ready to go forth with me
    To Gades or the Basques who spurn
Our empire still, or Syrtes' savage sea
    Where Moorish breakers churn;

May Tibur be the home of my old age,
    The town that Argives built of yore;
There would I end this weary pilgrimage
    Of roads and waves and war.

If cruel Fate forbids that goal, I'll seek
    The brook Galaesus, loved resort
Of coated flocks, the land where once the Greek
    Phalanthus held his court.

That nook of earth of all beneath the sky
    Allures me most, whose honey yields
Not to Hymettus, and whose olives vie
    With green Venafran fields;

There Spring is long and softly Winters fall
    By grace of Jove, and Aulon's vine
By Bacchus' blessing envies not at all
    Falernum's famous wine.

They call us both; those happy hills require
    Me and thee too: be there and lend
A tear to drop upon the glowing pyre
    Of me, thy bard and friend.

William Sinclair Marris (1912)

VII

O saepe mecum tempus in ultimum
deducte Bruto militiae duce,
   quis te redonavit Quiritem
    dis patriis Italoque caelo,

Pompei, meorum prime sodalium?   5
cum quo morantem saepe diem mero
   fregi coronatus nitentis
    malobathro Syrio capillos.

tecum Philippos et celerem fugam
sensi relicta non bene parmula,   10
   cum fracta virtus, et minaces
    turpe solum tetigere mento.

sed me per hostis Mercurius celer
denso paventem sustulit aëre:
   te rursus in bellum resorbens   15
    unda fretis tulit aestuosis.

ergo obligatam redde Iovi dapem
longaque fessum militia latus
   depone sub lauru mea, nec
    parce cadis tibi destinatis.   20

oblivioso levia Massico
ciboria exple; funde capacibus
   unguenta de conchis. quis udo
    deproperare apio coronas

curatve myrto? quem Venus arbitrum   25
dicet bibendi? non ego sanius
   bacchabor Edonis: recepto
    dulce mihi furere est amico.

7

O thou with whom I often faced
   The darkest days in Brutus's train,
Who has restored thee undisgraced
   To Roman skies and gods again?

Pompey, of all my comrades king!
   Oft I and thou at drink have beat
The lagging day, with wreaths of spring
   Upon our hair and perfumes sweet.

Philippi's wreck and rout we shared:
   My shield aside I basely thrust;
When even Valour's self despaired,
   And fiercest captains bit the dust.

But nimble Hermes hid me safe
   In thickest mist, and bore me far
From fears and foes: the ebbing wave
   Sucked thee into the surf of war.

Then pay to Jove the bounden feast,
   And stretch beneath my laurel tree
Thy limbs from weary war released
   Nor spare the pitchers nursed for thee.

Fill up the gleaming cups with wine
   That brings repose: let unguents fall
From spacious shells. Who runs to twine
   Soft parsley for our coronal,

Or myrtle? whom will Venus send
   To rule our cups? my madman's mood
Shall match the Bacchant's: when a friend
   Comes home, to play the fool is good.

William Sinclair Marris (1912)

VIII

Ulla si iuris tibi peierati
poena, Barine, nocuisset umquam,
dente si nigro fieres vel uno
    turpior ungui,

crederem. sed tu, simul obligasti   5
perfidum votis caput, enitescis
pulchrior multo iuvenumque prodis
    publica cura.

expedit matris cineres opertos
fallere et toto taciturna noctis   10
signa cum caelo gelidaque divos
    morte carentis.

ridet hoc, inquam, Venus ipsa, rident
simplices Nymphae, ferus et Cupido,
semper ardentis acuens sagittas   15
    cote cruenta.

adde quod pubes tibi crescit omnis,
servitus crescit nova, nec priores
impiae tectum dominae relinquunt,
    saepe minati.   20

te suis matres metuunt iuvencis,
te senes parci, miseraeque nuper
virgines nuptae, tua ne retardet
    aura maritos.

8

Did any punishment attend
    Thy former perjuries,
I should believe, a second time,
    Thy charming flatteries:
Did but one wrinkle mark thy face
Or hadst thou lost one single grace.

No sooner hast thou, with false vows,
    Provoked the powers above;
But thou art fairer than before
    And we are more in love.
Thus Heaven and Earth seem to declare
They pardon falsehood in the fair.

Sure 'tis no crime vainly to swear
    By every power on high,
And call our buried mother's ghost
    A witness to the lie!
Heaven at such perjury connives
And Venus with a smile forgives.

The nymphs and cruel Cupid too,
    Sharp'ning his pointed dart
On an old hone besmeared with blood,
    Forbear thy perjured heart.
Fresh youth grows up to wear thy chains
And the old slave no freedom gains.

Thee, mothers for their eldest sons,
    Thee, wretched misers fear,
Lest thy prevailing beauty should
    Seduce the hopeful heir;
New married virgins fear thy charms
Should keep their bridegrooms from their arms.

Sir Charles Sedley (1701)

IX

Non semper imbres nubibus hispidos
manant in agros aut mare Caspium
    vexant inaequales procellae
       usque, nec Armeniis in oris,

amice Valgi, stat glacies iners   5
mensis per omnis aut Aquilonibus
    querqueta Gargani laborant
       et foliis viduantur orni:

tu semper urges flebilibus modis
Mysten ademptum, nec tibi Vespero   10
    surgente decedunt amores
       nec rapidum fugiente solem.

at non ter aevo functus amabilem
ploravit omnis Antilochum senex
    annos, nec impubem parentes   15
       Troilon aut Phrygiae sorores

flevere semper. desine mollium
tandem querelarum, et potius nova
    cantemus Augusti tropaea
       Caesaris et rigidum Niphaten,   20

Medumque flumen gentibus additum
victis minores volvere vertices,
    intraque praescriptum Gelonos
       exiguis equitare campis.

9

Clouds do not always veil the skies,
 Nor showers immerse the verdant plain;
Nor do the billows always rise,
 No storms afflict the troubled main.

Nor, Valgius, on the Armenian shores,
 Do the chained waters always freeze;
Nor always furious Boreas roars,
 Or bends with violent force the trees.

But you are ever drowned in tears,
 For Mystes dead you ever mourn;
No setting sun can ease your cares,
 But finds you sad at his return.

The wise experienced Grecian sage
 Mourned not Antilochus so long:
Nor did King Priam's hoary age
 So much lament his slaughtered son.

Leave off at length these women's sighs,
 Augustus' num'rous trophies sing;
Repeat that prince's victories
 To whom all nations tribute bring.

Niphates rolls an humbler wave;
 At length th' undaunted Scythian yields,
Content to live the Romans' slave
 And scarce forsakes his native fields.

Samuel Johnson (published 1791)

X

Rectius vives, Licini, neque altum
semper urgendo neque, dum procellas
cautus horrescis, nimium premendo
    litus iniquum.

aptream quisquis mediocritatem   5
diligit, tutus caret obsoleti
sordibus tecti, caret invidenda
    sobrius aula.

saepius ventis agitatur ingens
pinus et celsae graviore casu   10
decidunt turres feriuntque summos
    fulgura montis.

sperat infestis, metuit secundis
alteram sortem bene praeparatum
pectus. informis hiemes reducit   15
    Iuppiter, idem

summovet. non, si male nunc, et olim
sic erit: quondam cithara tacentem
suscitat Musam neque semper arcum
    tendit Apollo.   20

rebus angustis animosus atque
fortis appare; sapienter idem
contrahes vento nimium secundo
    turgida vela.

10

Your ship will steer a straighter course
   If not to deepest channels held
And then, before the tempest's force,
   To hug unfriendly coasts compelled.

The man that loves the Golden Mean,
   Will neither take a tumble-down
Apartment, nor a mansion seen
   With envious eyes by half the Town.

The lightning strikes the highest peaks;
   The tallest towers furthest fall;
The wind that flays the forest seeks
   The loftiest tree-tops first of all.

Hearts well-conditioned hope in days
   Of stress – discount, in plenteous years,
Lean times to come. The scowling face
   Of Winter shows, and disappears,

As pleases Heaven. If things today
   Go ill, they will amend. Apollo
Unstrings at last his bow, to play
   The pleasant tunes the Muses follow.

Be bold of heart, and strong of mind,
   When wave run high – but have the wit
When in your wake a following wind
   Blows fresh, to trim your sails to it.

Lewis Evelyn Gielgud (1951)

XI

Quid bellicosus Cantaber et Scythes,
Hirpine Quincti, cogitet Hadria
   divisus obiecto, remittas
     quaerere, nec trepides in usum

poscentis aevi pauca: fugit retro   5
levis iuventas et decor, arida
   pellente lascivos amores
     canitie facilemque somnum.

non semper idem floribus est honor
vernis, neque uno Luna rubens nitet   10
   vultu: quid aeternis minorem
     consiliis animum fatigas?

cur non sub alta vel platano vel hac
pinu iacentes sic temere et rosa
   canos odorati capillos,   15
     dum licet, Assyriaque nardo

potamus uncti? dissipat Euhius
curas edaces. quis puer ocius
   restinguet ardentis Falerni
     pocula praetereunte lympha?   20

quis devium scortum eliciet domo
Lyden? eburna dic age cum lyra
   maturet in comptum Lacaenae
     more comas religata nodum.

11

What the Cantabrian stout, or Scythian think
Divided with opposèd Adria's brink,
Quintius Hirpinus, do not thou enquire;
Nor for life's use, which little doth desire,

Be thou too careful: smooth-faced youth apace
Doth backward fly, and with it beauty's grace,
Dry agèd hoariness with furrows deep,
Dispelling amorous fires, and gentle sleep.

The summer flowers keep not their native grace,
Nor shines the bright moon with a constant face.
Why dost thou tire thy mind, subordinate
Unto the counsels of eternal fate?

Why under this high plane, or pine-trees's shade
In discomposèd manner, careless laid,
Our hoary hair perfumed with fragrant rose,
And odours, which Assyria doth disclose,

Do we, anointed, not to drink prepare?
Free Bacchus dissipates consuming care:
But oh! what boy, Falernian wines' hot rage
Will soon for me, with gliding streams assuage?

Ah! who retirèd Lyde will require,
Hither to come? Boy, with her ivory lyre
Bid her make haste, and hair to tie not shame,
In careless knot, like a Laconian dame.

Sir Thomas Hawkins (1625)

XII

Nolis longa ferae bella Numantiae
nec durum Hannibalem nec Siculum mare
Poeno purpureum sanguine mollibus
    aptari citharae modis,

nec saevos Lapithas et nimium mero   5
Hylaeum domitosque Herculea manu
Telluris iuvenes, unde periculum
    fulgens contremuit domus

Saturni veteris; tuque pedestribus
dices historiis proelia Caesaris,   10
Maecenas, melius ductaque per vias
    regum colla minacium.

me dulces dominae Musa Licymniae
cantus, me voluit dicere lucidum
fulgentis oculos et bene mutuis   15
    fidum pectus amoribus,

quam nec ferre pedem dedecuit choris
nec certare ioco nec dare bracchia
ludentem nitidis virginibus sacro
    Dianae celebris die.   20

num tu quae tenuit dives Achaemenes
aut pinguis Phrygiae Mygdonias opes
permutare velis crine Licymniae,
    plenas aut Arabum domos,

cum flagrantia detorquet ad oscula   25
cervicem aut facili saevitia negat,
quae poscente magis gaudeat eripi,
    interdum rapere occupet?

12

Prince Hannibal – Numantia's endless war –
Sicilian waves imbrued with Punic gore –
Surely not these the themes you would desire,
    Maecenas, for my gentle lyre,

Nor those fierce Lapiths joined in furious brawls
With drunken Centaurs, nor Alcides armed
Against the Earth-born champions who alarmed
    Old Saturn in his shining halls;

And as for Caesar – you in your great prose
Will tell his battles better, and display
Proud kings with necks enchained, his vanquished foes,
    Led captive down the Sacred Way.

Me the sage Muse assigns an apter part,
To praise your fair Licymnia's radiant eyes,
Her thrilling voice that lifts you to the skies,
    The treasure of her faithful heart;

How all she does becomes her, the swift play
Of parrying wit, the dance of frolic grace
When with the bright-robed girls she takes her place
    To hymn Diana's festal day.

Friend, were you shown the wealth of Persia's heir,
The teeming riches of the Phrygian plain
And stored Arabian castles, would you deign
    To buy them with a single hair

Of her sweet head, when to your burning kisses
She bends her neck, and with a teasing mask
Of soon-surrendered pride denies the blisses
    She craves yet more than you that ask?

Sir Edward Marsh (1941)

XIII

Ille et nefasto te posuit die
quicumque primum, et sacrilega manu
   produxit, arbos, in nepotum
      perniciem opprobriumque pagi;

illum et parentis crediderim sui   5
fregisse cervicem et penetralia
   sparsisse nocturno cruore
      hospitis; ille venena Colcha

et quidquid usquam concipitur nefas
tractavit, agro qui statuit meo   10
   te triste lignum, te caducum
      in domini caput immerentis.

quid quisque vitet numquam homini satis
cautum est in horas: navita Bosphorum
   Poenus perhorrescit neque ultra   15
      caeca timet aliunde fata;

miles sagittas et celerem fugam
Parthi, catenas Parthus et Italum
   robur: sed improvisa leti
      vis rapuit rapietque gentis.   20

quam paene furvae regna Proserpinae
et iudicantem vidimus Aeacum
   sedesque discriptas piorum et
      Aeoliis fidibus querentem

Sappho puellis de popularibus,   25
et te sonantem plenius aureo,
   Alcaee, plectro dura navis,
      dura fugae mala, dura belli!

13

Shame of thy mother-soil! ill nurtured tree!
Set to the mischief of posterity,
That hand (whate'er it were) that was thy nurse
Was sacrilegious sure, or somewhat worse,
Black, as the day was dismal in whose sight
Thy rising top first stained the bashful light.
That man – I think – wrested the feeble life
From his old father; that man's barbarous knife
Conspired with darkness 'gainst the stranger's throat;
(Whereof the blushing walls took bloody note.)
Huge high flown poisons, ev'n of Colchis' breed
And whatso'er wild sins black thoughts do feed,
His hands have paddled in; his hands that found
Thy traitorous root a–dwelling in my ground.
Perfidious totterer! longing for the stains
Of thy kind master's well-deserving brains.
Man's daintiest care and caution cannot spy
The subtile point of his coy destiny
Which way it threats. With fear the merchant's mind
Is ploughed as deep as is the sea with wind
Roused in an angry tempest. Oh, the sea!
Oh, that's his fear! there floats his destiny.
While from another, unseen corner blows
The storm of fate to which his life he owes.
By Parthian's bow the soldier looks to die
(Whose hands are fighting while their feet do fly).
The Parthian starts at Rome's imperial name,
Fledged with her eagle's wing; the very shame
Of his captivity rings in his ears.
Thus, O thus fondly do we pitch our fears
Far distant from our fates, our fates that mock
Our giddy fears with an unlooked-for shock.
A little more and I had surely seen
Thy grisly majesty, Hell's blackest queen,
And Aeacus on his tribunal too,

utrumque sacro digna silentio
mirantur umbrae dicere; sed magis   30
    pugnas et exactos tyrannos
        densum umeris bibit aure vulgus.

quid mirum, ubi illis carminibus stupens
demittit atras belua centiceps
    auris et intorti capillis   35
        Eumenidum recreantur angues?

quin et Prometheus et Pelopis parens
dulci laborem decipitur sono,
    nec curat Orion leones
        aut timidos agitare lyncas.   40

Sifting the souls of guilt; and you, oh you,
You ever-blushing meads, where do the blest
Far from dark horror's home appeal to rest.
There amorous Sappho plains upon her lute
Her love's cross fortune; that the sad dispute
Runs murmuring on the strings. Alcaeus there
In high-built numbers wakes his golden lyre,
To tell the world how hard the matter went,
How hard, by sea, by war, by banishment.
There these brave souls deal to each wond'ring ear,
Such words so precious, as they may not hear
Without religious silence; above all
War's rattling tumults, or some tyrant's fall,
The thronging clotted multitude doth feast,
What wonder, when the hundred-headed beast
Hangs his black lugs, stroaked with those heavenly lines;
The Furies' curl'd snakes meet in gentle twines,
And stretch their cold limbs in a pleasing fire;
Prometheus' self, and Pelops' starvèd sire
Are cheated of their pains: Orion thinks
Of lions now no more, or spotted lynx.

Richard Crashaw (*c*.1640)

XIV

Eheu fugaces, Postume, Postume,
labuntur anni nec pietas moram
   rugis et instanti senectae
     adferet indomitaeque morti:

non si trecenis quotquot eunt dies,   5
amice, places illacrimabilem
   Plutona tauris, qui ter amplum
     Geryonen Tityonque tristi

compescit unda, scilicet omnibus,
quicumque terrae munere vescimur,   10
   enaviganda, sive reges
     sive inopes erimus coloni.

frustra cruento Marte carebimus
fractisque rauci fluctibus Hadriae,
   frustra per autumnos nocentem   15
     corporibus metuemus Austrum:

visendus ater flumine languido
Cocytos errans et Danai genus
   infame damnatusque longi
     Sisyphus Aeolides laboris: 20

linquenda tellus et domus et placens
uxor, neque harum quas colis arborum
   te praeter invisas cupressos
     ulla brevem dominum sequetur:

absumet heres Caecuba dignior   25
servata centum clavibus et mero
   tinget pavimentum superbo,
     pontificum potiore cenis.

14

How swiftly glide our flying years!
Alas! nor piety nor tears
 Can stop the fleeting day;
Deep-furrowed wrinkles, posting age,
And death's unconquerable rage,
 Are strangers to delay.

Though every day a bull should bleed
To Pluto, bootless were the deed,
 The monarch tearless reigns,
Where vulture-tortured Tityus lies,
And triple Geryon's monstrous size
 The gloomy wave detains.

Whoever tastes of earthly food
Is doomed to pass the joyless flood,
 And hear the Stygian roar;
The sceptred king, who rules the earth,
The labouring hind, of humbler birth,
 Must reach the distant shore.

The broken surge of Adria's main,
Hoarse-sounding, we avoid in vain,
 And Mars in blood-stained arms;
The southern blast in vain we fear,
And autumn's life-annoying air
 With idle fears alarms;

For all must see Cocytus flow,
Whose gloomy water sadly slow
 Strays through the dreary soil.
The guilty maids, an ill-famed train!
And, Sisyphus, thy labours vain,
 Condemned to endless toil.

Your pleasing consort must be left,
And you of villas, lands, bereft,
    Must to the shades descend;
The cypress only, hated tree!
Of all thy much-loved groves, shall thee,
    Its short-lived lord, attend.

Then shall your worthier heir discharge,
And set th' imprisoned casks at large,
    And dye the floor with wine,
So rich and precious, not the feasts
Of holy pontiffs cheer their guests
    With liquor more divine.

Philip Francis (1746)

XV

Iam pauca aratro iugera regiae
moles relinquent, undique latius
　　extenta visentur Lucrino
　　　　stagna lacu platanusque caelebs

evincet ulmos; tum violaria et　　　　　　　　　5
myrtus et omnis copia narium
　　spargent olivetis odorem
　　　　fertilibus domino priori;

tum spissa ramis laurea fervidos
excludet ictus. non ita Romuli　　　　　　　　10
　　praescriptum et intonsi Catonis
　　　　auspiciis veterumque norma.

privatus illis census erat brevis,
commune magnum: nulla decempedis
　　metata privatis opacam　　　　　　　　　15
　　　　porticus excipiebat Arcton,

nec fortuitum spernere caespitem
leges sinebant, oppida publico
　　sumptu iubentes et deorum
　　　　templa novo decorare saxo.　　　　　20

15

Soon princely palaces will make
Ploughed acres rare, and ponds will spread
As wide as is the Lucrine lake,
And lindens that no vine has wed

Will rout the elms; while gardens rich
In violet and myrtle pour
A world of scent o'er olives which
Gave elder owners goodly store,

And thickly-matted laurel boughs
Keep out the sun. Ah, other ways
Had Cato wrought and Romulus
In those untidy, good old days!

With them the state was rich, the man
Was poor – he had no colonnade
Set north and stretching many a span
To pamper him with air and shade.

Their laws allowed no man to scorn
The wayside turf for building; stone
The state provided to adorn
The temples and the towns alone.

William Sinclair Marris (1912)

XVI

Otium divos rogat in patenti
prensus Aegaeo, simul atra nubes
condidit lunam neque certa fulgent
    sidera nautis;

otium bello furiosa Thrace,   5
otium Medi pharetra decori,
Grosphe, non gemmis neque purpura ve-
    nale neque auro.

non enim gazae neque consularis
summovet lictor miseros tumultus   10
mentis et curas laqueata circum
    tecta volantis.

vivitur parvo bene, cui paternum
splendet in mensa tenui salinum
nec levis somnos timor aut cupido   15
    sordidus aufert.

quid brevi fortes iaculamur aevo
multa? quid terras alio calentis
sole mutamus? patriae quis exsul
    se quoque fugit?   20

scandit aeratas vitiosa navis
Cura nec turmas equitum relinquit,
ocior cervis et agente nimbos
    ocior Euro.

laetus in praesens animus quod ultra est   25
oderit curare et amara lento
temperet risu: nihil est ab omni
    parte beatum.

16

In storms when clouds the moon do hide,
And no kind stars the pilot guide,
Show me at sea the boldest there
Who does not wish for quiet here.

For quiet, friend, the soldier fights,
Bears weary marches, sleepless nights,
For this feeds hard and lodges cold,
Which can't be bought with hills of gold.

Since wealth and power too weak we find
To quell the tumults of the mind,
Or from the monarch's roofs of state
Drive thence the cares that round him wait,

Happy the man with little blest
Of what his father left possest;
No base desires corrupt his head,
No fears disturb him in his bed.

What then in life which soon must end
Can all our vain designs intend?
From shore to shore why should we run,
When none his tiresome self can shun?

For baneful care will still prevail,
And overtake us under sail,
'Twill dodge the great man's train behind,
Outrun the roe, outfly the wind.

If then thy soul rejoice today,
Drive far tomorrow's cares away,
In laughter let them all be drowned,
No perfect good is to be found.

abstulit clarum cita mors Achillem,
longa Tithonum minuit senectus,   30
et mihi forsan, tibi quod negarit,
    porriget hora.

te greges centum Siculaeque circum
mugiunt vaccae, tibi tollit hinnitum
apta quadrigis equa, te bis Afro   35
    murice tinctae

vestiunt lanae: mihi parva rura et
spiritum Graiae tenuem Camenae
Parca non mendax dedit et malignum
    spernere vulgus.   40

XVII

Cur me querelis exanimas tuis?
nec dis amicum est nec mihi te prius
    obire, Maecenas, mearum
        grande decus columenque rerum

a! te meae si partem animae rapit   5
maturior vis, quid moror altera,
    nec carus aeque nec superstes
        integer? ille dies utramque

ducet ruinam. non ego perfidum
dixi sacramentum: ibimus, ibimus,   10
    utcumque praecedes, supremum
        carpere iter comites parati.

me nec Chimaerae spiritus igneae
nec, si resurgat, centimanus Gyas
    divellet umquam: sic potenti   15
        Iustitiae placitumque Parcis.

One mortal feels fate's sudden blow,
Another's lingering death comes slow,
And what of life they take from thee
The gods may give to punish me.

Thy portion is a wealthy stock,
A fertile glebe, a fruitful flock,
Horses and chariots for thine ease,
Rich robes to deck and make thee please.

For me, a little cell I choose,
Fit for my mind, fit for my Muse,
Which soft content does best adorn,
Shunning the knaves and fools I scorn.

Thomas Otway (1684)

17

Why dost thou talk of dying so?
    Neither the gods nor I'm content,
Maecenas, that thou shouldst first go,
    My pillar and great ornament.

If thee, the one half of my soul,
    A riper fate snatch hence: alas!
What should I stay for, neither whole
    And but the dregs of what I was?

That day shall end us both: Come, come,
    I've sworn't, and will not break it neither.
March when thou wilt to thy long home,
    That journey we will make together.

Chimaera's flames, nor, where he rise
    Again, Briareus' hundred hands,
Should keep me back. 'Tis justice, this,
    And in the Book of Fate it stands.

seu Libra seu me Scorpios aspicit
formidulosus, pars violentior
   natalis horae, seu tyrannus
      Hesperiae Capricornus undae,   20

utrumque nostrum incredibili modo
consentit astrum: te Iovis impio
   tutela Saturno refulgens
      eripuit volucrisque Fati

tardavit alas, cum populus frequens   25
laetum theatris ter crepuit sonum:
   me truncus illapsus cerebro
      sustulerat, nisi Faunus ictum

dextra levasset, Mercurialium
custos virorum. reddere victimas   30
   aedemque votivam memento:
      nos humilem feriemus agnam.

Were I or under Libra born,
   Or Scorpio my ascendant be
With grim aspect, or Capricorn,
   The tyrant of the Latian sea;

Our stars do wondrously consent.
   Benigner Jove repriev'd thy breath
When Saturn was malevolent,
   And clip't the hasty wings of Death,

In frequent Theatre when thee
   Thrice the rejoicing people clap't,
A falling trunk had brainèd me,
   Between if Faunus had not step't,

The guardian of Mercurial men,
   Pay thou an ample sacrifice,
And build the chapel thou vow'dst then;
   For me an humble lambkin dies.

Sir Richard Fanshawe (1652)

XVIII

Non ebur neque aureum
mea renidet in domo lacunar,
　　non trabes Hymettiae
premunt columnas ultima recisas
　　Africa, neque Attali　　　　　　　　　　　5
ignotus heres regiam occupavi,
　　nec Laconicas mihi
trahunt honestae purpuras clientae:
　　at fides et ingeni
benigna vena est, pauperemque dives　　　10
　　me petit: nihil supra
deos lacesso nec potentem amicum
　　largiora flagito,
satis beatus unicis Sabinis.
　　truditur dies die,　　　　　　　　　　　15
novaeque pergunt interire lunae:
　　tu secanda marmora
locas sub ipsum funus et sepulcri
　　immemor struis domos
marisque Bais obstrepentis urges　　　　　20
　　summovere litora,
parum locuples continente ripa.
　　quid quod usque proximos
revellis agri terminos et ultra
　　limites clientium　　　　　　　　　　　25
salis avarus? pellitur paternos
　　in sinu ferens deos
et uxor et vir sordidosque natos.
　　nulla certior tamen
rapacis Orci fine destinata　　　　　　　　30
　　aula divitem manet
erum. quid ultra tendis? aequa tellus
　　pauperi recluditur
regumque pueris, nec satelles Orci
　　callidum Promethea　　　　　　　　　　35

18

No gilded roof nor ivory fret
For splendour in my house is set;
Nor are beams from Hymettus sought
To lie athwart rich columns brought
From Afric; nor I, heir unknown,
Make Attalus his wealth mine own.
No honest tenants' wives you see
Laconian purples weave for me.
A loyal heart and ready vein
Of wit I have, which doth constrain
Rome's richest men to seek the love
Of me, though poor: nor gods above
Do I invoke for larger store;
Nor of Maecenas ask I more.
To me my single Sabine field
Sufficient happiness doth yield.
One day thrusts on another fast,
And new moons to the wane do haste.
When death, perhaps, is near at hand,
Thou fairest marbles dost command
Be cut for use, yet dost neglect
Thy grave and houses still erect:
Nay, would'st abridge the vast sea's shore
Which loudly doth at Baiae roar:
Enrichèd little, less content,
With limits of the continent.
Why often pull'st thou up the bounds
T'enlarge the circuit of thy grounds,
Encroaching far from confines known
To make the neighbouring field thine own?
The husband, wife, and sordid brood,
With ancient household gods, that stood
In quiet peace, must be expelled.
Yet is not any mansion, held
For the rich landlord, so assured

revexit auro captus. hic superbum
    Tantalum atque Tantali
genus coercet, hic levare functum
    pauperem laboribus
vocatus atque non vocatus audit.   40

XIX

Bacchum in remotis carmina rupibus
vidi docentem – credite posteri –
    Nymphasque discentis et auris
      capripedum Satyrorum acutas.

Euhoe, recenti mens trepidat metu   5
plenoque Bacchi pectore turbidum
    laetatur: Euhoe, parce Liber,
      parce gravi metuende thyrso!

fas pervicaces est mihi Thyiadas
vinique fontem lactis et uberes   10
    cantare rivos atque truncis
      lapsa cavis iterare mella:

fas et beatae coniugis additum
stellis honorem tectaque Penthei
    disiecta non leni ruina   15
      Thracis et exitium Lycurgi.

As deep in hell to be immured.
Then whither do you further tend?
The indifferent earth, an equal friend,
As willingly opens her wide womb
For beggar's grave as prince's tomb.
Gold could of Charon not obtain
To bear Prometheus back again.
Proud Tantalus and all his stock
Death, with the bands of fate, doth lock
And, called or not called, ready stands
To free the poor from painful bands.

Sir Thomas Hawkins (1625)

19

In a blind corner jolly Bacchus taught
   The Nymphs and Satyrs poetry,
Myself (a thing scarce to be thought)
   Was at that time a stander-by.

And ever since the whim runs in my head,
   With heav'nly frenzy I'm on fire;
Dear Bacchus, let me not be punishèd
   For raving, when thou did'st inspire.

Ecstatically drunk, I now dare sing
   Thy bigot Thyades, and the source
Whence thy brisk wine, honey and milk did spring,
   Enchannell'd by thy sceptre's force.

Bold as I am, I dare yet higher fly,
   And sing bright Ariadne's crown,
Rejoice to see bold Pentheus' destiny,
   And grave Lycurgus tumbled down.

tu flectis amnis, tu mare barbarum,
tu separatis uvidus in iugis
   nodo coerces viperino
      Bistonidum sine fraude crinis: 20

tu, cum parentis regna per arduum
cohors Gigantum scanderet impia,
   Rhoetum retorsisti leonis
      unguibus horribilique mala;

quamquam choreis aptior et iocis   25
ludoque dictus non sat idoneus
   pugnae ferebaris: sed idem
      pacis eras mediusque belli.

te vidit insons Cerberus aureo
cornu decorum leniter atterens   30
   caudam et recedentis trilingui
      ore pedes tetigitque crura.

Rivers and seas thine empire all obey,
  When thou thy standard dost advance,
Wild mountaineers, thy vassals, trim and gay
  In tune and time stagger and dance.

Thou, when great Jove began to fear his throne
  (In no small danger then he was)
The mighty Rhoetus thou didst piss upon,
  And of that lion mad'st an ass.

'Tis true, thy talent is not war, but mirth;
  The fiddle, not the trumpet, thine;
Yet didst thou bravely lay about thee then,
  Great Moderator, God of wine.

And when to Hell in triumph thou didst ride
  O'er Cerberus thou didst prevail,
The silly cur thee for his master own'd,
  And, like a puppy, wagg'd his tail.

                              Thomas Flatman (1674)

XX

Non usitata nec tenui ferar
penna biformis per liquidum aethera
   vates, neque in terris morabor
     longius, invidiaque maior

urbis relinquam. non ego pauperum   5
sanguis parentum, non ego quem vocas,
   dilecte Maecenas, obibo
     nec Stygia cohibebor unda.

iam iam residunt cruribus asperae
pelles, et album mutor in alitem   10
   superne, nascunturque leves
     per digitos umerosque plumae.

iam Daedaleo notior Icaro
visam gementis litora Bospori
   Syrtisque Gaetulas canorus   15
     ales Hyperboreosque campos.

me Colchus et qui dissimulat metum
Marsae cohortis Dacus et ultimi
   noscent Geloni, me peritus
     discet Hiber Rhodanique potor.   20

absint inani funere neniae
luctusque turpes et querimoniae;
   compesce clamorem ac sepulcri
     mitte supervacuos honores.

20

Now with no weak unballast wing
   A poet double-formed I rise;
From th' envious world with scorn I spring,
   And cut with joy the wond'ring skies.

Though from no princes I descend,
   Yet shall I see the blest abodes,
Yet, great Maecenas, shall your friend
   Quaff nectar with th'immortal Gods.

See! how the mighty change is wrought!
   See how whate'er remained of man
By plumes is veiled; see! quick as thought
   I pierce the clouds a tuneful swan.

Swifter than Icarus I'll fly
   Where Libya's swarthy offspring burns,
And where beneath th' inclement sky
   The hardy Scythian ever mourns.

My works shall propagate my fame,
   To distant realms and climes unknown,
Nations shall celebrate my name
   That drink the Phasis or the Rhone.

Restrain your tears and cease your cries,
   Nor grace with fading flowers my hearse;
I without funeral elegies
   Shall live for ever in my verse.

Samuel Johnson (c.1726)

NOTES TO BOOK TWO

1

Cato: Cato the Younger, who committed suicide after the battle of Thapsus (46 BC; see I, xii).

Juno: tutelary goddess of Carthage.

Jugurth: Jugurtha, a tribal chief in north Africa, long held out against the Romans at the end of the second century BC. Horace means that the Romans killed in Africa during the civil war have appeased Jugurtha's ghost.

Daunian: Latin, or Roman.

in Dioneïan cell: in a grotto sacred to Venus, or love.

2

Proculeius: a contemporary, who divided his property with his two brothers.

both the Carthages: Carthage in north Africa and in southern Spain (Carthagena).

Phraates: king of Parthia, restored to his throne after a period of exile.

Cyrus: the king who united Media and Persia in the 6th century BC.

3

The ferry-boat: in which Charon rows the souls of the dead across the river Styx to the underworld.

4

Briseïs: captive given as a prize to Achilles. See Book 1 of Homer's *Iliad*.

Telamonian: son of Telamon.

Atrides: Agamemnon.

a girl, his prize: Cassandra, daughter of Priam, king of Troy.

5

Gyges: king of Lydia in the 7th century BC.

6

Gades: Cadiz.

Syrtes: dangerous shoals off the coast of north Africa.

Argives: Greeks.

Galaesus: a river that flows into the Gulf of Tarentum.

coated flocks: the sheep of Tarentum wore pelts to protect their valuable wool.

Phalanthus: legendary founder of Tarentum.

Aulon's vine: from the valley of Aulon, near Tarentum.

7

Pompeius Varus (see Table of Contents): *fought on the Republican side with Brutus; returned to Italy under an amnesty from Augustus.*

9

Boreas: the north wind.

the Grecian sage: Nestor, eldest of the Greek warriors at Troy, whose son, Antilochus, was killed.

his slaughtered son: Troilus, youngest son of Priam.

Niphates: a river in Armenia.

11

Cantabrian: Spanish tribesman.

Adria: the Adriatic.

Laconian: Spartan.

12

Numantia: town in central Spain, taken by the Romans from the Carthaginians after a long siege in 133 BC.

Lapiths: mythological Thracian tribe.

Sacred Way: Rome's principal thoroughfare.

Alcides . . . Earth-born champions . . . Old Saturn: Hercules (Alcides) fought the Giants, offspring of the earth, when they rebelled against Saturn and the gods of Olympus.

Licymnia: possibly Maecenas' wife, or mistress.

13

Colchis: on the Black Sea, home of the sorceress, Medea.

Aeacus: a judge in the underworld.

Sappho: the poetess.

Alcaeus . . . banishment: the poet Alcaeus was banished from Lesbos for his opposition to the tyrant Myrsilus.

hundred-headed beast: Cerberus, the monstrous hound guarding the underworld.

Pelops' starvèd sire: Tantalus; see **1**, 28.

Orion: a renowned hunter.

14

Pluto: god of the underworld.

Tityus; triple Geryon: giants subjected to Pluto's control. Geryon had three bodies.

the gloomy wave: the river Styx.

hind: peasant

Cocytus: river in the underworld.

the guilty maids: the daughters of king Danaüs, who all murdered their husbands.

Sisyphus: condemned in the underworld to push a rock forever uphill.

15

Lucrine Lake: a shallow lagoon close to the Bay of Naples. Famous for its oysters.

lindens that no vine has wed will rout the elms: vines were normally trained on (wed to) elms. Linden trees were unsuitable for viticulture.

Cato: Cato the Elder, well-known for his republican frugality.

17

Chimaera: a fire-breathing monster.

Briareus: a giant with a hundred hands.

the rejoicing people clap't: see **1**, 20.

a falling trunk: see **2**, 13 'To a Falling Tree which nearly killed him.'

Faunus: Roman god of forests and the countryside; often identified with the Greek god Pan.

Mercurial men: favoured by Mercury.

18

Attalus: king of Pergamum, bequeathed his riches to the Roman people in 133 BC.

Baiae: fashionable resort on the bay of Naples.

Charon: boatman who rowed the dead across the river Styx to the underworld.

Tantalus and all his stock: for Tantalus, see note on **1**, 28. His descendants included Pelops, Atreus and Thyestes, Agamemnon and Menelaus, all ill-fated.

19

Thyades: followers of Bacchus.

Ariadne's crown: Bacchus turned the crown of his wife, Ariadne, into a constellation.

Pentheus; Lycurgus: punished for opposing Bacchus.

Rhoetus: one of the giants cast into the underworld for rebelling against Jupiter.

And when to Hell . . . thou didst ride: Bacchus rescued his mother, Semele, from the underworld.

20

Icarus: enabled to fly on wings made of wax, which melted when he approached the sun.

Phasis: river in Colchis, on the Black Sea.

BOOK THREE

I

Odi profanum vulgus et arceo;
favete linguis: carmina non prius
   audita Musarum sacerdos
     virginibus puerisque canto.

regum timendorum in proprios greges,   5
reges in ipsos imperium est Iovis,
   clari Giganteo triumpho,
     cuncta supercilio moventis.

est ut viro vir latius ordinet
arbusta sulcis, hic generosior   10
   descendat in Campum petitor,
     moribus hic meliorque fama

contendat, illi turba clientium
sit maior: aequa lege Necessitas
   sortitur insignis et imos: 15
     omne capax movet urna nomen.

destrictus ensis cui super impia
cervice pendet, non Siculae dapes
   dulcem elaborabunt saporem,
     non avium citharaeque cantus   20

somnum reducent: somnus agrestium
lenis virorum non humilis domos
   fastidit umbrosamque ripam,
     non Zephyris agitata Tempe.

desiderantem quod satis est neque   25
tumultuosum sollicitat mare
   nec saevus Arcturi cadentis
     impetus aut orientis Haedi,

1

I count no common man my friend.
　I serve the Muses, and increase
　The volume of my verse, to please
Young men and maidens. Peace! Attend.

As Kings their Peoples' shepherds are,
　So He the Shepherd is of Kings
　Who won the Heavenly War. All things
The Lord can make, the Lord can mar.

One squire a richer crop may grow
　On acres wider, than another –
　One advocate his learned brother
By birth or worth may overthrow,

Or distance in repute or wit:
　Fate casts the dice for high and low,
　Unweighted; Luck directs the throw
For all, and there's an end of it.

Above the sinner's head, the blade
　For ever hangs. His appetite
　No dainty dishes may excite.
No song of birds, no music played,

May bring him sleep. But Sleep is kind
　To humble countryfolk, and comes
　By shady rills to rustic homes
In valleys ruffled by the wind.

The man with soul exempt from greed,
　Tempestuous seas, and stars that presage
　Approaching gales, or bear the message
Of gathering storms, will never heed.

non verberatae grandine vineae
fundusque mendax, arbore nunc aquas   30
    culpante, nunc torrentia agros
      sidera, nunc hiemes iniquas.

contracta pisces aequora sentiunt
iactis in altum molibus; huc frequens
    caementa demittit redemptor   35
      cum famulis dominusque terrae

fastidiosus: sed Timor et Minae
scandunt eodem quo dominus, neque
    decedit aerata triremi et
      post equitem sedet atra Cura.   40

quodsi dolentem nec Phrygius lapis
nec purpurarum sidere clarior
    delenit usus nec Falerna
      vitis Achaemeniumque costum,

cur invidendis postibus et novo   45
sublime ritu moliar atrium?
    cur valle permutem Sabina
      divitias operosiores?

II

Angustam amice pauperiem pati
robustus acri militia puer
    condiscat et Parthos feroces
      vexet eques metuendus hasta

vitamque sub divo et trepidis agat   5
in rebus. illum ex moenibus hosticis
    matrona bellantis tyranni
      prospiciens et adulta virgo

When hops by hail are lashed and lost,
 Or orchards fail, he will not bother,
 But leave the trees to tell each other
Their tales of drought, or floods, or frost.

Vast piers obstruct the watery ways
 Of fishes, where the builders' men
 Have trespassed on the sea – but when
My Lord, who scorned his home to raise

On honest earth, ascends his stair,
 Disquiet with him climbs, and Dread;
 Aboard his yacht, brass-riveted,
And on his horse, sits cruel Care.

No rest he gets, and no relief,
 From marble halls and rich apparel;
 And port and sherry by the barrel
Are helpless to assuage his grief.

Why then should I draw envious eyes
 By building like a millionaire,
 And spend what I would gladly spare
And lose my rural Paradise?

Lewis Evelyn Gielgud (1951)

2

Train up a boy to walk the way
 Of hardship – train him up to fight,
 To ride and fence, and put to flight
The enemy, and win the day,

Defying alien suns, and swords!
 The maids and mothers of the foe
 Shall watch him from the walls, and go
In terror for their savage Lords,

suspiret, eheu, ne rudis agminum
sponsus lacessat regius asperum 10
   tactu leonem, quem cruenta
     per medias rapit ira caedis.

dulce et decorum est pro patria mori:
mors et fugacem persequitur virum,
   nec parcit imbellis iuventae 15
     poplitibus timidove tergo.

Virtus repulsae nescia sordidae
intaminatis fulget honoribus,
   nec sumit aut ponit securis
     arbitrio popularis aurae. 20

Virtus, recludens immeritis mori
caelum, negata temptat iter via,
   coetusque vulgaris et udam
     spernit humum fugiente penna.

est et fideli tuta silentio 25
merces: vetabo, qui Cereris sacrum
   vulgarit arcanae, sub isdem
     sit trabibus fragilemque mecum

solvat phaselon; saepe Diespiter
neglectus incesto addidit integrum: 30
   raro antecedentem scelestum
     deseruit pede Poena claudo.

And call to warn them: 'Have a care!
   Yon warrior has a lion's mood.
   He rages in the ranks for blood,
And lays about him – oh, beware!'

A soldier's death is death well-met
   And worthy. Cowards also die,
   For though with knocking knees they fly,
Old Death will overtake them yet.

But Valour, master of Dismay,
   Such honour wins as shall not fade –
   Not honours which to-day are made
And voted void another day.

And Valour, opening Heaven's Gate
   To dauntless men Death dares not spoil,
   Makes haste to fly from sodden soil,
And holds the common crowd in hate.

Discretion, too, deserves reward –
   But he that published or revealed
   Reports for which his lips were sealed
Finds me from home, nor will I board

A boat with him. Though Justice halt,
   No rogue escapes her, in the end,
   And oftentimes a guiltless friend
May suffer for his neighbour's fault.

Lewis Evelyn Gielgud (1951)

III

Iustum et tenacem propositi virum
non civium ardor prava iubentium,
   non vultus instantis tyranni
      mente quatit solida neque Auster,

dux inquieti turbidus Hadriae,   5
nec fulminantis magna manus Iovis:
   si fractus illabatur orbis,
      impavidum ferient ruinae.

hac arte Pollux et vagus Hercules
enisus arces attigit igneas,   10
   quos inter Augustus recumbens
      purpureo bibit ore nectar.

hac te merentem, Bacche pater, tuae
vexere tigres indocili iugum
   collo trahentes; hac Quirinus   15
      Martis equis Acheronta fugit,

gratum elocuta consiliantibus
Iunone divis: 'Ilion, Ilion
   fatalis incestusque iudex
      et mulier peregrina vertit   20

in pulverem, ex quo destituit deos
mercede pacta Laomedon, mihi
   castaeque damnatum Minervae
      cum populo et duce fraudulento.

iam nec Lacaenae splendet adulterae   25
famosus hospes nec Priami domus
   periura pugnaces Achivos
      Hectoreis opibus refringit,

3

The man resolved and steady to his trust,
Inflexible to ill, and obstinately just,
May the rude rabble's insolence despise,
Their senseless clamours and tumultuous cries;
    The tyrant's fierceness he beguiles,
And the stern brow, and the harsh voice defies,
    And with superior greatness smiles.
Not the rough whirlwind that deforms
Adria's black gulf, and vexes it with storms,
The stubborn virtue of his soul can move;
Nor the red arm of angry Jove,
That flings the thunder from the sky,
And gives it rage to roar, and strength to fly.
Should the whole frame of Nature round him break,
    In ruin and confusion hurled,
He, unconcerned, would hear the mighty crack,
    And stand secure amidst a falling world.
Such were the godlike arts that led
    Bright Pollux to the blessed abodes;
Such did for great Alcides plead,
    And gained a place amongst the gods;
Where now Augustus, mixed with heroes, lies,
And to his lips the nectar bowl applies:
His ruddy lips the purple tincture show,
And with immortal stains divinely glow.
By arts like these did young Lyaeus rise:
His tigers drew him to the skies;
    Wild from the desert, and unbroke,
In vain they foamed, in vain they stared,
In vain their eyes with fury glared;
He tamed them to the lash, and bent them to the yoke.
    Such were the paths that Rome's great founder trod,
When in a whirlwind snatched on high,
He shook off dull mortality,
    And lost the monarch in the god.

nostrisque ductum seditionibus
bellum resedit. protinus et gravis 30
   iras et invisum nepotem
      Troica quem peperit sacerdos,

Marti redonabo: illum ego lucidas
inire sedes, ducere nectaris
   sucos et adscribi quietis 35
      ordinibus patiar deorum.

dum longus inter saeviat Ilion
Romamque pontus, qualibet exsules
   in parte regnanto beati;
      dum Priami Paridisque busto 40

insultet armentum et catulos ferae
celent inultae, stet Capitolium
   fulgens triumphatisque possit
      Roma ferox dare iura Medis.

horrenda late nomen in ultimas 45
extendat oras, qua medius liquor
   secernit Europen ab Afro,
      qua tumidus rigat arva Nilus,

aurum irrepertum et sic melius situm,
cum terra celat, spernere fortior 50
   quam cogere humanos in usus
      omne sacrum rapiente dextra.

quicumque mundo terminus obstitit,
hunc tanget armis, visere gestiens,
   qua parte debacchentur ignes, 55
      qua nebulae pluviique rores.

Bright Juno then her awful silence broke,
And thus th' assembled deities bespoke:
'Troy,' says the goddess, 'perjured Troy has felt
The dire effects of her proud tyrant's guilt;
The towering pile, and soft abodes,
Walled by the hand of servile gods,
Now spreads its ruins all around,
And lies inglorious on the ground.
An umpire partial and unjust,
And a lewd woman's impious lust
Lay heavy on her head, and sank her to the dust.
Since false Laomedon's tyrannic sway
That durst defraud th' immortals of their pay,
Her guardian gods renounced their patronage,
    Nor would the fierce invading foe repel;
To my resentment, and Minerva's rage,
    The guilty king and the whole people fell.
And now the long-protracted wars are o'er,
The soft adulterer shines no more;
No more does Hector's force the Trojans shield,
That drove whole armies back, and singly cleared the
    field.
My vengeance sated, I at length resign
To Mars his offspring of the Trojan line:
Advanced to godhead, let him rise,
And take his station in the skies:
There entertain his ravished sight
With scenes of glory, fields of light:
Quaff with the gods immortal wine,
And see adoring nations crowd his shrine.
    The thin remains of Troy's afflicted host
In distant realms may seats unenvied find,
    And flourish on a foreign coast;
But far be Rome from Troy disjoined,
Removed by seas from the disastrous shore,
May endless billows rise between, and storms unnum-
    bered roar.
Still let the cursed detested place
Where Priam lies, and Priam's faithless race,

sed bellicosis fata Quiritibus
hac lege dico, ne nimium pii
   rebusque fidentes avitae
      tecta velint reparare Troiae.   60

Troiae renascens alite lugubri
fortuna tristi clade iterabitur,
   ducente victrices catervas
      coniuge me Iovis et sorore.

ter si resurgat murus aeneus   65
auctore Phoebo, ter pereat meis
   excisus Argivis, ter uxor
      capta virum puerosque ploret.'

non hoc iocosae conveniet lyrae:
quo Musa, tendis? desine pervicax   70
   referre sermones deorum et
      magna modis tenuare parvis.

Be covered o'er with weeds, and hid in grass.
There let the wanton flocks unguarded stray
  Or, while the lonely shepherd sings,
Amidst the mighty ruins play,
  And frisk upon the tombs of kings.
May tigers there, and all the savage kind
Sad solitary haunts and deserts find;
In gloomy vaults and nooks of palaces,
May th' unmolested lioness
Her brindled whelps securely lay,
Or, couched, in dreadful slumbers waste the day.
While Troy in heaps of ruins lies,
Rome and the Roman Capitol shall rise;
Th' illustrious exiles unconfined
Shall triumph far and near, and rule mankind.
In vain the sea's intruding tide
Europe from Afric shall divide,
And part the severed world in two:
  Through Afric's sands their triumphs they shall spread,
And the long train of victories pursue
  To Nile's yet undiscovered head.
Riches the hardy soldiers shall despise,
And look on gold with undesiring eyes,
Nor the disbowelled earth explore
In search of the forbidden ore;
Those glittering ills, concealed within the mine
Shall lie untouched, and innocently shine.
To the last bounds that nature sets
The piercing colds and sultry heats,
The godlike race shall spread their arms;
Now fill the polar circle with alarms,
Till storms and tempests their pursuits confine;
Now sweat for conquest underneath the line.
This only law the victor shall restrain;
On these conditions shall he reign:
If none his guilty hand employ
To build again a second Troy,
If none the rash design pursue,
Nor tempt the vengeance of the gods anew.

IV

Descende caelo et dic age tibia
regina longum Calliope melos,
   seu voce nunc mavis acuta,
     seu fidibus citharave Phoebi.

auditis an me ludit amabilis   5
insania? audire et videor pios
   errare per lucos, amoenae
     quos et aquae subeunt et aurae.

me fabulosae Vulture in Apulo
nutricis extra limen Apuliae   10
   ludo fatigatumque somno
     fronde nova puerum palumbes

A curse there cleaves to the devoted place,
That shall the new foundations raze;
Greece shall in mutual leagues conspire
To storm the rising town with fire,
And at their armies' head myself will show
What Juno, urged to all her rage, can do.
Thrice should Apollo's self the city raise,
And line it round with walls of brass;
Thrice should my favourite Greeks his works confound,
And hew the shining fabric to the ground:
Thrice should her captive dames to Greece return,
And their dead sons and slaughtered husbands mourn.'
But hold, my muse, forbear thy towering flight,
Nor bring the secrets of the gods to light:
In vain would thy presumptuous verse
Th' immortal rhetoric rehearse;
The mighty strains, in lyric numbers bound,
Forget their majesty, and lose the sound.

Joseph Addison (1709)

4

Come from heaven, come and sing
    Some many-linkèd melody;
If the glad voice loud and clear,
Or the wood-reed please thine ear,
Or Apollo's cittern be more dear,
    O Queen Calliope!
Do ye hear? oh, can it be,
A sweet deceiving ecstasy!
I seem to hear, I seem to roam
Through some spirit-haunted home,
Where beneath the leaves dark hushing,
The pleasant winds, and streams are gushing!
Alone upon the Vultur-mount,
    From fond Apulia's threshold straying,
The doves the dewy foliage wound

texere, mirum quod foret omnibus,
quicumque celsae nidum Acherontiae
   saltusque Bantinos et arvum   15
      pingue tenent humilis Forenti,

ut tuto ab atris corpore viperis
dormirem et ursis, ut premerer sacra
   lauroque collataque myrto,
      non sine dis animosus infans.   20

vester, Camenae, vester in arduos
tollor Sabinos, seu mihi frigidum
   Praeneste seu Tibur supinum
      seu liquidae placuere Baiae.

vestris amicum fontibus et choris   25
non me Philippis versa acies retro,
   devota non exstinxit arbos,
      nec Sicula Palinurus unda.

utcumque mecum vos eritis, libens
insanientem navita Bosporum   30
   temptabo et urentis harenas
      litoris Assyrii viator,

visam Britannos hospitibus feros
et laetum equino sanguine Concanum,
   visam pharetratos Gelonos   35
      et Scythicum inviolatus amnem.

vos Caesarem altum, militia simul
fessas cohortis abdidit oppidis,
   finire quaerentem labores
      Pierio recreatis antro.   40

vos lene consilium et datis et dato
gaudetis almae. scimus ut impios
   Titanas immanemque turbam
      fulmine sustulerit caduco,

qui terram inertem, qui mare temperat   45
ventosum, et urbes regnaque tristia

The weary poet-child around,
    Worn out with sleep and playing.
And wonder woke in every breast,
On Acherontia's crownèd crest,
And through the Bantine fields, and where
Forentum looketh green and fair –
That I, untouched by prowling bear,
    Or viper black, should sleep,
A spirit-guarded, gleeful boy,
    Upon that sacred myrtle heap!
Daughters of music! I am borne
    Into your towering Sabine hills,
Or 'mid Praeneste's cooling leaves,
Or where its path the Tiber weaves,
Or Baia's crystal rills.
Dance beside me, and I go
    A sailor on the stormy sea,
Or over Syria's burning sands,
    A pilgrim journeying joyfully.
I will see the Briton's dwelling,
    The Spaniard banqueting on gore;
I will behold the quivered Scythian,
    Wandering on the desert shore.
When mighty Caesar, victory-crowned,
A home among the towns hath found
    For his legions tired with fight,
His grief-forgetting heart your songs
    In the Pierian cave delight.
With gentle counsel, singers sweet,
Rejoicing in your gifts, ye greet.
    A tale is in my memory:
The Titans and the giant-band,
Scattered by the thunder-hand,
Whose sceptred might is over all –
    The earth, its towns, the wind-shook sea,
    And Hades with its agony.
Alike that fearful hand doth fall
    On man, and immortality!

divosque mortalisque turmas
　　imperio regit unus aequo.

magnum illa terrorem intulerat Iovi
fidens iuventus horrida bracchiis   50
　　fratresque tendentes opaco
　　　　Pelion imposuisse Olympo.

sed quid Typhoeus et validus Mimas,
aut quid minaci Porphyrion statu,
　　quid Rhoetus evulsisque truncis   55
　　　　Enceladus iaculator audax

contra sonantem Palladis aegida
possent ruentes? hinc avidus stetit
　　Vulcanus, hinc matrona Iuno et
　　　　numquam umeris positurus arcum,   60

qui rore puro Castaliae lavit
crinis solutos, qui Lyciae tenet
　　dumeta natalemque silvam,
　　　　Delius et Patareus Apollo.

vis consili expers mole ruit sua: 65
vim temperatam di quoque provehunt
　　in maius; idem odere viris
　　　　omne nefas animo moventis.

testis mearum centimanus Gyas
sententiarum, notus et integrae   70
　　temptator Orion Dianae,
　　　　virginea domitus sagitta.

iniecta monstris Terra dolet suis
maeretque partus fulmine luridum
　　missos ad Orcum; nec peredit   75
　　　　impositam celer ignis Aetnen,

incontinentis nec Tityi iecur
reliquit ales, nequitiae additus
　　custos; amatorem trecentae
　　　　Pirithoum cohibent catenae.   80

A thought the rebel-brothers woke
   Of terror in the monarch's breast,
As glorying in their arms, they strove to fling
   Pelion upon Olympus' forky crest.
Vain boasters! – Typhon, mighty Mimas,
   Porphyrion with the threatening form,
Or Rhoetus, or the demon-hurler
   Of trees uprooted, like a storm;
Feebly they rushed, untaught to yield,
Against Minerva's sounding shield.
Here eager Vulcan stood, and there
The matron Juno, proudly fair;
And he whose bow is ever on his back;
Who bathes his wild locks in the dew
Of Castaly, and roameth through
The Lycian plain, his native glen –
Apollo, the many-named of men!
Brute strength, if wisdom guide it not,
By its own strength to earth is pressed;
But thought-restrained, the gods exalt
Its weakness into power: they hate the breast
Where sin abides a busy guest.
Bear witness to my story, thou,
Gyas! the hundred-handed king;
And, thou, whose tongue unchilled by fear,
Hath whispered love in Dian's ear,
Within thy soul the virgin's dart is quivering!
Earth upon the monsters thrown,
Sadly weepeth for her own,
Mourning for her children sent
Unto hell's lurid element;
Not yet the rapid flame doth leap
Through Etna's fast upgathered heap.
By Tityus' heart the vulture sitteth,
A watcher sleeping never;
And hell about the cloud-born lover
Hath bound its manacles for ever!

John Wilmot (*c*.1670)

V

Caelo tonantem credidimus Iovem
regnare: praesens divus habebitur
   Augustus adiectis Britannis
      imperio gravibusque Persis.

milesne Crassi coniuge barbara   5
turpis maritus vixit et hostium –
   pro curia inversique mores!
      consenuit socerorum in armis

sub rege Medo Marsus et Apulus,
anciliorum et nominis et togae   10
   oblitus aeternaeque Vestae,
      incolumi Iove et urbe Roma?

hoc caverat mens provida Reguli
dissentientis condicionibus
   foedis et exemplo trahentis   15
      perniciem veniens in aevum,

si non periret immiserabilis
captiva pubes. 'signa ego Punicis
   adfixa delubris et arma
      militibus sine caede' dixit   20

'derepta vidi; vidi ego civium
retorta tergo bracchia libero
   portasque non clausas et arva
      Marte coli populata nostro.

auro repensus scilicet acrior   25
miles redibit. flagitio additis
   damnum: neque amissos colores
      lana refert medicata fuco,

5

[From his thunder we believe that Jupiter
reigns above: Augustus will be acknowledged
as a god on earth, with the annexation of the
Britons and fearsome Parthians to the empire.]

And so Rome's soldier settles down
   At ease beneath an alien sky,
Marries an alien wife and lives
   Contented in the Persian sty?

A Persian master for his lord,
   A Persian grandsire for his son –
Is it so easy to forget
   The regiment and the name of Rome?

Too easy. Rome's ambassador
   Foresaw, and prayed Rome not to sign
A shameful treaty, precedent
   Of treason to all future time.

'Better to let the young men die
   Captive. I saw our standards bow
Before their altars, saw the swords
   Our men flung down without a blow.

'I saw our Romans with their arms
   Bound behind backs that once were free.
Driven through the open gates to till
   The fields they fought on yesterday.

'You say the men will fight again,
   Gold-bought? Aye, bargain with disgrace,
So wool once dyed, turns white again?
   So courage, fallen from her place,

nec vera virtus, cum semel excidit,
curat reponi deterioribus.   30
    si pugnat extricata densis
        cerva plagis, erit ille fortis

qui perfidis se credidit hostibus,
et Marte Poenos proteret altero,
    qui lora restrictis lacertis   35
        sensit iners timuitque mortem.

hic unde vitam sumeret inscius,
pacem duello miscuit. o pudor!
    o magna Carthago, probrosis
        altior Italiae ruinis!'   40

fertur pudicae coniugis osculum
parvosque natos ut capitis minor
    ab se removisse et virilem
        torvus humi posuisse vultum,

donec labantis consilio patres   45
firmaret auctor numquam alias dato,
    interque maerentis amicos
        egregius properaret exsul.

atqui sciebat quae sibi barbarus
tortor pararet; non aliter tamen   50
    dimovit obstantis propinquos
        et populum reditus morantem

quam si clientum longa negotia
diiudicata lite relinqueret,
    tendens Venafranos in agros   55
        aut Lacedaemonium Tarentum.

'Will cringe to be propped up again?
If the stag, shivering in the snare,
Will stand as resolute at bay,
Then will the soldier do and dare,

'And fight with Carthage once again,
Who trusted in their lying breath,
Whose arms have felt the twisted thongs,
And struck no blow, and quailed at death.

'What's peace? What's war? What market's bad
Where a man buys security?
– O mighty Carthage, towering high
Above dishonoured Italy!'

Then as a man who has no more the right
   To live a citizen, he put aside
His wife's dear kiss, his little clinging sons,
   Nor from the ground would lift his haughty head

Until his high resolve, unparalleled,
   Steadied the quavering senators of Rome.
Then, glorious, self-exiled, amid the fears
   Of men that loved him, turned his face from home.

He knew the torture that awaited him,
   The thing that Carthage would prepare,
Yet put aside his kinsmen staying him,
   The anxious townsfolk, with as light a care

As though, his client's long-drawn business done,
   And judgement given, he set out that day
For green Venafrum in its olive groves,
   Seaward Tarentum, for a holiday.

Helen Waddell (1980)

VI

Delicta maiorum immeritus lues
Romane, donec templa refeceris
    aedesque labentis deorum et
        foeda nigro simulcra fumo.

dis te minorem quod geris, imperas: 5
hinc omne principium, huc refer exitum:
    di multa neglecti dederunt
        Hesperiae mala luctuosae.

iam bis Monaeses et Pacori manus
non auspicatos contudit impetus   10
    nostros et adiecisse praedam
        torquibus exiguis renidet.

paene occupatam seditionibus
delevit urbem Dacus et Aethiops,
    hic classe formidatus, ille   15
        missilibus melior sagittis.

fecunda culpae saecula nuptias
primum inquinavere et genus et domos;
    hoc fonte derivata clades
        in patriam populumque fluxit.   20

motus doceri gaudet Ionicos
matura virgo et fingitur artibus
    iam nunc et incestos amores
        de tenero meditatur ungui;

mox iuniores quaerit adulteros   25
inter mariti vina, neque eligit
    cui donet impermissa raptim
        gaudia luminibus remotis,

sed iussa coram non sine conscio
surgit marito, seu vocat institor   30
    seu navis Hispanae magister,
        dedecorum pretiosus emptor.

6

Those ills your ancestors have done,
Romans! are now become your own:
    And they will cost you dear,
    Unless you soon repair
The falling temples, which the gods provoke,
And statues, sullied yet with sacrilegious smoke.
Propitious Heaven, that raised your fathers high
    For humble grateful piety,
  (As it rewarded their respect)
  Hath sharply punished your neglect.
  All empires on the gods depend,
Begun by their command, at their command they end.
Let Crassus' ghost and Labienus tell
How twice, by Jove's revenge, our legions fell
    And with insulting pride,
Shining in Roman spoils, the Parthian victors ride.
  The Scythian and Egyptian scum
    Had almost ruined Rome,
  While our seditions took their part,
Filled each Egyptian sail, and winged each Scythian dart.
    First these flagitious times
    (Pregnant with unknown crimes)
  Conspire to violate the nuptial bed,
    From which polluted head
Infectious streams of crowding sins began,
And through the spurious breed and guilty nation ran.
  Behold a fair and melting maid
  Bound 'prentice to a common trade:
Ionian artists, at a mighty price,
Instruct her in the mysteries of vice,
What nets to spread, where subtle baits to lay
And, with an early hand, they form the tempered clay.
  'Tis not the spawn of such as these,
That dyed with Punic blood the conquered seas,
  And quashed the stern Aeacides;

non his iuventus orta parentibus
infecit aequor sanguine Punico,
    Pyrrhumque et ingentem cecidit   35
        Antiochum Hannibalemque dirum,

sed rusticorum mascula militum
proles, Sabellis docta ligonibus
    versare glebas et severae
        matris ad arbitrium recisos   40

portare fustis, sol ubi montium
mutaret umbras et iuga demeret
    bobus fatigatis, amicum
        tempus agens abeunte curru.

damnosa quid non imminuit dies?   45
aetas parentum peior avis tulit
    nos nequiores, mox daturos
        progeniem vitiosiorem.

VII

Quid fles, Asterie, quem tibi candidi
primo restituent vere Favonii
    Thyna merce beatum,
        constantis iuvenem fide

Gygen? ille Notis actus ad Oricum   5
post insana Caprae sidera frigidas
    noctes non sine multis
        insomnis lacrimis agit.

atqui sollicitae nuntius hospitae,
suspirare Chloen et miseram tuis   10
    dicens ignibus uri,
        temptat mille vafer modis.

Made the proud Asian monarch feel
How weak his gold was against Europe's steel;
 Forced e'en dire Hannibal to yield,
And won the long disputed world, at Zama's fatal field.
 But soldiers of a rustic mould,
 Rough, ready, seasoned, manly, bold;
 Either they dug the stubborn ground,
Or, through hewn woods, their weighty strokes did
   sound;
 And after the declining sun
Had changed the shadows, and their task was done,
Home with their weary team they took their way,
And drowned in friendly bowls the labour of the day.
 Time sensibly all things impairs;
 Our fathers have been worse than theirs;
 And we than ours; next age will see
 A race more profligate than we,
With all the pains we take, have skill enough to be.

Wentworth Dillon, Earl of Roscommon (1684)

7

 For constant Gyges why dost thou complain,
 Asterie, whom soft winds will bring again,
 Fraught with Bithynian merchandise,
 When the first beauties of the spring arise?

 He, driv'n to Oricus by southern storm,
 Whilst the Goat's furious sign doth seas alarm,
 Wastes solitary nights alone,
 Turmoiled, alas, with frequent moan.

 Meanwhile the messenger of busy love
 Tries many wily ways how him to move,
 Saying Chloe sighs with heart's desire
 And burneth with thy proper fire.

ut Proetum mulier perfida credulum
falsis impulerit criminibus nimis
    casto Bellerophontae   15
       maturare necem refert:

narrat paene datum Pelea Tartaro,
Magnessam Hippolyten dum fugit abstinens;
    et peccare docentis
       fallax historias monet.   20

frustra: nam scopulis surdior Icari
voces audit adhuc integer. at tibi
    ne vicinus Enipeus
       plus iusto placeat cave;

quamvis non alius flectere equum sciens   25
aeque conspicitur gramine Martio,
    nec quisquam citus aeque
       Tusco denatat alveo.

prima nocte domum claude neque in vias
sub cantu querulae despice tibiae,   30
    et te saepe vocanti
       duram difficilis mane.

He telleth how a treach'rous woman brought
The credulous Proetus, by feigned treason wrought,
Into unripened death to cast
Bellerophon the purely chaste.

He shows how Peleus Hell approachèd nigh,
While he, unstained, Hippolyte doth fly,
And witty stories bringeth in
That teach the ready way to sin.

In vain: for he, more deaf than hardest rocks,
Unmoved at all, his ear from passion locks.
But take good heed, lest more than sit,
Thou, love of Enipeus, admit.

Thou well in Martian field we understand,
His horse none manageth with more command;
Or any dares, who best can swim
In Tuscan stream, compete with him.

Shut in thy doors when first it groweth dark,
Nor from thy window to shrill music hark;
And still be of obdurate mind
To him, who says thou are unkind.

Sir Thomas Hawkins (1625)

VIII

Martiis caelebs quid agam Kalendis,
quid velint flores et acerra turis
plena miraris positusque carbo in
    caespite vivo,

docte sermones utriusque linguae?   5
voveram dulcis epulas et album
Libero caprum prope funeratus
    arboris ictu.

hic dies anno redeunte festus
corticem adstrictum pice dimovebit   10
amphorae fumum bibere institutae
    consule Tullo.

sume, Maecenas, cyathos amici
sospitis centum et vigiles lucernas
perfer in lucem: procul omnis esto   15
    clamor et ira.

mitte civilis super urbe curas:
occidit Daci Cotisonis agmen,
Medus infestus sibi luctuosis
    dissidet armis,   20

servit Hispanae vetus hostis orae
Cantaber sera domitus catena,
iam Scythae laxo meditantur arcu
    cedere campis.

neglegens ne qua populus laboret   25
parce privatus nimium cavere et
dona praesentis cape laetus horae ac
    linque severa.

8

Learned Maecenas, wonder not that I
(A bachelor) invoke that deity,
Which at this feast the married rout adore,
            And yearly do implore.

They pray the gods to make their burden light,
And that their yoke-fellows may never fight:
I praise them, not for giving me a wife,
            But saving of my life.

By heav'n redeem'd, I 'scap'd a falling tree,
And yearly own that strange delivery,
Yearly rejoice, and drink the briskest wine,
            Nor spill it at their shrine.

Come (my Maecenas) let us drink, and thus
Cherish that life, those powers have given us:
A thousand cups to midwife this new birth
            With inoffensive mirth.

No state affairs near my Maecenas come,
Since all are fall'n that fought victorious Rome.
By civil broils the Medes, our foes, will fall,
            The weakest to the wall.

Our fierce and ancient enemy of Spain
Is now subdu'd, and tamely bears our chain.
The savage Scythian too begins to yield,
            About to quit the field.

Bear they the load of government that can;
Thou, since a private, and good-natur'd man,
Enjoy th' advantage of the present hour,
            For why should'st thou look sour?

Thomas Flatman (1674)

IX

'Donec gratus eram tibi
nec quisquam potior bracchia candidae
　　cervici iuvenis dabat,
Persarum vigui rege beatior.'

'donec non alia magis　　　　　　　　　　5
arsisti neque erat Lydia post Chloen,
　　multi Lydia nominis
Romana vigui clarior Ilia.'

'me nunc Thressa Chloe regit,
dulcis docta modos et citharae sciens,　　　10
　　pro qua non metuam mori,
si parcent animae fata superstiti.'

'me torret face mutua
Thurini Calais filius Ornyti,
　　pro quo bis patiar mori,　　　　　　　15
si parcent puero fata superstiti.'

'quid si prisca redit Venus
diductosque iugo cogit aëneo,
　　si flava excutitur Chloe
reiectaeque patet ianua Lydiae?'　　　　　20

'quamquam sidere pulchrior
ille est, tu levior cortice et improbo
　　iracundior Hadria,
tecum vivere amem, tecum obeam libens.'

9

Horace: Whilst, Lydia, I was loved of thee,
      And 'bout thy ivory neck no youth did fling
         His arms, more acceptably free,
      I thought me richer than the Persian king.

Lydia: Whilst Horace loved no mistress more,
      Nor after Chloe did his Lydia sound,
         In name I went all names before,
      The Roman Ilia was not more renowned.

Horace: 'Tis true I'm Thracian Chloe's – I,
      Who sings so sweet, and with such cunning plays,
         As, for her, I'd not fear to die,
      So Fate would give her life and longer days.

Lydia: And I am mutually on fire
      With gentle Calaïs, Thurine Ornith's son,
         For whom I doubly would expire,
      So Fate would let the boy a long thread run.

Horace: But say old love return should make
      And us disjoined force to her brazen yoke;
         That I bright Chloe off should shake
      And to left Lydia now the door stand ope'?

Lydia: Though he be fairer than a star,
      Thou lighter than the bark of any tree,
         And than rough Adria angrier far;
      Yet would I wish to love, live, die with thee.

                         Ben Jonson (1640)

X

Extremum Tanain si biberes, Lyce,
saevo nupta viro, me tamen asperas
porrectum ante foris obicere incolis
    plorares Aquilonibus.

audis quo strepitu ianua, quo nemus   5
inter pulchra satum tecta remugiat
ventis, et positas ut glaciet nives
    puro numine Iuppiter?

ingratam Veneri pone superbiam,
ne currente retro funis eat rota.   10
non te Penelopen difficilem procis
    Tyrrhenus genuit parens.

O quamvis neque te munera nec preces
nec tinctus viola pallor amantium
nec vir Pieria paelice saucius   15
    curvat, supplicibus tuis

parcas, nec rigida mollior aesculo
nec Mauris animum mitior anguibus.
non hoc semper erit liminis aut aquae
    caelestis patiens latus.   20

10

See, Madam, see, how your poor lover lies
Before your doors, neglected and forlorn,
Expos'd to the rage of weather and your scorn,
  Both unrelenting enemies.
  And can you still so cruel be
As to behold all this, and yet not pity me?

Hark how the north-wind blusters 'gainst your doors,
Hark how amongst the neighbouring trees it roars;
See how the earth's all covered o'er with snow,
  And like your heart is frozen too.
  Away with this disdain, away,
For what is my case now, may b' yours another day.

Sure, you were ne'er so cruel bred or born,
What though with gifts I ne'er did bribe your love;
  Nor could for it look wan and pale,
  I knew you did such fool'ries scorn;
  Yet let my constancy prevail.
  Will nothing your compassion move?
Fie, fie, you're more inflexible, I swear,
Than the tough oak, cruel as serpents are.
  What shall I do? I cannot sure
These heats and colds of love for ever thus endure.

Richard Newcourt (1671)

XI

Mercuri – nam te docilis magistro
movit Amphion lapides canendo –
tuque testudo resonare septem
    callida nervis,

nec loquax olim neque grata, nunc et   5
divitum mensis et amica templis,
dic modos, Lyde quibus obstinatas
    applicet auris,

quae velut latis equa trima campis
ludit exsultim metuitque tangi,   10
nuptiarum expers et adhuc protervo
    cruda marito.

tu potes tigris comitesque silvas
ducere et rivos celeris morari;
cessit immanis tibi blandienti   15
    ianitor aulae,

Cerberus, quamvis furiale centum
muniant angues caput eius atque
spiritus taeter saniesque manet
    ore trilingui.   20

quin et Ixion Tityosque vultu
risit invito, stetit urna paulum
sicca, dum grato Danai puellas
    carmine mulces.

audiat Lyde scelus atque notas   25
virginum poenas et inane lymphae
dolium fundo pereuntis imo,
    seraque fata,

11

Mercury – for, taught by thy song,
Amphion drew the stones along –
And thou, o lute, which now affords
Sweet airy strains on sev'n-fold chords;

Erst silent, and by all refused,
But now in feasts and temples used,
Notes dictate, which th' obdurate ear
Of Lyde, may attentive hear,

Who, as a colt in open plains,
Wantonly skips, nor entertains
The touch of man, or marriage-awe,
As yet for sportive husband raw.

Thou tigers canst tame with thy lay,
Make woods to wait, swift rivers stay;
To thy soft notes in tuneful verse
Loud Cerberus, Hell's porter fierce,

Submits, although his direful head
With hundred snakes 's encompassèd,
And noisome breath with bloody drops
Flow from his triple-tonguèd chaps.

Nay Tityus and Ixion smile
Against their wills, whilst you beguile
Danaus' daughters with soft rime:
Their tubs stand empty for a time.

Let Lyde hear the wicked stain
And virgins' most deservèd pain;
Their urn unfillèd, labour crossed,
And water in the bottom lost;

quae manent culpas etiam sub Orco.
impiae – nam quid potuere maius? –   30
impiae sponsos potuere duro
    perdere ferro.

una de multis face nuptiali
digna periurum fuit in parentem
splendide mendax et in omne virgo   35
    nobilis aevum,

'surge,' quae dixit iuveni marito,
'surge, ne longus tibi somnus, unde
non times, detur; socerum et scelestas
    falle sorores,   40

quae velut nactae vitulos leaenae
singulos eheu lacerant: ego illis
mollior nec te feriam neque intra
    claustra tenebo.

me pater saevis oneret catenis,   45
quod viro clemens misero peperci:
me vel extremos Numidarum in agros
    classe releget.

i pedes quo te rapiunt et aurae,
dum favet nox et Venus, i secundo   50
omine et nostri memorem sepulcro
    scalpe querelam.'

And punishment ensuing tell,
Which waits on ugly sin in Hell.
Oh wicked ones! What greater ill?
Caitiffs! They durst their husbands kill.

One, 'mongst the rest, worthy the style
Of married wife, did well beguile
Her perjured father, and shall be
Famous to all posterity,

Who to her husband said, 'Arise,
Nor let a long sleep shut thy eyes,
Of which thou dost no fear conceive;
Sisters and wicked sire deceive,

Who are as lionesses bent
Piecemeal surprisèd calves to rent:
But I, much better rectified,
Will thee nor kill, nor closely hide.

For tho' my father chains prepare,
'Cause I a forlorn husband spare:
Let him to rough seas me convey,
In far Numidian fields to stray.

Go thou where speed and winds permit,
Whilst night and Venus favour it;
Go prosp'rously, and be thy doom
To write this story on my tomb.'

Sir Thomas Hawkins (1625)

XII

Miserarum est neque amori dare ludum neque dulci
mala vino lavere, aut exanimari metuentis
   patruae verbera linguae.

tibi qualum Cythereae puer ales, tibi telas
operosaeque Minervae studium aufert, Neobule,   5
   Liparaei nitor Hebri,

simul unctos Tiberinis umeros lavit in undis,
eques ipso melior Bellerophonte, neque pugno
   neque segni pede victus:

catus idem per apertum fugientis agitato   10
grege cervos iaculari et celer arto latitantem
   fruticeto excipere aprum.

12

No more Love's subjects, but his slaves they be,
That dare not o'er a glass of wine be free,
But quit, for fear of friends, their liberty.

Fond Neobulë! thou art lazy grown,
Away thy needle, web and distaff thrown,
Thou hop'st thy work by Hebrus will be done,

A sturdy youth, and a rank rider he,
Can run a race, and box most manfully,
Swim like a duck, and caper like a flea.

He hunts the stag, and all the forest o'er
With strength and craft pursues the savage boar:
He minds the sport, and thou desir'st no more.

Thomas Flatman (1671)

XIII

O fons Bandusiae splendidior vitro
dulci digne mero non sine floribus,
   cras donaberis haedo,
      cui frons turgida cornibus

primis et venerem et proelia destinat;   5
frustra: nam gelidos inficiet tibi
   rubro sanguine rivos
      lascivi suboles gregis.

te flagrantis atrox hora Caniculae
nescit tangere, tu frigus amabile   10
   fessis vomere tauris
      praebes et pecori vago.

fies nobilium tu quoque fontium,
me dicente cavis impositam ilicem
   saxis, unde loquaces   15
      lymphae desiliunt tuae.

13

O more than crystal bright, Bandusian Spring,
Worthy sweet wine, with flowers withal the morn
    A kidling thee shall bring,
        Whose front of budding horns

E'en now encounter lustful or of fight
Premeditates! unwitting! thy cold streams
    With the red blood shall tinge
        The youngling of the goats.

Thee the hot noon of Dogstar flaming fierce,
Knows not to touch: from thee delicious cool,
    Bulls wearied from the share
        Receive; and wandering herds.

Of the famed fountains thee too one shall make
Thy poet's verse, that tells thine ilex crowning
    The impendent rocks, from whence
        Thy babbling waters leap.

Arthur Hugh Clough (1847)

XIV

Herculis ritu modo dictus, o plebs,
morte venalem petiisse laurum
Caesar Hispana repetit penatis
    victor ab ora.

unico gaudens mulier marito   5
prodeat iustis operata divis,
et soror clari ducis et decorae
    supplice vitta

virginum matres iuvenumque nuper
sospitum. vos, o pueri et puellae   10
iam virum expertae, male ominatis
    parcite verbis.

hic dies vere mihi festus atras
eximet curas; ego nec tumultum
nec mori per vim metuam tenente   15
    Caesare terras.

i pete unguentum, puer, et coronas
et cadum Marsi memorem duelli,
Spartacum si qua potuit vagantem
    fallere testa.   20

dic et argutae properet Neaerae
murreum nodo cohibere crinem
si per invisum mora ianitorem
    fiet, abito.

lenit albescens animos capillus   25
litium et rixae cupidos protervae;
non ego hoc ferrem calidus iuventa
    consule Planco.

14

Great Caesar, who is said to go
Like Hercules against his foe,
To purchase bays by death, again
victorious is returned from Spain.

The wife that's with one husband pleased,
Let her come forth, the gods appeased:
Octavia, Caesar's sister, haste,
And mothers with your daughters chaste,

Attired in modest veil appear,
And sons, returnèd safe, draw near.
You boys, and you new-married train
Of wives, from evil words abstain.

From me this new-made holiday
Black sullen cares shall take away;
Nor fear I, in great Caesar's reign,
By force or tumult to be slain.

Boy! crowns and unguents now prepare,
And vessel kept since Marsian war,
If any such concealed hath been,
By wand'ring Spartacus not seen.

Let hither shrill Neaera hie,
And hair perfumed in tresses tie;
But if the porter make delay
With churlish answer, haste away.

White hoary hairs temper the mind,
To brawls and quarrels erst inclined;
This in youth's heat I could not brook,
When Plancus charge of consul took.

Sir Thomas Hawkins (1625)

XV

Uxor pauperis Ibyci,
tandem nequitiae fige modum tuae
    famosisque laboribus:
maturo propior desine funeri
    inter ludere virgines   5
et stellis nebulam spargere candidis.
    non, si quid Pholoen satis,
et te, Chlori, decet: filia rectius
    expugnat iuvenum domos,
pulso Thyias uti concita tympano.   10
    illam cogit amor Nothi
lascivae similem ludere capreae:
    te lanae prope nobilem
tonsae Luceriam, non citharae decent
    nec flos purpureus rosae   15
nec poti vetulam faece tenus cadi.

15

For shame, for shame, give o'er
   Thou over–ridden whore!
Thou play the wanton? Fie!
   Thou that e're long must die!
Thou merry with the maids? For shame!
   Thy ice will freeze their flame.
Think'st thou to please a man
   Because thy daughters can?
Few youngsters will knock at
   An old, a rotten gate.
Wish thy young daughter luck;
   Thou'dst better spin than —.
Drink brandy, then, and hope
   No garland, but a rope.

Thomas Flatman (1671)

XVI

Inclusam Danaen turris aenea
robustaeque fores et vigilum canum
tristes excubiae munierant satis
　　nocturnis ab adulteris,

si non Acrisium virginis abditae　　　　　　　5
custodem pavidum Iuppiter et Venus
risissent: fore enim tutum iter et patens
　　converso in pretium deo.

aurum per medios ire satellites
et perrumpere amat saxa potentius　　　　　　10
ictu fulmineo: concidit auguris
　　Argivi domus ob lucrum

demersa exitio: diffidit urbium
portas vir Macedo et subruit aemulos
reges muneribus; munera navium　　　　　　　15
　　saevos illaqueant duces.

crescentem sequitur cura pecuniam
maiorumque fames. iure perhorrui
late conspicuum tollere verticem,
　　Maecenas, equitum decus.　　　　　　　　20

quanto quisque sibi plura negaverit,
ab dis plura feret: nil cupientium
nudus castra peto et transfuga divitum
　　partis linquere gestio,

contemptae dominus splendidior rei　　　　　25
quam si quidquid arat impiger Apulus
occultare meis dicerer horreis,
　　magnas inter opes inops.

16

Doors strongly barr'd, and brazen tower,
With careful guard of waking dogs, had power
From night-adulterers to have secured
Fair Danaë, in stony walls immured,

Had not sly Jove and Venus both betrayed
Acrisius, fearful keeper of the maid:
For they the way knew safe, open the hold,
Were but the god once turnèd into gold.

More strong than thunder, gold, through armèd foes,
Through guarded towers of stone, and bulwarks, goes:
The Argive augur's house, with all his state,
Desire of gain did wholly ruinate;

With gifts the Macedonian did subdue
Strong city gates, and proud kings overthrew;
Seamen are snared with gifts and golden store.
Care-growing wealth pursues with thirst of more.

Then, dear Maecenas, well may I detest
To vaunt myself with high erected crest.
How much the more man doth himself deny,
So much the more the gods will him supply.

I, poor in state, seek those that nought desire,
And, flying, far from rich men's tents retire,
And better live, lord of a slender store,
Than were I said to hoard upon my floor

What the Apulian painfully hath tilled,
And in great wealth be poor, and never filled.
My stream of waters pure, my little copse,
My certain hope of happy fruitful crops,

purae rivus aquae silvaque iugerum
paucorum et segetis certa fides meae   30
fulgentem imperio fertilis Africae
    fallit sorte beatior.

quamquam nec Calabrae mella ferunt apes
nec Laestrygonia Bacchus in amphora
languescit mihi nec pinguia Gallicis   35
    crescunt vellera pascuis,

importuna tamen pauperies abest
nec, si plura velim, tu dare deneges.
contracto melius parva cupidine
    vectigalia porrigam,   40

quam si Mygdoniis regnum Alyattei
campis continuem. multa petentibus
desunt multa: bene est, cui deus obtulit
    parca quod satis est manu.

He understands not, as a better chance,
Who empire in rich Afric doth advance.
Though me Calabrian bees no honey give,
Nor wines in Laestrygonian vessels, live

Till age make good the taste; though no man knows
That my rich fleece in fertile Gallia grows;
Yet from me craving poverty doth fly,
Nor, should I ask you more, would you deny.

I better will, with limited desire,
Pay Caesar little tributes, than aspire
By greatness, to unite the Phrygian plain,
To Allyat's ample state and princely reign.

Who much desire, want much: he richly lives
T' whom God, with sparing hand, sufficient gives.

Sir Thomas Hawkins (1625)

XVII

Aeli vetusto nobilis ab Lamo, –
quando et priores hinc Lamias ferunt
   denominatos et nepotum
     per memores genus omne fastus,

auctore ab illo ducis originem,   5
qui Formiarum moenia dicitur
   princeps et innantem Maricae
     litoribus tenuisse Lirim

late tyrannus – cras foliis nemus
multis et alga litus inutili   10
   demissa tempestas ab Euro
     sternet, aquae nisi fallit augur

annosa cornix. dum potes, aridum
compone lignum: cras Genium mero
   curabis et porco bimestri   15
     cum famulis operum solutis.

17

Aelius, from ancient Lamus sprung
(Who first Campania's hills among
Founded the Formian walls of old,
And used in sovereign right to hold
Those fertile tracts where Liris pours
His stream upon Marica's shores),
Unless yon croaking raven's throat
Deceive me with its boding note,
Tomorrow's rising sun shall see
The shattered limbs of many a tree,
When the wild tempest whirling by
Tumultuous from the Eastern sky
Shall strip the leaves and strew the strand
With tangled weed and drifted sand.
Now while 'tis dry, fetch in the store
Of fuel ready at your door;
Tomorrow you may cheer your soul
With bumpers from the genial bowl,
And feast on chine of fatted pork,
Releasing all your slaves from work.

Lord Ravensworth (1851)

XVIII

Faune, Nympharum fugientum amator,
per meos finis et aprica rura
lenis incedas abeasque parvis
    aequus alumnis,

si tener pleno cadit haedus anno,   5
larga nec desunt Veneris sodali
vina craterae, vetus ara multo
    fumat odore.

ludit herboso pecus omne campo,
cum tibi Nonae redeunt Decembres;   10
festus in pratis vacat otioso
    cum bove pagus;

inter audaces lupus errat agnos;
spargit agrestis tibi silva frondis;
gaudet invisam pepulisse fossor   15
    ter pede terram.

18

Faunus, who after Nymphs dost range,
Thorough my precincts and fruitful grange
Pass gently, and propitious be
       To flocks, and me.

A tender kid the year shall end;
Full cups of liquor (Venus' friend)
We'll pay; fumes shall on altars fly
       In odours, high.

Beasts, when December's Nones appear,
In grazy grounds make sportive cheer;
The jocund clown in meads doth feast,
       The ox doth rest.

The wolf 'mongst fearless lambs doth stray,
Woods strew thee leaves upon this day,
The ditcher joys with measured mirth
       To tread the earth.

Sir Thomas Hawkins (1625)

XIX

    Quantum distet ab Inacho
Codrus pro patria non timidus mori,
   narras et genus Aeaci
et pugnata sacro bella sub Ilio.
    quo Chium pretio cadum   5
mercemur, quis aquam temperet ignibus
   quo praebente domum et quota
Paelignis caream frigoribus, taces.
    da lunae propere novae,
da noctis mediae, da, puer, auguris   10
   Murenae: tribus aut novem
miscentur cyathis pocula commodis.
    qui Musas amat imparis,
ternos ter cyathos attonitus petet
   vates: tris prohibet supra   15
rixarum metuens tangere Gratia
   nudis iuncta sororibus.
insanire iuvat: cur Berecyntiae
   cessant flamina tibiae?
cur pendet tacita fistula cum lyra?   20
   parcentis ego dexteras
odi: sparge rosas: audiat invidus
   dementem strepitum Lycus
et vicina seni non habilis Lyco.
    spissa te nitidum coma,   25
puro te similem, Telephe, Vespero,
   tempestiva petit Rhode:
me lentus Glycerae torret amor meae.

19

No history, please! Work out some other time
The pedigree of Aeacus,
Settle the dates of Inachus
And Codrus, in his death sublime.
Even your outline of the Trojan War,
Just now, would be a bore.
Far sooner would we have you say
What price a cask of Chian is today,
Or where, and what o'clock, we dine,
Who warms the water for the wine,
And shields us from this Arctic winter's nip.
Now, boy, the toasts! Murena's augurship!
New Moon! and Midnight! shall the bumpers be
Nine ladlefuls, or three?
Our frenzied bard, the Muses' votary,
Will plump, of course, for nine;
While they who, like the Graces, hate a riot,
Choose three, to keep the table quiet.
Now we'll go berserk – let the binge begin!
Pipe up, thou Berecynthian flute!
Down from your pegs, ye lyre and lute!
I hate a stingy host like sin.
More roses! wake the neighbours with the din –
Crusty old Lycus and his Pretty Poll,
Who has no use for him at all.
Here Love be lord! flushed Rhoda find her heaven
In Bassus, shining like the star of even
With his bright curly hair; while I,
Burning for Chloe, lingeringly die.

Sir Edward Marsh (1941)

XX

Non vides quanto moveas periclo,
Pyrrhe, Gaetulae catulos leaenae?
dura post paulo fugies inaudax
    proelia raptor,

cum per obstantis iuvenum catervas   5
ibit insignem repetens Nearchum,
grande certamen, tibi praeda cedat
    maior an illi.

interim, dum tu celeris sagittas
promis, haec dentis acuit timendos,   10
arbiter pugnae posuisse nudo
    sub pede palmam

fertur et leni recreare vento
sparsum odoratis umerum capillis,
qualis aut Nireus fuit aut aquosa   15
    raptus ab Ida.

20

Pyrrhus, how dang'rous 'tis, confess,
To take whelps from a lioness;
Straight thou scarred ravisher wilt run
    When battle's done.

When she through crowds of youthful men
Shall to Nearchus turn again,
Great question 'tis, who bears away
    The greater prey.

As thou prepar'st thy speedy piles,
She whets her dreadful tusks the whiles;
He, th' umpire, trampled down, they say,
    The victor's bay.

And wafted his sweet 'shevelled hair
With gentle blasts: like Nireus fair,
Or Ganymede, snatched up from fount-
    full Ida's mount.

Barten Holyday (1652)

XXI

O nata mecum consule Manlio,
seu tu querelas sive geris iocos
    seu rixam et insanos amores
        seu facilem, pia testa, somnum,

quocumque lectum nomine Massicum   5
servas, moveri digna bono die,
    descende, Corvino iubente
        promere languidiora vina.

non ille, quamquam Socraticis madet
sermonibus, te negleget horridus: 10
    narratur et prisci Catonis
        saepe mero caluisse virtus.

tu lene tormentum ingenio admoves
plerumque duro; tu sapientium
    curas et arcanum iocoso   15
        consilium retegis Lyaeo;

tu spem reducis mentibus anxiis,
virisque et addis cornua pauperi
    post te neque iratos trementi
        regum apices neque militum arma.   20

te Liber et, si laeta aderit, Venus
segnesque nodum solvere Gratiae
    vivaeque producent lucernae,
        dum rediens fugat astra Phoebus.

21

Kind Brother Butt! as old, and brisk, as I,
For we had both the same nativity;
 Whether to mirth, to brawls, or desperate love,
  Or sleep, thy gentle power do 's move;

By what, or name or title, dignified,
Thou need'st not fear the nicest test t' abide,
 Corvinus' health since we may not refuse,
  Give down amain thy generous juice.

Corvinus, though a Stoic, will not balk
Thy charms, for he can drink, as well as talk;
 Old Cato, though he often were morose,
  Yet he would sometimes take a dose.

O Wine! Thou mak'st the thick-skulled fellow soft,
Easest the statesman, vext with cares full oft;
 Unriddlest all intrigues with a free bowl,
  Thou arrant pick-lock of the soul!

Thou dost our gasping, dying hopes revive,
To peasants, souls as big as princes, give;
 Inspired by thee, they scorn their slavish fears,
  And bid their rulers shake their ears.

All this, and more, great Bacchus, thou canst do,
But if kind Venus be assistant too,
 Then bring more candles to expel the night,
  Till Phoebus puts the stars to flight.

Thomas Flatman (1671)

XXII

Montium custos nemorumque, Virgo,
quae laborantis utero puellas
ter vocata audis adimisque leto,
    diva triformis,

imminens villae tua pinus esto,   5
quam per exactos ego laetus annos
verris obliquum meditantis ictum
    sanguine donem.

XXIII

Caelo supinas si tuleris manus
nascente Luna, rustica Phidyle,
    si ture placaris et horna
        fruge Lares avidaque porca,

nec pestilentem sentiet Africum   5
fecunda vitis nec sterilem seges
    robiginem aut dulces alumni
        pomifero grave tempus anno.

nam quae nivali pascitur Algido
devota quercus inter et ilices   10
    aut crescit Albanis in herbis
        victima pontificum securis

cervice tinget: te nihil attinet
temptare multa caede bidentium
    parvos coronantem marino   15
        rore deos fragilique myrto.

22

O Maid, who watchest wood and fell
  And thrice invoked dost hear the moan
Of girls in need, and guard them well;
  Queen, that art three yet one!

Be thine the pine above my cot:
  There gladly as each year doth go
I'll slay a boar who yet has not
  Achieved his side-long blow.

William Sinclair Marris (1912)

23

If with the new moon thou to the sky above
Spread forth thy hands, O villager Pheidyle,
  And with the frankincense, the new year's
    Corn, and a young pig appease the Lares,

No sickly wind shall breathing from Africa
Infect the vineyard, nor i' the corn be seen
  Mildew, nor Autumn-days of fruitage
    Come with a plague to the tender younglings.

He, whom (a vowed thing) oak-tree and ilices,
Feed where the snows lie thick upon Algidus,
  Or whom Albano's pasture rears for
    Offering, unto the priestly axes

His neck shall render. Thee it availeth not
With overweening slaughter to supplicate
  Those humble Gods, for whose adornment
    Rosemary mixed with the myrtle serveth.

immunis aram si tetigit manus,
non sumptuosa blandior hostia
   mollivit aversos Penatis
     farre pio et saliente mica.   20

XXIV

   Intactis opulentior
thesauris Arabum et divitis Indiae
   caementis licet occupes
Tyrrhenum omne tuis et mare Apulicum,
   si figit adamantinos   5
summis verticibus dira Necessitas
   clavos, non animum metu,
non mortis laqueis expedies caput.
   campestres melius Scythae,
quorum plaustra vagas rite trahunt domos,   10
   vivunt et rigidi Getae,
immetata quibus iugera liberas
   fruges et Cererem ferunt,
nec cultura placet longior annua,
   defunctumque laboribus   15
aequali recreat sorte vicarius.
   illic matre carentibus
privignis mulier temperat innocens,
   nec dotata regit virum
coniunx nec nitido fidit adultero.   20
   dos est magna parentium
virtus et metuens alterius viri
   certo foedere castitas:
et peccare nefas aut pretium est mori.
   o quisquis volet impias   25
caedis et rabiem tollere civicam,

Hand laid on altar simply and holily
No costly gifts can make more effectual;
   'Twill soothe the adverse powers as well with
      Consecrate meal and the leaping salt-grain.

Arthur Hugh Clough (1847)

24

Though richer than the treasuries
   Untouched in Araby or Ind
And though thy rubble fills the seas,
   When dread Necessity has pinned

Her talons wrought of adamant
   Upon thy roof, thou shalt draw breath
No longer without fears to daunt,
   Nor free thee from the nets of Death.

Better the Scythians of the plain,
   Whose wagons draw their wandering homes,
Whose fields unparcelled yield them grain,
   And better where the Getan roams,

Who does not care to cultivate
   His acres longer than a year.
Another comes, and his estate
   Is worked in his turn. Women here

Care for their stepsons faithfully,
   The children that have lost their mother.
No rich wife rules her husband; she
   Never trusts falsely to another.

Great is their dowry, virtue got
   From parents, and the faith that fears
Another man, and that will not
   Transgress, or death ends their careers.

    si quaeret 'pater urbium'
subscribi statuis, indomitam audeat
    refrenare licentiam,
clarus postgenitis: quatenus – heu nefas!–   30
    virtutem incolumem odimus,
sublatam ex oculis quaerimus invidi.
    quid tristes querimoniae,
si non supplicio culpa reciditur,
    quid leges sine moribus   35
vanae proficiunt, si neque fervidis
    pars inclusa caloribus
mundi nec Boreae finitimum latus
    durataeque solo nives
mercatorem abigunt, horrida callidi   40
    vincunt aequora navitae,
magnum pauperies opprobrium iubet
    quidvis et facere et pati
virtutisque viam deserit arduae?
    vel nos in Capitolium,   45
quo clamor vocat et turba faventium,
    vel nos in mare proximum
gemmas et lapides, aurum et inutile,
    summi materiem mali,
mittamus, scelerum si bene paenitet.   50
    eradenda cupidinis
pravi sunt elementa et tenerae nimis
    mentes asperioribus
formandae studiis. nescit equo rudis
    haerere ingenuus puer   55
venarique timet, ludere doctior
    seu Graeco iubeas trocho
seu malis vetita legibus alea,
    cum periura patris fides
consortem socium fallat et hospites,   60
    indignoque pecuniam
heredi properet. scilicet improbae
    crescunt divitiae; tamen
curtae nescio quid semper abest rei.

O who will care to put an end
   To slaughter and to civil war,
To have inscribed The City's Friend
   Upon his statues, let him dare

To curb unchecked licentiousness,
   To be in after-ages famed,
Since virtue lost is sought no less
   Than it was, when amongst us, blamed.

But what can these complaints avail
   If there is nought to punish crime?
For without morals laws must fail,
   If thus the world's most torrid clime,

Nor that part bordering the North
   Where on the earth lies frozen snow,
Deter no merchant if the wrath
   Of waters by the men that know

A seaman's work is overcome;
   If to do aught and suffer aught
By poverty's opprobrium
   We are compelled, and set at nought

Virtue's hard way. Where many call
   Let us into the temple go
With all our useless gold and all
   Our gems, the matter of much woe,

Or cast them in the nearest sea.
   If of our sins we will repent
The rudiments of greed must be
   Uprooted, and soft minds be bent

By harder study. Free young boys
   Are ignorant of how to ride,
They fear to hunt and all their joys
   Are in the Grecian hoops they guide,

XXV

Quo me, Bacche, rapis tui
plenum? quae nemora aut quos agor in specus
velox mente nova? quibus
antris egregii Caesaris audiar
aeternum meditans decus   5
stellis inserere et consilio Iovis?
dicam insigne recens adhuc
indictum ore alio. non secus in iugis
exsomnis stupet Euhias
Hebrum prospiciens et nive candidam   10
Thracen ac pede barbaro
lustratam Rhodopen, ut mihi devio
ripas et vacuum nemus
mirari libet. o Naiadum potens
Baccharumque valentium   15
proceras manibus vertere fraxinos,
nil parvum aut humili modo,
nil mortale loquar. dulce periculum est,
o Lenaee, sequi deum
cingentem viridi tempora pampino.   20

Or with the dice the laws forbid,
    While their false fathers cheat their friends,
Their partners and whoever did
    Put trust in them, their only ends

To pile up riches for base heirs.
    Dishonest riches surely grow;
And yet some lack is always theirs,
    And what it is I do not know.

Lord Dunsany (1947)

25

Whither, Bacchus, thy votary
Lead'st thou? what be the woods, what be the grots to which
    Borne in frenzy I come? and what
Caves shall hear me, the while musing a mighty theme,
    Caesar's infinite glory I
Fain would mix with the stars, fain with the deities?
    A song lofty and new! a song
No tongue else hath essayed! So on the hills doth a
    Sleepless Bacchanal stand at the
Sight of Hebrus amazed, sight of the snowy-white
    Thrace, and where the barbarians
Range o'er Rhodope hill: as in my wilderment
    Bank and forest and solitude
I with wonder behold. Lord of the Naiades
    Thou, and lord of Bacchantes; who
From its roots with the hand rend up a lofty ash!
    No light thing, or in littleness,
No thing human I speak! Sweet the adventure is,
    O Lenaean, to follow thee,
Thee with sprays of the vine wreathing thy holy brows.

Arthur Hugh Clough (1847)

XXVI

Vixi puellis nuper idoneus
et militavi non sine gloria;
   nunc arma defunctumque bello
     barbiton hic paries habebit,

laevum marinae qui Veneris latus   5
custodit. hic, hic ponite lucida
   funalia et vectis et arcus
     oppositis foribus minaces.

O quae beatam diva tenes Cyprum et
Memphin carentem Sithonia nive,   10
   regina, sublimi flagello
     tange Chloen semel arrogantem.

XXVII

Impios parrae recinentis omen
ducat et praegnas canis aut ab agro
rava decurrens lupa Lanuvino
   fetaque vulpes:

rumpat et serpens iter institutum   5
si per obliquum similis sagittae
terruit mannos: ego cui timebo
   providus auspex,

antequam stantis repetat paludes
imbrium divina avis imminentum,   10
oscinem corvum prece suscitabo
   solis ab ortu.

26

We loved of yore, in warfare bold,
  Nor laurelless. Now all must go;
  Let this left wall of Venus show
The arms, the tuneless lyre of old.

Here let them hang, the torches cold,
  The portal-bursting bar, the bow,
                We loved of yore.

But thou, who Cyprus sweet dost hold,
  And Memphis free from Thracian snow,
  Goddess and queen, with vengeful blow,
Smite, – smite but once that pretty scold
                We loved of yore!

                                Austin Dobson (1877)

27

May sinners meet all omens ill!
  The bitch with cubs; the owlet's tongue;
The dun wolf stalking down the hill;
  The vixen great with young;

May adders o'er the roadway glide
  And scare their steeds with arrowy dart
But I, diviner eagle-eyed
  For her who hath my heart,

Will pray the raven, e'er he hies
  Back to the stagnant marshes where
He calls the rain, at morning-rise
  To croak an omen fair.

sis licet felix ubicumque mavis,
et memor nostri, Galatea, vivas,
teque nec laevus vetet ire picus   15
    nec vaga cornix.

sed vides quanto trepidet tumultu
pronus Orion. ego quid sit ater
Hadriae novi sinus et quid albus
    peccet Iapyx.   20

hostium uxores puerique caecos
sentiant motus orientis Austri et
aequoris nigri fremitum et trementis
    verbere ripas.

sic et Europe niveum doloso   25
credidit tauro latus et scatentem
beluis pontum mediasque fraudes
    palluit audax.

nuper in pratis studiosa florum et
debitae Nymphis opifex coronae,   30
nocte sublustri nihil astra praeter
    vidit et undas.

quae simul centum tetigit potentem
oppidis Creten, 'pater, o relictum
filiae nomen, pietasque' dixit   35
    'victa furore!

unde quo veni? levis una mors est
virginum culpae. vigilansne ploro
turpe commissum, an vitiis carentem
    ludit imago   40

vana, quae porta fugiens eburna
somnium ducit? meliusne fluctus
ire per longos fuit, an recentis
    carpere flores?

Be happy, wheresoe'er thou art,
   And think on me, my lady, still;
No roaming crow delay thy start,
   No daw that bodeth ill!

Yet see, Orion sinks and reels
   With tempest. Well I know the mien
Of inky Adria, when it feels
   The west wind lashing keen.

For wives and children of our foes
   Such terrors be! when Auster roars
And whips the surges black, whose blows
   Convulse the solid shores.

E'en bold Europe, when she gave
   Her snowy limbs to yon false bull,
Grew pale, beholding ocean's wave
   Of beasts and terrors full.

Of late intent on meadow flowers,
   She plaited wreaths the Nymphs to please:
Now she discerns through Night's dim hours
   Only the stars and seas.

Anon to mighty Crete she came
   With all its hundred towns, and cried
'O Sire! I may not speak thy name,
   Since folly love defied.

'O whence, O where? mere death – no more –
   Were doom too light for maid's offence:
Am I awake and sinning sore,
   Or all in innocence

' By phantoms from the ivory gate
   Bemocked? To pluck the buds new-blown,
Or wander o'er yon weary strait –
   Ah, which were better done?

si quis infamem mihi nunc iuvencum   45
dedat iratae, lacerare ferro et
frangere enitar modo multum amati
    cornua monstri.

impudens liqui patrios Penatis,
impudens Orcum moror. o deorum   50
si quis haec audis, utinam inter errem
    nuda leones!

antequam turpis macies decentis
occupet malas teneraeque sucus
defluat praedae, speciosa quaero   55
    pascere tigris.

"vilis Europe," pater urget absens:
"quid mori cessas? potes hac ab orno
pendulum zona bene te secuta
    laedere collum.   60

sive te rupes et acuta leto
saxa delectant, age te procellae
crede veloci, nisi erile mavis
    carpere pensum

regius sanguis, dominaeque tradi   65
barbarae paelex." ' aderat querenti
perfidum ridens Venus et remisso
    filius arcu.

mox, ubi lusit satis: 'abstineto'
dixit 'irarum calidaeque rixae,   70
cum tibi invisus laceranda reddet
    cornua taurus.

uxor invicti Iovis esse nescis:
mitte singultus, bene ferre magnam
disce fortunam; tua sectus orbis   75
    nomina ducet.'

'Give me that steer of ill-repute
    To hew in pieces with the sword,
To wrench the horns from off the brute
    That once I so adored!

'Shameless I left my father's home,
    Shameless I shrink from death. This prayer
Hear, some kind god, and let me roam
    'Mid lions, lone and bare!

'Ere wasting mars my comely cheek,
    Ere withers all my sap away,
While I am seemly yet, I seek
    To be the tigers' prey.

' "Die, die! thou base Europe, haste!
    (Far off my father chideth me)
For noose, the good zone at thy waist,
    For gibbet, yon tall tree.

' "Or haply climb yon airy scaur,
    And fling thee on the jagged rock
To death; unless it likes thee more,
    Thou child of kingly stock,

' "To card thy wool the slaves among,
    And serve a foreign master's dame." '
Now Cupid, with his bow unstrung,
    And Venus mocked her shame;

Till, tired of jibes, the goddess spake:
    'Refrain from rage and railing, when
Thy hated bull shall bring thee back
    His horns to rend again,

'Wife of unconquered Jove thou art,
    And know'st it not! learn not to shame
Thy honours: hush thy sobs; a part
    Of Earth shall bear thy name.'

William Sinclair Marris (1912)

XXVIII

Festo quid potius die
Neptuni faciam? prome reconditum,
    Lyde, strenua Caecubum
munitaeque adhibe vim sapientiae.
        inclinare meridiem   5
sentis ac, veluti stet volucris dies,
    parcis deripere horreo
cessantem Bibuli consulis amphoram.
        nos cantabimus invicem
Neptunum et viridis Nereidum comas;   10
    tu curva recines lyra
Latonam et celeris spicula Cynthiae,
    summo carmine, quae Cnidon
fulgentisque tenet Cycladas et Paphum
        iunctis visit oloribus;   15
dicetur merita Nox quoque nenia.

XXIX

Tyrrhena regum progenies, tibi
non ante verso lene merum cado
    cum flore, Maecenas, rosarum et
        pressa tuis balanus capillis

iamdudum apud me est. eripe te morae,   5
nec semper udum Tibur et Aefulae
    declive contempleris arvum et
        Telegoni iuga parricidae.

28

How more suitably celebrate
        Neptune's festival day? Out with it quickly now,
that long-mellowing Caecuban,
        Lyde, storm the secure forts of Philosophy!

Though you know that the sun is well
        past its zenith, as if vanishing day had stopped,
still you leave on the store-room shelf
        what's been loitering since Bibulus' consulship.

First we'll chant in alternate strains
        Neptune's realm and the green locks of the Nereids;
you shall then to the curving lyre
        sing Latona and swift Cynthia's darting shafts;

last that queen who, in Carian
        Cnidos throned and the white-shimmering Cyclades,
visits Paphos in swan-drawn car,
        we'll commemorate; Night too in a fitting close.

James Blair Leishman (1956)

29

Maecenas, – sprung from Tuscan kings – for thee,
Mild wine in vessels never touched, I keep:
   Here roses and sweet odours be
     Whose dew thy hair shall steep.

O stay not, let moist Tibur be disdained,
And Aefulae's declining fields and hills
   Where once Telegonus remained –
     Whose hand his father kills.

fastidiosam desere copiam et
molem propinquam nubibus arduis.   10
   omitte mirari beatae
      fumum et opes strepitumque Romae.

plerumque gratae divitibus vices
mundaeque parvo sub lare pauperum
   cenae sine aulaeis et ostro   15
      sollicitam explicuere frontem.

iam clarus occultum Andromedae pater
ostendit ignem, iam Procyon furit
   et stella vesani Leonis,
      sole dies referente siccos: 20

iam pastor umbras cum grege languido
rivumque fessus quaerit et horridi
   dumeta Silvani, caretque
      ripa vagis taciturna ventis.

tu civitatem quis deceat status   25
curas et Urbi sollicitus times
   quid Seres et regnata Cyro
      Bactra parent Tanaisque discors.

prudens futuri temporis exitum
caliginosa nocte premit deus,   30
   ridetque si mortalis ultra
      fas trepidat. quod adest memento

componere aequus; cetera fluminis
ritu feruntur, nunc medio alveo
   cum pace delabentis Etruscum   35
      in mare, nunc lapides adesos

stirpesque raptas et pecus et domos
volventis una non sine montium
   clamore vicinaeque silvae,
      cum fera diluvies quietos   40

Forsake that height where loathsome plenty cloys,
And towers which to the lofty clouds aspire;
   The smoke of Rome, her wealth and noise
     Thou wilt not here admire.

In pleasing change the rich man takes delight,
And frugal meals in homely seats allows,
   Where hangings want, and purple bright,
     He clears his care-full brows.

Now Cepheus plainly shows his hidden fire,
The Dogstar now his furious heat displays,
   The Lion spreads his raging ire,
     The sun brings parching days.

The shepherd now his sickly flock restores
With shades and rivers, and the thickets finds
   Of rough Silvanus; silent shores
     Are free from playing winds.

To keep the state in order is thy care,
Solicitous for Rome, thou fear'st the wars
   Which barbarous eastern troops prepare,
     And Tanais, used to jars.

The wise Creator from our knowledge hides
The end of future times in darksome night;
   False thoughts of mortals he derides
     When them vain toys affright.

With mindful temper present hours compose,
The rest are like a river, which with ease
   Sometimes within its channel flows
     Into Etrurian seas.

Oft stones, trees, flocks, and houses it devours,
With echoes from the hills and neighb'ring woods
   When some fierce deluge, raised by showers,
     Turns quiet brooks to floods.

irritat amnis. ille potens sui
laetusque deget, cui licet in diem
    dixisse 'vixi: cras vel atra
        nube polum Pater occupato

vel sole puro.' non tamen irritum,   45
quodcumque retro est, efficiet neque
    diffinget infectumque reddet,
        quod fugiens semel hora vexit.

Fortuna saevo laeta negotio et
ludum insolentem ludere pertinax   50
    transmutat incertos honores,
        nunc mihi, nunc alii benigna.

laudo manentem; si celeris quatit
pennas, resigno quae dedit et mea
    virtute me involvo probamque   55
        pauperiem sine dote quaero.

non est meum, si mugiat Africis
malus procellis, ad miseras preces
    decurrere et votis pacisci
        ne Cypriae Tyriaeque merces   60

addant avaro divitias mari.
tunc me biremis praesidio scaphae
    tutum per Aegaeos tumultus
        aura feret geminusque Pollux.

He, master of himself, in mirth may live
Who saith, 'I rest well pleased with former days,
   Let God from heaven tomorrow give
     Black clouds or sunny rays.'

No force can make that void, which once is past,
Those things are never altered, or undone,
   Which from the instant rolling fast
     With flying moments run.

Proud Fortune, joyful sad affairs to find,
Insulting in her sport, delights to change
   Uncertain honours: quickly kind,
     And straight again as strange.

I praise her stay; but if she stir her wings,
Her gifts I leave, and to myself retire,
   Wrapt in my virtue: honest things
     In want no dower require.

When Libyan storms the mast in pieces shake
I never God with prayers and vows implore,
   Lest precious wares addition make
     To greedy Neptune's store.

Then I, contented with a little boat,
Am through Aegean waves by winds conveyed,
   Where Pollux makes me safely float,
     And Castor's friendly aid.

Sir John Beaumont (1603)

XXX

Exegi monumentum aere perennius
regalique situ pyramidum altius,
quod non imber edax, non Aquilo impotens
possit diruere aut innumerabilis
annorum series et fuga temporum.   5
non omnis moriar, multaque pars mei
vitabit Libitinam: usque ego postera
crescam laude recens, dum Capitolium
scandet cum tacita virgine pontifex.
dicar, qua violens obstrepit Aufidus   10
et qua pauper aquae Daunus agrestium
regnavit populorum, ex humili potens
princeps Aeolium carmen ad Italos
deduxisse modos. sume superbiam
quaesitam meritis et mihi Delphica   15
lauro cinge volens, Melpomene, comam.

30

A monument by me is brought to pass,
Outliving pyramids, or lasting brass,
The sepulchre of kings; which eating rain,
Nor the fierce northern tempest can restrain,
Nor years though numberless, nor Time's swift start.
I will not wholly die; my better part
Shall 'scape the sullen hearse: bright fame shall raise
My memory renewed, with future praise,
While in the Capitol the priest ascends
With Vestals pure, whom silence so commends.
I, though of humble strain, will be declared
The first, and able most, that ever dared
Unto Italian proportion's use,
Aeolian antique measures to reduce,
Where Aufidus with wrathful streams doth roar
Or Daunus, poor in waters, reigneth o'er
Rough barbarous nations. Take to thee a name,
Which best, Melpomene, may suit thy fame;
And, willingly, thy Poet doth request
My hair with delphic laurels thou invest.

Barten Holyday (1652)

NOTES TO BOOK THREE

1

the blade forever hangs: the sword of Damocles, which he saw above his head at a banquet, suspended by a single horse-hair.

2

reports for which his lips were sealed: mysteries and rites connected with the worship of the goddess Ceres.

3

Adria: the Adriatic.

Alcides: Hercules.

Lyaeus: Bacchus.

Rome's great founder: Romulus.

an umpire partial and unjust, and a lewd woman's impious lust: Paris, whose judgment in favour of Venus was induced by her bribing him with the love of Helen, wife of Menelaus, king of Sparta.

false Laomedon . . . the guilty king: Laomedon, king of Troy, refused to pay Apollo and Neptune what he had promised them for building the walls of Troy.

the soft adulterer: Paris.

his offspring of the Trojan line: Romulus, son of Mars.

flourish on a foreign coast: The Trojan prince Aeneas, fleeing from the sack of Troy, journeyed to Italy and founded Rome.

a second Troy: Juno forbade Troy to be rebuilt.

4

Calliope: the muse of epic poetry.

Vultur-mount: mountain near Horace's birthplace of Venusia.

Acherontia: town on the summit of Vultur.

Bantine fields: the district of Bantia, a town near Venusia.

Forentum: town near Venusia.

Praeneste: town twenty miles east-south-east of Rome.

Baia: Baiae, on the gulf of Naples.

the Pierian cave: housed a spring sacred to the muses.

the Titans: gods overthrown by Jupiter.

Pelion: mountain range in Thessaly.

Typhon (Typhoeus); Mimas; Porphyrion; Rhoetus; the demon-hurler of trees (Enceladus): rebellious giants who tried to invade heaven and were cast by Jupiter into the underworld.

he whose bow is ever on his back: Apollo.

Castaly: the Castalian spring sacred to the muses.

Gyas: a giant with a hundred arms.

thou, whose tongue: Orion.

Tityus: a giant, punished by having two vultures forever tearing at his liver.

the cloud-born lover: Pirithous, who attempted to abduct Proserpina from the underworld, was doomed to remain there forever, bound to a rock.

5

Rome's soldier settles down: In 53 BC a Roman army under Crassus suffered catastrophic defeat by the Parthians at Carrhae. The survivors, taken prisoner, settled in Parthia and married local women.

Rome's ambassador: During the First Punic War the Roman commander, Regulus, was captured with his men by the Carthaginians and sent to Rome with peace proposals, which included ransoming the Roman prisoners. Regulus urged the Senate to reject the terms, and returned to Carthage to meet his death by torture.

6

Crassus; Labienus: defeated by the Parthians in 53 BC and 39 BC respectively.

Scythian and Egyptian: Archers from Dacia fought on the Egyptian side at the battle of Actium.

Punic: Carthaginian.

Aeacides: Pyrrhus, king of Epirus after the death of Alexander the Great, claimed descent from Achilles, the grandson of Aeacus. See note to 3,19.

the proud Asian monarch: Antiochus, king of Syria, was defeated in 188 BC.

Zama's fatal field: Hannibal and the Carthaginians were finally defeated at the battle of Zama in 202 BC.

7

Bithynian: from the province of Bithynia, on the southern coast of the Black Sea.

Oricus: port in western Greece.

the Goat's furious sign: the goat-star rises in September.

the credulous Proetus: When Bellerophon rejected the advances of king Proetus' wife, she told Proetus that he had raped her. Bellerophon survived all attempts by Proetus to have him murdered.

Peleus: was falsely accused of rape by Hippolyte, wife of king Acastus of Thessaly. He narrowly escaped death when Acastus stole his sword, leaving him a prey to centaurs.

8

that deity, which at this feast the married rout adore: March 1 was the festival of married women, whose deity was Juno.

I 'scap'd a falling tree: see 2, 13.

9

the Roman Ilia: mother of Romulus.

Calaïs, Thurine Ornith's son: Calais, the son of Ornytus, from Thurii, in southern Italy.

Adria: the Adriatic.

11

Amphion: Amphion built the walls of Thebes by charming the stones with his lyre.

Cerberus . . . submits: tamed by Orpheus' lute when the latter entered the underworld to rescue Eurydice.

Tityus and Ixion: condemned to eternal punishment in the underworld, Tityus continually at the mercy of two vultures, Ixion tied to a rotating wheel.

Danaus' daughters: for murdering their husbands, the daughters of Danaus were condemned in the underworld to constantly filling a water-jar ('tub') perforated at the bottom.

13

Bandusian spring: a fountain near Venusia, Horace's birthplace.

Dogstar flaming fierce: the Dogstar rises in late July, a time of heatwave.

14

like Hercules against his foe: Hercules passed through Italy after slaying the giant Geryon in Spain.

The wife: Livia, wife of Augustus. By 'one husband' (*unico marito*) Horace means 'unique, peerless'.

Marsian war: between Rome and her Italian allies 90–88 BC.

Spartacus: leader of a slave rebellion 73–71 BC.

Plancus: Plancus was consul in 42 BC, the year of the battle of Philippi, when Horace was twenty-three.

16

Danaë: told by an oracle that he would be killed by his grandson, Acrisius immured his only child, Danaë, in a bronze tower. However, she conceived by Jupiter, disguised as a shower of gold, and her son, Perseus, later killed Acrisius.

the Argive augur's house: Amphiaraus, a priest (augur) of Argos, knew that he would die if he joined the expedition against Thebes; but he succumbed to the bribe of a golden necklace, and duly perished, as did his wife, murdered by their son, who then went mad.

the Macedonian: King Philip of Macedon.

wines in Laestrygonian vessels: wines from Formiae, a city associated with the Laestrygonians, a race of giants.

Gallia: Gaul, France.

Allyat: Alyattes, a wealthy king of Lydia.

17

Lamus: king of the Laestrygonians. See note to 3,16.

Liris: river near Formiae.

Marica: a nymph of the river Liris.

raven: bird of ill omen.

18

December's Nones: December 5, the feast of Faunus. Faunus was the god of forests and the countryside, the Roman equivalent of the Greek god Pan.

19

Aeacus: legendary king of Aegina, and judge in the underworld. See 4,8.

Inachus: legendary king of Argos

Codrus, in his death sublime: Codrus, last king of Athens, provoked his own death in battle with the Dorians on learning from an oracle that only thus could Athens be saved.

augurship: important priestly office.

Berecynthian flute: Mount Berecynthus was sacred to the eastern goddess Cybele and her frenzied rituals.

20

Nireus: reputedly one of the handsomest of the Greeks at Troy.

Ganymede . . . Ida's mount: Ganymede, a handsome Trojan prince, was abducted by Jupiter from Mount Ida, near Troy, to be cupbearer to the gods.

21

Corvinus: general under Brutus at Philippi, then served Mark Antony, and later Augustus.

Old Cato: Cato the Elder, renowned for his austerity.

22

three yet one: Diana was goddess of the woodlands on earth, of the moon in heaven, and of the underworld. She also presided over childbirth.

23

Lares: the household gods.

Algidus . . . Albano's pasture: Algidus, a peak near the Alban hills, south-east of Rome.

24

Getan: Thracian tribesman.

The City's Friend: Augustus accepted honours as a municipal benefactor. He eventually took the title 'Father of his Country'.

Grecian hoops: hoops propelled with sticks. These Greek toys are here scorned as effeminate.

25

Hebrus; Rhodope: river and mountain in Thrace.

Naiades: water-nymphs.

Lenaean: Lenaeus was another name for Bacchus.

26

the arms: dedicated to Venus and hung on the wall of her temple.

27

Auster: the south wind.

Europe: Europa, a Phoenician princess, was enticed by Jupiter, disguised as a bull, to climb on his back. He then swam with her to Crete, where he ravished her.

the ivory gate: false dreams and visions pass from the underworld through an ivory gate.

zone: belt, sash.

28

Neptune's festival day: July 23.

Bibulus' consulship: 59 BC.

Nereids: sea-nymphs.

Latona: mother of Apollo and Diana.

Cynthia: Diana.

that queen: Venus.

29

Aefulae: town between Tibur and Praeneste.

Telegonus: killed his father Ulysses in ignorance.

Cepheus; the Dogstar; the Lion: stars which rise in July.

Silvanus: forest-god, similar to Faunus.

Tanais: the river Don.

jars: troubles, disturbances.

30

Aeolian measures: Greek verse.

Aufidus: the river which flowed through Venusia, Horace's birth-place.

Daunus: Apulia was reputedly founded by Daunus, a Greek.

Melpomene: the muse of Tragedy.

BOOK FOUR

I

Intermissa, Venus, diu
rursus bella moves? parce precor, precor.
   non sum qualis eram bonae
sub regno Cinarae. desine, dulcium
   mater saeva Cupidinum, 5
circa lustra decem flectere mollibus
   iam durum imperiis: abi
quo blandae iuvenum te revocant preces.
   tempestivius in domum
Pauli purpureis ales oloribus 10
   comissabere Maximi,
si torrere iecur quaeris idoneum:
   namque et nobilis et decens
et pro sollicitis non tacitus reis
   et centum puer artium 15
late signa feret militiae tuae,
   et, quandoque potentior
largi muneribus riserit aemuli,
   Albanos prope te lacus
ponet marmoream sub trabe citrea. 20
   illic plurima naribus
duces tura, lyraeque et Berecyntiae
   delectabere tibiae
mixtis carminibus non sine fistula;
   illic bis pueri die 25
numen cum teneris virginibus tuum
   laudantes pede candido
in morem Salium ter quatient humum.
   me nec femina nec puer
iam nec spes animi credula mutui 30
   nec certare iuvat mero
nec vincire novis tempora floribus.
   sed cur heu, Ligurine, cur
manat rara meas lacrima per genas?

1

No more of war; dread Cytherea, cease;
   Thy feeble soldier sues for peace.
Alas, I am not now that man of might,
   As when fair Cinara bade me fight.
Leave, Venus, leave! Consider my gray hairs,
   Snowed on by fifty tedious years.
My forts are slighted, and my bulwarks down:
   Go, and beleaguer some strong town.
Make thy attempts on Maximus: there's game
   To entertain thy sword and flame.
There peace and plenty dwell: he's of the Court,
   Ignorant what 'tis to storm a fort.
There sound a charge: he's generous and young,
   He's unconcern'd, lusty and strong.
He of thy silken banners will be proud,
   And of thy conquests talk aloud.
His bags are full: the lad thou may'st prefer
   To be thy treasurer in war.
He may erect gold statues to thy name,
   And be the trumpet of thy fame.
Thy deity the zealous youth will then invoke,
   And make thy beauteous altars smoke.
With voice and instruments thy praise shall sound;
   Division he, and love the ground.
There, twice a day the gamesome company
   Of lads and lasses in devoir to thee,
Like Mars's priests, their numbers shall advance,
   And sweetly sing, and nimbly dance.
But as for me, I'm quite dispirited,
   I court nor maid, nor boy to bed!
I cannot drink, nor bind a garland on,
   Alas! my dancing days are done!
But hold – why do these tears steal from my eye?
   My lovely Ligurinus, why?

cur facunda parum decoro   35
inter verba cadit lingua silentio?
    nocturnis ego somniis
iam captum teneo, iam volucrem sequor
    te per gramina Martii
campi, te per aquas, dure, volubilis.   40

II

Pindarum quisquis studet aemulari,
Iule, ceratis ope Daedalea
nititur pennis vitreo daturus
    nomina ponto.

monte decurrens velut amnis, imbres   5
quem super notas aluere ripas,
fervet immensusque ruit profundo
    Pindarus ore,

laurea donandus Apollinari,
seu per audaces nova dithyrambos   10
verba devolvit numerisque fertur
    lege solutis,

seu deos regesque canit, deorum
sanguinem, per quos cecidere iusta
morte Centauri, cecidit tremendae   15
    flamma Chimaerae,

sive quos Elea domum reducit
palma caelestis pugilemve equumve
dicit et centum potiore signis
    munere donat,   20

flebili sponsae iuvenemve raptum
plorat et viris animumque moresque
aureos educit in astra nigroque
    invidet Orco.

Why does my falt'ring tongue disguise my voice
   With rude and inarticulate noise?
O Ligurin! 'tis thou that break'st my rest,
   Methinks I grasp thee in my breast;
Then I pursue thee in my passionate dreams
   O'er pleasant fields and purling streams.

Thomas Flatman (1671)

2

Who thinks to equal Pindar, tries
With waxen wings to reach the skies,
Like him that, falling, a name gave
   T' his wat'ry grave.

As a proud stream that, swoll'n with rain,
Comes pouring down the hills amain,
So Pindar flows, and fears no drouth,
   Such his deep mouth;

Worthy the bays, whether he pour
From unexhausted springs a shower
Of lawless dithyrambs, and thunders
   In bolder numbers;

Or sings of gods and heroes, seed
Of gods, whose just swords did outweed
The Centaurs, and Chimaera stout
   Her flames put out;

Or mourns some youth, from his sad spouse
Unkindly torn, whose strength and prowess
And golden mind he lifts to th' sky,
   And lets not die.

This Theban swan, when he will sing
Among the clouds, raises his wing
On a stiff gale: I, like the bee
   Of Calabrie,

multa Dircaeum levat aura cycnum,   25
tendit, Antoni, quotiens in altos
nubium tractus: ego apis Matinae
   more modoque

grata carpentis thyma per laborem
plurimum circa nemus uvidique   30
Tiburis ripas operosa parvus
   carmina fingo.

concines maiore poeta plectro
Caesarem, quandoque trahet feroces
per sacrum clivum merita decorus   35
   fronde Sygambros,

quo nihil maius meliusve terris
fata donavere bonique divi
nec dabunt, quamvis redeant in aurum
   tempora priscum.   40

concines laetosque dies et Urbis
publicum ludum super impetrato
fortis Augusti reditu forumque
   litibus orbum.

tum meae, si quid loquar audiendum,   45
vocis accedet bona pars, et, 'o Sol
pulcher! o laudande!' canam, recepto
   Caesare felix.

teque, dum procedis, io Triumphe,
non semel dicemus, io Triumphe,   50
civitas omnis, dabimusque divis
   tura benignis.

te decem tauri totidemque vaccae,
me tener solvet vitulus, relicta
matre qui largis iuvenescit herbis   55
   in mea vota,

fronte curvatos imitatus ignis
tertium lunae referentis ortum,
qua notam duxit, niveus videri,
   cetera fulvus.   60

Which, toiling, sucks beloved flowers
About the thymy groves and scours
Of fount-well Tibur, from a terse
    But humble verse.

Thou, Antony, in higher strains
Chant Caesar, when he leads in chains
Fierce Germans, his victorious brows
    Crowned with bay-boughs;

Than whom a greater thing, or good,
Heaven hath not lent the earth, nor should,
Though it refined the age to th' old
    Saturnian gold.

Thou shalt sing to the public plays
For his return, and holidays
For our prayers heard, and wrangling pleas,
    Bound to the peace.

Then I, if I may then be heard,
Happy in my restorèd lord,
Will join i' th' close, and 'O', I'll say,
    O sun-shine day!

And, thou proceeding, we'll all sing,
'Io Triumphe!' and again
'Io Triumphe!' at each turning
    Incense burning.

A hecatomb's required of thee,
And weanèd calf excuses me,
In high grass fat and frisking now,
    To pay my vow;

Resembled in whose shining horns
The increasing moon his brow adorns,
Save a white feather in his head,
    All sorrel red.

Sir Richard Fanshawe (1652)

III

   Quem tu, Melpomene, semel
nascentem placido lumine videris,
   illum non labor Isthmius
clarabit pugilem, non equus impiger
    curru ducet Achaico   5
victorem, neque res bellica Deliis
   ornatum foliis ducem,
quod regum tumidas contuderit minas,
   ostendet Capitolio:
sed quae Tibur aquae fertile praefluunt   10
   et spissae nemorum comae
fingent Aeolio carmine nobilem.
   Romae principis urbium
dignatur suboles inter amabilis
    vatum ponere me choros,   15
et iam dente minus mordeor invido.
   o, testudinis aureae
dulcem quae strepitum, Pieri, temperas,
   o mutis quoque piscibus
donatura cycni, si libeat, sonum,   20
   totum muneris hoc tui est,
quod monstror digito praetereuntium
   Romanae fidicen lyrae:
quod spiro et placeo, si placeo, tuum est.

3

He on whose birth the lyric Queen
    Of numbers smiled, shall never grace
The Isthmian gauntlet, or be seen
    First in the famed Olympic race.
He shall not, after toils of war,
    And humbling haughty monarchs' pride,
With laurelled brows, conspicuous far,
    To Jove's Tarpeian Temple ride.
But him, the streams that warbling flow,
    Rich Tibur's fertile meads along,
And shady groves, his haunts, shall know
    The master of th' Aeolian song.
The sons of Rome, majestic Rome!
    Have placed me in the poets' choir,
And envy now, or dead or dumb,
    Forbears to blame what they admire.
Goddess of the sweet-sounding lute!
    Which thy harmonious touch obeys;
Who canst the finny race, though mute,
    To cygnets' dying accents raise;
Thy gift it is, that all, with ease,
    Me, prince of Roman lyrics, own;
That while I live, my numbers please,
    If pleasing be thy gift alone.

Francis Atterbury (1743)

IV

Qualem ministrum fulminis alitem,
cui rex deorum regnum in avis vagas
    permisit expertus fidelem
        Iuppiter in Ganymede flavo,

olim iuventas et patrius vigor   5
nido laborum protulit inscium,
    vernique iam nimbis remotis
        insolitos docuere nisus

venti paventem, mox in ovilia
demisit hostem vividus impetus,   10
    nunc in reluctantis dracones
        egit amor dapis atque pugnae,

qualemve laetis caprea pascuis
intenta fulvae matris ab ubere
    iam lacte depulsum leonem   15
        dente novo peritura vidit,

videre Raeti bella sub Alpibus
Drusum gerentem Vindelici – quibus
    mos unde deductus per omne
        tempus Amazonia securi   20

dextras obarmet, quaerere distuli,
nec scire fas est omnia – sed diu
    lateque victrices catervae
        consiliis iuvenis revictae

sensere, quid mens rite, quid indoles   25
nutrita faustis sub penetralibus
    posset, quid Augusti paternus
        in pueros animus Nerones.

fortes creantur fortibus et bonis;
est in iuvencis, est in equis patrum   30
    virtus, neque imbellem feroces
        progenerant aquilae columbam;

4

The eagle, when he carried off
   Fair Ganymede, was faithful found,
Wherefore he guards the bolts of Jove
   And king of roving birds is crowned:

Like him – as fledgeling yet he plies
   In pride of blood a callow wing,
Till April winds and sunny skies
   Allure him to more daring spring,

When swooping down with blinding flight
   Havoc among the pens he makes,
Until he lusts for feast and fight
   And grapples with the writhing snakes;

Or as a grazing kid espies
   A lion's cub that ne'er before
Has left his tawny dam, and dies
   By teeth till then unflushed with gore;

So Drusus to the Vandals' sight
   Appeared, as 'neath the Alps he warred,
And wise in counsel, bold in fight,
   Destroyed their long triumphant horde.

(They arm themselves like Amazons
   With axes in their hands: but why
Or whence the ancient customs runs,
   I know not: 'tis a mystery.)

And taught the power of soul and brain
   Developed 'neath a godly roof,
And what the Nero striplings twain
   Owed to their foster-father's love.

When sires are good and brave, the child
   Is brave: in cattle and in steeds
Blood proves itself: the eagle wild
   The timorous ring-dove never breeds:

doctrina sed vim promovet insitam,
rectique cultus pectora roborant;
    utcumque defecere mores,   35
        indecorant bene nata culpae.

quid debeas, o Roma, Neronibus,
testis Metaurum flumen et Hasdrubal
    devictus et pulcher fugatis
        ille dies Latio tenebris,   40

qui primus alma risit adorea,
dirus per urbis Afer ut Italas
    ceu flamma per taedas vel Eurus
        per Siculas equitavit undas.

post hoc secundis usque laboribus   45
Romana pubes crevit, et impio
    vastata Poenorum tumultu
        fana deos habuere rectos,

dixitque tandem perfidus Hannibal
'cervi, luporum praeda rapacium,   50
    sectamur ultro, quos opimus
        fallere et effugere est triumphus.

gens, quae cremato fortis ab Ilio
iactata Tuscis aequoribus sacra
    natosque maturosque patres   55
        pertulit Ausonias ad urbis,

duris ut ilex tonsa bipennibus
nigrae feraci frondis in Algido,
    per damna, per caedis, ab ipso
        ducit opes animumque ferro.   60

non hydra secto corpore firmior
vinci dolentem crevit in Herculem,
    monstrumve submisere Colchi
        maius Echioniaeve Thebae.

Yet ordered training nerves the brain
   And teaching betters Nature's worth;
For, failing virtue, many a stain
   Disfigures those of spotless birth.

Thy debt to Nero's house, O Rome,
   Metaurus' river testifies
And Hasdrubal's defeat, when gloom
   Was swept from our Italian skies,

The first of days that glowed benign,
   Since the dread foe through Italy
Careered, like flame through woods of pine,
   Or Eurus o'er Sicilian sea.

Thenceforth our youth have grown unstayed
   In prosperous toils, and temples wrecked
By Carthage in her godless raid
   Have held their gods again erect,

Till faithless Hannibal spoke out:
   'We are as stags amid a pack
Of wolves: 'twere boast enough to flout
   The foe; 'tis madness to attack.

'That race that braved the Trojan fires
   And carried tossed on Tuscan sea
Its gods, its children, and its sires
   Unto the towns of Italy,

'Like oak that biting bill-hook rives
   Where Algidus stands deep in shade,
E'en through its ghastly wounds derives
   New strength and spirit from the blade.

'The Hydra thriving at each thrust
   Of foiled and angry Hercules,
The monsters Thebes and Colchis loosed
   Were never prodigy like these.

merses profundo: pulchrior evenit: 65
luctere: multa proruet integrum
   cum laude victorem geretque
      proelia coniugibus loquenda.

Carthagini iam non ego nuntios
mittam superbos: occidit, occidit   70
   spes omnis et fortuna nostri
      nominis Hasdrubale interempto.'

nil Claudiae non perficiunt manus,
quas et benigno numine Iuppiter
   defendit et curae sagaces   75
      expediunt per acuta belli.

V

Divis orte bonis, optime Romulae
custos gentis, abes iam nimium diu;
maturum reditum pollicitus patrum
   sancto concilio, redi.

lucem redde tuae, dux bone, patriae: 5
instar veris enim vultus ubi tuus
adfulsit populo, gratior it dies
   et soles melius nitent.

ut mater iuvenem, quem Notus invido
flatu Carpathii trans maris aequora   10
cunctantem spatio longius annuo
   dulci distinet a domo,

votis ominibusque et precibus vocat,
curvo nec faciem litore dimovet:
sic desideriis icta fidelibus   15
   quaerit patria Caesarem.

'Submerged awhile, more fair she soars:
    Close-gripped, she hurls her victor down,
And wives shall chatter of the wars
    She yet will wage with high renown.

'No couriers proud will speed apace
    Henceforth to Carthage. Fallen all
The hope and fortune of our race:
    They died – they died with Hasdrubal.'

The Neros' daring who can stay?
    For Jove hath blessed them with his might,
And skill and forethought guide their way
    Along the thorny paths of fight.

William Sinclair Marris (1912)

5

Propitious to the sons of earth
    (Best guardian of the Roman state),
The heavenly powers beheld thy birth,
    And form'd thee glorious, good and great;
Rome and her holy fathers cry, thy stay
Was promised short, ah! wherefore this delay?

Come then, auspicious prince, and bring
    To thy long gloomy country light,
For in thy countenance the spring
    Shines forth to cheer thy people's sight;
Then hasten thy return for, thou away,
Nor lustre has the sun, nor joy the day.

As a fond mother views with fear
    The terrors of the rolling main,
While envious winds beyond his year,
    From his loved home her son detain;
To the good gods with fervent prayer she cries,
And catches every omen as it flies;

tutus bos etenim rura perambulat,
nutrit rura Ceres almaque Faustitas,
pacatum volitant per mare navitae,
    culpari metuit fides,   20

nullis polluitur casta domus stupris,
mos et lex maculosum edomuit nefas,
laudantur simili prole puerperae,
    culpam poena premit comes.

quis Parthum paveat, quis gelidum Scythen,   25
quis Germania quos horrida parturit
fetus, incolumi Caesare? quis ferae
    bellum curet Hiberiae?

condit quisque diem collibus in suis,
et vitem viduas ducit ad arbores;   30
hinc ad vina redit laetus et alteris
    te mensis adhibet deum;

te multa prece, te prosequitur mero
defuso pateris et Laribus tuum
miscet numen, uti Graecia Castoris   35
    et magni memor Herculis.

'longas o utinam, dux bone, ferias
praestes Hesperiae!' dicimus integro
sicci mane die, dicimus uvidi,
    cum sol Oceano subest.   40

Then anxious listens to the roar
    Of winds, that loudly sweep the sky;
Nor, fearful, from the winding shore
    Can ever turn her longing eye:
Smit with as faithful, and as fond desires,
Impatient Rome her absent lord requires.

Safe by thy cares her oxen graze,
    And yellow Ceres clothes her fields:
The sailor ploughs the peaceful seas,
    And Earth her rich abundance yields;
While nobly conscious of unsullied fame,
Fair Honour dreads th' imputed sense of blame.

By thee our wedded dames are pure
    From foul adultery's embrace:
The conscious father views secure
    His own resemblance in his race:
Thy chaste example quells the spotted deed,
And to the guilt thy punishments succeed.

Who shall the faithless Parthian dread,
    The freezing armies of the north,
The enormous youth, to battle bred,
    Whom horrid Germany brings forth?
Who shall regard the war of cruel Spain,
If Caesar live secure, if Caesar reign!

Safe in his vineyard toils the hind,
    Weds to the widow'd elm his vine,
Till the sun sets his hill behind;
    Then hastens joyful to his wine,
And in his gayer hours of mirth implores
Thy godhead to protect and bless his stores.

To thee he chants the sacred song,
    To thee the rich libation pours;
Thee, placed his household gods among,
    With solemn, daily prayer adores;
So Castor and great Hercules of old
Were with her gods by grateful Greece enroll'd.

VI

Dive, quem proles Niobea magnae
vindicem linguae Tityosque raptor
sensit et Troiae prope victor altae
    Phthius Achilles,

ceteris maior, tibi miles impar,   5
filius quamvis Thetidis marinae
Dardanas turris quateret tremenda
    cuspide pugnax.

ille, mordaci velut icta ferro
pinus aut impulsa cupressus Euro,   10
procidit late posuitque collum in
    pulvere Teucro.

ille non inclusus equo Minervae
sacra mentito male feriatos
Troas et laetam Priami choreis   15
    falleret aulam;

sed palam captis gravis, heu nefas! heu!
nescios fari pueros Achivis
ureret flammis, etiam latentem
    matris in alvo,   20

Gracious and good, beneath thy reign
    May Rome her happy hours employ,
And grateful hail thy just domain
    With pious hymns and festal joy!
Thus, with the rising sun we sober pray,
    Thus, in our wine, beneath his setting ray.

Philip Francis (1746)

6

Apollo, by whose hand the boasted brood
Of Niobe, and Tityos ravisher,
Were smitten down, and he who came so near
    To vanquish Troy in battle proud —

Achilles, first of men, no match for thee,
Though from her cavern Thetis gave her son
A spear imbued with magic of the sea
    To shake the towers of Ilion!

He, as a pine the biting axe hath hewed,
Or cypress by the furious East o'erthrown,
In majesty brought low fell where he stood,
    And in Troy's dust his neck laid down.

No trickster he, to pass the leaguered wall
Crouched in the Horse, feigned gift to Pallas' shrine,
Surprise the jubilant townsmen at their wine,
    And dash the feast in Priam's hall.

Frank was his barbarous rigour, stern to doom
His miserable captives; he had given
The tenderest babes to the Argive flames, him even
    Yet sleeping in his mother's womb,

ni tuis victus Venerisque gratae
vocibus divum pater adnuisset
rebus Aeneae potiore ductos
    alite muros.

doctor argutae fidicen Thaliae,   25
Phoebe, qui Xantho lavis amne crines,
Dauniae defende decus Camenae,
    levis Agyieu.

spiritum Phoebus mihi, Phoebus artem
carminis nomenque dedit poetae.   30
virginum primae puerique claris
    patribus orti,

Deliae tutela deae fugaces
lyncas et cervos cohibentis arcu,
Lesbium servate pedem meique   35
    pollicis ictum,

rite Latonae puerum canentes,
rite crescentem face Noctilucam,
prosperam frugum celeremque pronos
    volvere mensis.   40

nupta iam dices 'ego dis amicum,
saeculo festas referente luces,
reddidi carmen, docilis modorum
    vatis Horati.'

Had not the Almighty Father, by thy pleas
And Venus' soft cajoling moved to grace,
Vouchsafed Aeneas favouring auspices
    The walls of his new town to trace.

Clear-voiced instructor of the tuneful Nine,
Smooth-brow'd Agyieus, who in Lycian dews
Dost bathe thy tresses, lend thine aid benign
    To uphold the younger Daunian Muse.

'Twas Phoebus granted me the sacred fire,
The skill of melody, the poet's name.
Fair youths and damsels of my novice choir,
    Best heirs of Rome's ancestral fame,

Wards of the Delian Queen, whose arrows fleet
Subdue the stags and lynxes to her sway!
Keep strict the Lesbian measure, and obey
    My downward finger's guiding beat,

While in your ritual song ye duly praise
Latona's son, and her who rules the night,
Ripening the corn, and with her crescent light
    Fulfils the monthly round of days.

Each maid hereafter, wedded many a year,
Shall tell the tale: 'In the great thanksgiving
I chanted with the rest, while Heaven gave ear,
    And Horace 'twas who bade me sing.'

Sir Edward Marsh (1941)

VII

Diffugere nives, redeunt iam gramina campis
    arboribusque comae;
mutat terra vices, et decrescentia ripas
    flumina praetereunt;
Gratia cum Nymphis geminisque sororibus audet   5
    ducere nuda choros.
immortalia ne speres, monet annus et almum
    quae rapit hora diem:
frigora mitescunt Zephyris, ver proterit aestas
    interitura simul   10
pomifer Autumnus fruges effuderit, et mox
    bruma recurrit iners.
damna tamen celeres reparant caelestia lunae:
    nos ubi decidimus
quo pater Aeneas, quo Tullus dives et Ancus,   15
    pulvis et umbra sumus.
quis scit an adiciant hodiernae crastina summae
    tempora di superi?
cuncta manus avidas fugient heredis, amico
    quae dederis animo.   20
cum semel occideris et de te splendida Minos
    fecerit arbitria,
non, Torquate, genus, non te facundia, non te
    restituet pietas;
infernis neque enim tenebris Diana pudicum   25
    liberat Hippolytum,
nec Lethaea valet Theseus abrumpere caro
    vincula Pirithoo.

7

The snows are fled away, leaves on the shaws
   And grasses in the mead renew their birth,
The river to the river-bed withdraws,
   And altered is the fashion of the earth.

The Nymphs and Graces three put off their fear
   And unapparelled in the woodland play.
The swift hour and the brief prime of the year
   Say to the soul, *Thou wast not born for aye.*

Thaw follows frost; hard on the heel of spring
   Treads summer sure to die, for hard on hers
Comes autumn, with his apples scattering;
   Then back to wintertide, when nothing stirs.

But oh, whate'er the sky-led seasons mar,
   Moon upon moon rebuilds it with her beams:
Come *we* where Tullus and where Ancus are,
   And good Aeneas, we are dust and dreams.

Torquatus, if the gods in heaven shall add
   The morrow to the day, what tongue has told?
Feast then thy heart, for what thy heart has had
   The fingers of no heir will ever hold.

When thou descendest once the shades among,
   The stern assize and equal judgment o'er,
Not thy long lineage nor thy golden tongue,
   No, nor thy righteousness, shall friend thee more.

Night holds Hippolytus the pure of stain,
   Diana steads him nothing, he must stay;
And Theseus leaves Pirithöus in the chain
   The love of comrades cannot take away.

Alfred Edward Housman (1897)

VIII

Donarem pateras grataque commodus,
Censorine, meis, aera sodalibus,
donarem tripodas, praemia fortium
Graiorum, neque tu pessima munerum
ferres, divite me scilicet artium   5
quas aut Parrhasius protulit aut Scopas,
hic saxo, liquidis ille coloribus
sollers nunc hominem ponere, nunc deum.
sed non haec mihi vis, non tibi talium
res est aut animus deliciarum egens.   10
gaudes carminibus; carmina possumus
donare et pretium dicere muneri.
non incisa notis marmora publicis,
per quae spiritus et vita redit bonis
post mortem ducibus, non celeres fugae   15
reiectaeque retrorsum Hannibalis minae,
non incendia Carthaginis impiae
eius, qui domita nomen ab Africa
lucratus rediit, clarius indicant
laudes quam Calabrae Pierides: neque,   20
si chartae sileant quod bene feceris,
mercedem tuleris. quid foret Iliae
Mavortisque puer, si taciturnitas
obstaret meritis invida Romuli?
ereptum Stygiis fluctibus Aeacum   25
virtus et favor et lingua potentium
vatum divitibus consecrat insulis.
dignum laude virum Musa vetat mori:
caelo Musa beat. sic Iovis interest
optatis epulis impiger Hercules,   30

8

My friends I would accommodate
With goblets, Grecian tripods, plate
Of Corinth brass; and Censorine,
The worst of these should not be thine:
That is to say, if I were rich
In those same antique pieces which
Parrhasius and Scopas fame;
He skill'd to paint, in stone to frame
This, now a God, a mortal now.
But I have not the means; nor thou
A mind, or purse, that wants such knacks.
Verse thou dost love. Thou shalt not lack
For verse. And hear me what 'tis worth.
Not inscrib'd marbles planted forth
To public view, which give new breath
To great and good men after death:
Not the swift flight of Hannibal,
And his threats turn'd to his own wall;
Not perjur'd Carthage wrapt in flame,
By which young Scipio brought a name
From conquer'd Affrick; speak his praise
So loud, as the Pierian lays.
Nor, were books silenc'd couldst thou gain
The guerdon of thy virtuous pain
What had become of Ilia's child
She bare to Mars, had darkness veil'd
The merits of our Romulus?
From Stygian waters Aeacus,
Virtue and fav'ring verse assails,
And consecrates to the blest isles.
A man that hath deserv'd t' have praise,
The Muse embalms. She keeps Heav'n's keys.
Thus Hercules (his labours past)
With Jupiter takes wished repast:

clarum Tyndaridae sidus ab infimis
quassas eripiunt aequoribus ratis,
ornatus viridi tempora pampino
Liber vota bonos ducit ad exitus.

IX

Ne forte credas interitura, quae
longe sonantem natus ad Aufidum
non ante vulgatas per artis
verba loquor socianda chordis:

non, si priores Maeonius tenet   5
sedes Homerus, Pindaricae latent
Ceaeque et Alcaei minaces
Stesichorive graves Camenae;

nec, si quid olim lusit Anacreon,
delevit aetas; spirat adhuc amor   10
vivuntque commissi calores
Aeoliae fidibus puellae.

non sola comptos arsit adulteri
crinis et aurum vestibus illitum
mirata regalisque cultus   15
et comites Helene Lacaena,

primusve Teucer tela Cydonio
direxit arcu; non semel Ilios
vexata; non pugnavit ingens
Idomeneus Sthenelusve solus   20

dicenda Musis proelia; non ferox
Hector vel acer Deiphobus gravis
excepit ictus pro pudicis
coniugibus puerisque primus.

The sons of Leda stars are made,
And give the sinking sea-man aid;
Good Bacchus, crownèd with vine leaves,
His drooping votaries relieves.

Sir Richard Fanshawe (1652)

9

Verses immortal (as my bays) I sing,
    When suited to my trembling string:
When by strange art both voice and lyre agree
    To make one pleasant harmony.
All poets are by their blind captain led,
    (For none e'er had the sacrilegious pride
To tear the well-placed laurel from his aged head).
    Yet Pindar's rolling dithyrambic tide
Hath still this praise, that none presume to fly
Like him, but flag too low, or soar too high.
    Still does Stesichorus his tongue
Sing sweeter than the bird which on it hung.
    Anacreon ne'er too old can grow,
    Love from every verse does flow:
    Still Sappho's strings do seem to move,
    Instructing all her sex to love.

    Golden rings of flowing hair
    More than Helen did ensnare ;
    Others a prince's grandeur did admire,
    And wond'ring, melted to desire.
    Not only skilful Teucer knew
    To direct arrows from the bending yew.
    Troy more than once did fall,
Though hireling gods rebuilt its nodding wall.
Was Sthenelus the only valiant he,
A subject fit for lasting poetry?

vixere fortes ante Agamemnona 25
multi; sed omnes illacrimabiles
   urgentur ignotique longa
     nocte carent quia vate sacro.

paulum sepultae distat inertiae
celata virtus. non ego te meis 30
   chartis inornatum sileri,
     totve tuos patiar labores

impune, Lolli, carpere lividas
obliviones. est animus tibi
   rerumque prudens et secundis 35
     temporibus dubiisque rectus,

vindex avarae fraudis et abstinens
ducentis ad se cuncta pecuniae,
   consulque non unius anni,
     sed quotiens bonus atque fidus 40

iudex honestum praetulit utili,
reiecit alto dona nocentium
   vultu, per obstantis catervas
     explicuit sua victor arma.

non possidentem multa vocaveris 45
recte beatum: rectius occupat
   nomen beati, qui deorum
     muneribus sapienter uti

duramque callet pauperiem pati
peiusque leto flagitium timet, 50
   non ille pro caris amicis
     aut patria timidus perire.

Was Hector that prodigious man alone,
Who, to save others' lives, exposed his own?
Was only he so brave to dare his fate
And be the pillar of a tott'ring state?
   No, others buried in oblivion lie
     As silent as their grave,
Because no charitable poet gave
Their well-deservèd immortality.

Virtue with sloth, and cowards with the brave,
Are levell'd in the impartial grave,
    If they no poet have.
   But I will lay my music by,
And bid the mournful strings in silence lie;
Unless my songs begin and end with you,
To whom my strings, to whom my songs are due.
No pride does with your rising honours grow ,
You meekly look on suppliant crowds below.
Should fortune change your happy state,
You could admire, yet envy not, the great.
Your equal hand holds an unbiass'd scale,
Where no rich vices, gilded bait, prevail.
You with a generous honesty despise
What all the meaner world so dearly prize.
Nor does your virtue disappear
With the small circle of one short-lived year.
Others, like comets, visit and away ;
Your lustre, great as theirs, finds no decay,
But with the constant sun makes an eternal day.

We barbarously call those bless'd
Who are of largest tenements possess'd,
Whilst swelling coffers break their owner's rest.
   More truly happy those, who can
   Govern the little empire, man:
Bridle their passions, and direct their will
Through all the glitt'ring paths of charming ill;

X

O crudelis adhuc et Veneris muneribus potens,
insperata tuae cum veniet pluma superbiae,
et, quae nunc umeris involitant, deciderint comae,
nunc et qui color est puniceae flore prior rosae,
mutatus Ligurinum in faciem verterit hispidam,   5
dices 'heu' quotiens te speculo videris alterum,
'quae mens est hodie, cur eadem non puero fuit,
vel cur his animis incolumes non redeunt genae?'

Who spend their treasure freely, as 'twas given
By the large bounty of indulgent Heaven;
Who in a fix'd unalterable state,
   Smile at the doubtful tide of Fate,
And scorn alike her friendship and her hate;
   Who poison less than falsehood fear,
   Loth to purchase life so dear;
But kindly for their friend embrace cold death,
And seal their country's love with their departing breath.

George Stepney (1689)

10

Cruel and fair! when this soft down
   (Thy youth's bloom) shall to bristles grow
And these fair curls thy shoulders crown,
   Shall shed or cover'd be with snow;

When those bright roses that adorn
   Thy cheeks shall wither quite away,
And in the glass (now made time's scorn)
   Thou shalt thy changèd face survey:

Then, ah then! (sighing) thou'lt deplore
   Thy ill-spent youth; and wish, in vain,
Why had I not those thoughts before?
   Or come not my first looks again?

Sir Edward Sherburne (1651)

XI

Est mihi nonum superantis annum
plenus Albani cadus; est in horto,
Phylli, nectendis apium coronis;
   est hederae vis

multa, qua crinis religata fulges;   5
ridet argento domus; ara castis
vincta verbenis avet immolato
   spargier agno;

cuncta festinat manus, huc et illuc
cursitant mixtae pueris puellae;   10
sordidum flammae trepidant rotantes
   vertice fumum.

ut tamen noris quibus advoceris
gaudiis, Idus tibi sunt agendae,
qui dies mensem Veneris marinae   15
   findit Aprilem,

iure sollemnis mihi sanctiorque
paene natali proprio, quod ex hac
luce Maecenas meus adfluentis
   ordinat annos.   20

Telephum, quem tu petis, occupavit
non tuae sortis iuvenem puella
dives et lasciva tenetque grata
   compede vinctum.

terret ambustus Phaethon avaras   25
spes, et exemplum grave praebet ales
Pegasus terrenum equitem gravatus
   Bellerophontem,

semper ut te digna sequare et ultra
quam licet sperare nefas putando   30
disparem vites. age iam, meorum
   finis amorum –

11

Come Phyllis, gentle Phyllis! prithee come,
I have a glass of rich old wine at home,
And in my garden curious flowers do grow,
    That languish to adorn thy brow.

The ivy, and the yellow crowfoot there
With verdant chaplets wait to braid thy hair;
With silver goblets all my house does shine,
    And vervain round my altar twine,

On which the best of all my flock shall bleed.
Come, and observe with what officious speed
Each lad and lass of all my house attends
    Till to my roof the smoke ascends.

If thou would'st know why thou must be my guest,
I tell thee, 'tis to celebrate a feast,
The Ides of April, which have ever been
    Devoted to the Cyprian Queen.

A day more sacred, and more fit for mirth
Than that which gave me, worthless mortal, birth:
For on that day Maecenas first saw light,
    Born for our wonder and delight.

My Phyllis, since thy years come on apace,
Substitute me in Telephus his place;
He's now employed by one more rich, more fair,
    And proudly does her shackles wear.

Remember what became of Phaethon;
Remember what befell Bellerophon;
That by ambition from his father's throne,
    And this, by Pegasus thrown down.

Content thyself with what is fit for thee,
Happy that couple that in years agree!
Shun others, and accept my parity,
    And I will end my loves with thee.

non enim posthac alia calebo
femina – condisce modos, amanda
voce quos reddas: minuentur atrae   35
    carmine curae.

XII

Iam veris comites, quae mare temperant,
impellunt animae lintea Thraciae;
iam nec prata rigent nec fluvii strepunt
    hiberna nive turgidi.

nidum ponit Ityn flebiliter gemens   5
infelix avis et Cecropiae domus
aeternum opprobrium, quod male barbaras
    regum est ulta libidines.

dicunt in tenero gramine pinguium
custodes ovium carmina fistula   10
delectantque deum cui pecus et nigri
    colles Arcadiae placent.

adduxere sitim tempora, Vergili;
sed pressum Calibus ducere Liberum
si gestis, iuvenum nobilium cliens,   15
    nardo vina merebere.

nardi parvus onyx eliciet cadum,
qui nunc Sulpiciis accubat horreis,
spes donare novas largus amaraque
    curarum eluere efficax.   20

ad quae si properas gaudia, cum tua
velox merce veni: non ego te meis
immunem meditor tingere poculis,
    plena dives ut in domo.

Thou art the last whom I intend to court,
Come then; and, to prepare thee for the sport,
Learn prick-song, and my merry odes rehearse;
    Many a care is charmed by verse.

Thomas Flatman (1671)

12

South winds, the spring attending still,
Now seas becalm and sails do fill;
Now frosts make not the meadows hoar,
Nor winter-snow swoll'n rivers roar.

The luckless bird her nest doth frame,
Bewailing Itys, and the shame
Of Cecrops' house, and that so ill
On kings' rude lust she wrought her will.

The shepherds of rich flocks rehearse,
And to their pipes chant rural verse,
Seeking his god-head to appease,
Whom flocks and hills Arcadian please.

These times do thirsty seasons send,
But if thou, Virgil, Caesar's friend,
Calenian wines desir'st to try,
To me with fragrant unguents hie,

And purchase, with a little box,
Wine, which Sulpicius safely locks,
New hopes most powerful to create
And bitter cares to dissipate.

To which content if thou agree,
Stay not, but quickly come to me:
I'll not, free-cost, my cups carouse,
As rich men in a plenteous house.

verum pone moras et studium lucri,   25
nigrorumque memor. dum licet, ignium
misce stultitiam consiliis brevem:
   dulce est desipere in loco.

XIII

Audivere, Lyce, di mea vota, di
audivere, Lyce: fis anus, et tamen
   vis formosa videri
     ludisque et bibis impudens

et cantu tremulo pota Cupidinem   5
lentum sollicitas. ille virentis et
   doctae psallere Chiae
     pulchris excubat in genis.

importunus enim transvolat aridas
quercus et refugit te, quia luridi   10
   dentes te, quia rugae
     turpant et capitis nives.

nec Coae referunt iam tibi purpurae
nec cari lapides tempora quae semel
   notis condita fastis   15
     inclusit volucris dies.

quo fugit Venus, heu, quove color? decens
quo motus? quid habes illius, illius,
   quae spirabat amores,
     quae me surpuerat mihi,   20

felix post Cinaram notaque et artium
gratarum facies? sed Cinarae brevis
   annos fata dederunt,
     servatura diu parem

Then leave delays, and gain's desire,
And mindful of black funeral fire,
Short folly mix with counsels best:
'Tis sweet sometimes to be in jest.

Sir Thomas Hawkins (1625)

13

My prayers are heard, O Lyce, now
They're heard; years write thee aged, yet thou,
   Youthful and green in will,
   Putt'st in for handsome still,
And shameless dost intrude among
The sports and feastings of the young.

There, thawed with wine, thy ragged throat
To Cupid shakes some feeble note,
   To move unwilling fires,
   And rouse our lodged desires,
When he still wakes in Chia's face,
Chia, that's fresh and sings with grace.

For he, choice god, doth in his flight
Skip sapless oaks, and will not light
   Upon thy cheek or brow,
   Because deep wrinkles now,
Grey hairs, and teeth decayed and worn,
Present thee foul, and fit for scorn,

Neither thy Coan purple's lay,
Nor that thy jewel's native day
   Can make thee backwards live,
   And those lost years retrieve
Which wingèd time unto our known
And public annals once hath thrown.

cornicis vetulae temporibus Lycen,   25
possent ut iuvenes visere fervidi
    multo non sine risu
      dilapsam in cineres facem.

XIV

Quae cura patrum quaeve Quiritium
plenis honorum muneribus tuas,
    Auguste, virtutes in aevum
      per titulos memoresque fastus

aeternet, o, qua sol habitabilis   5
illustrat oras, maxime principum?
    quem legis expertes Latinae
      Vindelici didicere nuper,

quid Marte posses. milite nam tuo
Drusus Genaunos, implacidum genus,   10
    Breunosque veloces et arces
      Alpibus impositas tremendis

Whither is now that softness flown?
Whither that blush, that motion gone?
 Alas, what now in thee
 Is left of all that she —
That she that loves did breathe and deal?
That Horace from himself did steal?

Thou wert awhile the cried-up face
Of taking arts, and catching grace,
 My Cynara being dead;
 But my fair Cynara's thread
Fates broke, intending thine to draw
Till thou contest with the aged daw;

That those young lovers once thy prey,
Thy zealous eager servants, may
 Make thee their common sport,
 And to thy house resort
To see a torch that proudly burned
Now into colder ashes turned.

William Cartwright (1638)

14

How shall the Senate's or the people's care
 With honours worthy of thy titles raise
 Fit monument, O Caesar, to thy praise?
Or how extol thy fame and virtues rare,
Greatest of princes! o'er each land supreme,
Where'er the sun displays his universal beam?

Late the Vindelic savage felt thy sword,
 When Drusus his undaunted legions led
'Gainst tribes that ne'er had owned a Roman lord,
 And Breuni swift and fierce Genaunian bled,
And Alpine cliffs re-echoed to the sound
Of rock-built castles levelled to the ground.

deiecit acer plus vice simplici:
maior Neronum mox grave proelium
   commisit immanisque Raetos 15
      auspiciis pepulit secundis,

spectandus in certamine Martio,
devota morti pectora liberae
   quantis fatigaret ruinis,
      indomitas prope qualis undas 20

exercet Auster, Pleiadum choro
scindente nubes, impiger hostium
   vexare turmas et frementem
      mittere equum medios per ignis.

sic tauriformis volvitur Aufidus, 25
qui regna Dauni praefluit Apuli,
   cum saevit horrendamque cultis
      diluviem meditatur agris,

ut barbarorum Claudius agmina
ferrata vasto diruit impetu 30
   primosque et extremos metendo
      stravit humum sine clade victor,

te copias, te consilium et tuos
praebente divos. nam tibi, quo die
   portus Alexandrea supplex 35
      et vacuam patefecit aulam,

fortuna lustro prospera tertio
belli secundos reddidit exitus,
   laudemque et optatum peractis
      imperiis decus arrogavit. 40

te Cantaber non ante domabilis
Medusque et Indus, te profugus Scythes
   miratur, o tutela praesens
      Italiae dominaeque Romae.

Nor less the elder Nero dared,
   When rushing to the fight
He smote the Rhaetian's giant guard
With their devoted bosoms bared
   To death for Freedom's right.

Conspicuous in the martial fray
What ghastly ruin marked his way
When urging on his maddened horse
   Against the foeman's chivalry,
Through blood and flame he held his course,
   As Auster rides the raging sea
Beneath the Pleiad's stormy light,
That cleaves the rolling clouds in bleak November's
                         night.

Or like the bull-formed Aufidus
   When swoln with rain his torrents sweep
Past Daunia's realm impetuous,
   Threatening the ripened grain and sheep
That graze upon his yielding banks;
So Claudius the barbarian ranks,
Though closely wedged and iron-bound,
With might resistless scattered round,
And mowed down front and rear heaped on the
                    crimson ground;

Himself unhurt! for thou hadst given
   The warrior band, the counsel sage,
The favour of propitious Heaven
   That smiles upon th' Augustan age!
Since from that memorable day
   When Alexandria oped her gates
And did her vacant halls display,
   For lustres three the kindly Fates
Have granted still success in war,
And Fortune's ever-beaming star
On thee hath poured from hour to hour
Increase of glory still, with still increasing power.

te, fontium qui celat origines,   45
Nilusque et Hister, te rapidus Tigris,
   te beluosus qui remotis
     obstrepit Oceanus Britannis,

te non paventis funera Galliae
duraeque tellus audit Hiberiae,   50
   te caede gaudentes Sygambri
     compositis venerantur armis.

XV

Phoebus volentem proelia me loqui
victas et urbis increpuit lyra,
   ne parva Tyrrhenum per aequor
     vela darem. tua, Caesar, aetas

fruges et agris rettulit uberes,   5
et signa nostro restituit Iovi
   derepta Parthorum superbis
     postibus et vacuum duellis

Ianum Quirini clausit et ordinem
rectum evaganti frena licentiae   10
   iniecit emovitque culpas
     et veteres revocavit artis,

Cantabria's tribes long unsubdued,
The Mede and India's multitude,
    And Scythia's nomad horde,
Confess thy tutelary hand
Stretched o'er the world in proud command
    From Italy its lord.
Thee Nile, who hides his secret source,
And Tigris in his rapid course,
    And Ister's stream obey;
Thee Britain for her monarch hails
Girt by those seas where giant whales
    In stormy whirlpools play.
Th' intrepid Gaul who fears not death,
And proud Castile with bated breath,
    Thy clemency implore;
And Thee, Sygambrian chiefs who stood
And revelled in the battle's blood
    With arms reversed, adore.

Lord Ravensworth (1858)

15

Phoebus rebuked me when I wished to sing
    Of battles and of cities overthrown,
Lest on the Tuscan Sea I dare to bring
    My little sails. The seasons that have known

Thee, Caesar, have restored our crops to us
    And brought our standards back from Parthian
                                        doors
And closed the temple's gates, which Romulus
    To Janus built, and there are no more wars.

They've curbed inordinate licentiousness
    That overpassed the bounds that should restrain,
And stopped all evils by which men transgress,
    And called the ancient virtues back again,

per quas Latinum nomen et Italae
crevere vires, famaque et imperi
   porrecta maiestas ad ortus   15
     solis ab Hesperio cubili.

custode rerum Caesare non furor
civilis aut vis exiget otium,
   non ira, quae procudit ensis
     et miseras inimicat urbis.   20

non qui profundum Danuvium bibunt
edicta rumpent Iulia, non Getae,
   non Seres infidive Persae,
     non Tanain prope flumen orti.

nosque et profestis lucibus et sacris   25
inter iocosi munera Liberi
   cum prole matronisque nostris,
     rite deos prius apprecati,

virtute functos more patrum duces
Lydis remixto carmine tibiis   30
   Troiamque et Anchisen et almae
     progeniem Veneris canemus.

Whence grew the name of Rome and all the strength
  Of Italy, and out of which was drawn
The majesty of empire, all the length
  Of land between the sunset and the dawn.

While Caesar rules us neither civil rage
  Nor violence shall break tranquillity,
Nor wrath, which forges swords, till cities wage
  War on each other all unhappily.

Not where they drink out of the Danube deep
  Break they the Julian edicts, nor the bands
Of Getae, Persians, Seres, they who keep
  Not treaties, nor those born upon the lands

Watered by Tanais. On festal days
  And workdays, with the merry gift of wine,
First having given to the gods due praise,
  We shall with wife and family combine

To sing of heroes, as our fathers did,
  Mingling our singing with the Lydian horn,
And then of Troy and of the Aeneid,
  And of the progeny to Venus born.

Lord Dunsany (1947)

NOTES TO BOOK FOUR

1

Cytherea: Venus.

2

Pindar: Greek lyric poet of the fifth century BC.

watery grave: The Icarian sea, named after Icarus, who drowned in it after his wax wings melted.

lawless dithyrambs: choral odes in unconventional metres.

Theban swan: Pindar.

Calabrie: Calabria, the heel of Italy.

th' old Saturnian gold: the mythical golden age of Saturn.

Io Triumphe!: a Latin cry of victory.

3

the Isthmian gauntlet: a festival of games held on the Isthmus of Corinth.

Jove's Tarpeian Temple: the Capitol.

Aeolian song: Greek poetry in the style of Alcaeus and Sappho.

numbers: verses.

4

Ganymede: Ganymede, Jupiter's cup-bearer and favourite, was borne aloft to heaven by an eagle, who became king of birds.

Vandals: the Vindelici, an Alpine tribe.

the Nero striplings twain: Augustus' step-sons, Drusus and his elder brother Tiberius (Augustus' eventual successor). Their paternal cognomen Nero retained favourable associations until the reign of the emperor Nero (AD 54–68).

Thy debt to Nero's house; Metaurus' river; Hasdrubal: in 207 BC Gaius Claudius Nero, an ancestor of Drusus and Tiberius, defeated Hasdrubal, brother of Hannibal, on the river Metaurus.

Eurus: the south-east wind.

Algidus: mountain near Praeneste.

The Hydra: multi-headed serpent attacked by Hercules, which sprouted two heads for each one severed by him.

the monsters Thebes and Colchis loosed: mythological serpents.

5

holy fathers: the Senators.

Ceres: goddess of harvests.

weds to the widowed elm: vines were trained on elms. Elms without vines were called 'widowed'.

6

brood of Niobe: Niobe, mother of fourteen children, boasted her superiority to Latona, who had only two, Apollo and Diana. They avenged Latona by slaughtering Niobe's children.

Tityos or Tityus: giant, punished by Apollo for attempting to ravish Apollo's mother, Latona.

Achilles: was slain by Apollo at Troy.

Ilion: Troy.

the Horse: the wooden horse of Troy concealed a detachment of Greeks. The Trojans, misled into supposing the horse to be a gift to Minerva (Pallas), dragged it into the city. While they celebrated unawares, the Greeks descended from the horse, unlocked the gates and admitted the Greek army, who put the city to fire and sword.

Argive flames: the flames of Troy, set on fire by the Greeks (Argives).

Aeneas: the son of Venus, escaped from Troy, and (as narrated in Virgil's epic, the *Aeneid*), became the eventual founder of the Roman people.

Agyieus: an alias of Apollo.

Daunian Muse: Muse of southern Italy. Horace is alluding to himself.

Fair youths and damsels: Horace addresses a mixed choir who are to sing the 'Centennial Hymn'.

Delian Queen: Diana.

Lesbian measure: Sapphics, the metre used by the poetess Sappho, who lived on the island of Lesbos in the 6th century BC.

Latona's son, and her who rules the night: Apollo and Diana.

the great thanksgiving: the Centennial Games of 17 BC, for which Horace wrote the 'Centennial Hymn' (*Carmen Saeculare*).

7

where Tullus and where Ancus are: in the underworld. Tullus and Ancus were early kings of Rome.

the stern assize: the judgment of Minos in the underworld.

Hippolytus: a devotee of the goddess Diana, Hippolytus was sent to the underworld having been falsely accused of raping his stepmother.

Theseus leaves Pirithous in the chain: Theseus and his friend Pirithous tried to abduct Proserpina from the underworld. Both were caught by Pluto and chained to a rock. Theseus escaped, but was unable to release Pirithous.

8

Parrhasius: Athenian painter, 5th century BC.

Scopas: 4th century BC sculptor, born in Paros.

threats turned to his own wall: threats turned against himself and Carthage.

young Scipio: in fact Scipio the Elder, who defeated Hannibal at the battle of Zama in 202 BC, bringing the last Carthaginian war to an end. He was honoured with the title 'Africanus'.

the Pierian lays: the epic poems of Ennius.

Ilia's child: Romulus.

Aeacus: legendary king of Aegina, and judge in the underworld.

the sons of Leda: Castor and Pollux.

9

Pindar; Stesichorus; Anacreon: Sappho: Greek poets of the sixth to fifth century BC.

Teucer: Greek warrior skilled in archery.

Sthenelus: a Greek commander in the Trojan war.

Hector: son of Priam, king of Troy.

with the small circle of one short-lived year: i.e. during Lollius' consulship in 21 BC.

11

the Ides of April: April 13.

the Cyprian Queen: Venus.

Phaethon: the sun-god allowed his son, Phaethon, to drive his heavenly chariot across the skies. Phaethon was killed by a thunderbolt from Jupiter.

Bellerophon: was killed by a fall from his winged horse, Pegasus, when he attempted to ride to heaven.

prick-song: musical scores.

12

The luckless bird . . . bewailing Itys: Procne and Philomela were
sisters, daughters of the Athenian house of Cecrops. Procne married
Tereus, king of Thrace, by whom she had a son, Itys. Tereus later
ravished Philomela, and to prevent her from telling what had
happened, cut out her tongue. Philomela informed Procne of what
had befallen her by means of a tapestry. The sisters took their revenge
by murdering Itys and feeding his flesh to his father, Tereus.
Eventually the gods turned the sisters into birds: Philomela became a
nightingale, and Procne a swallow, with a cry of 'Itys! Itys!'
Sulpicius: a warehouse-owner.

13

Coan purples: silks from the island of Cos.

14

the Vindelic savage; Breuni; Genaunian; Rhaetians: Alpine tribes.
Drusus: Augustus' step-son (see **4**, 4).
the elder Nero: Tiberius Claudius Nero, elder brother of Drusus
(see **4**, 4).
Auster: the south wind.
Aufidus: river near Venusia, Horace's birthplace.
Daunia: south-east Italy.
Claudius: Tiberius.
Alexandria oped her gates: Alexandria surrendered to Augustus
after his victory at Actium in 31 BC.
Cantabria: Spain.
Ister: the Danube.
Sygambrian: a German tribe.

15

brought our standards back from Parthian doors: Augustus
recovered from the Parthians the standards captured from Crassus in
53 BC.
closed the temple's gates, which Romulus to Janus built: the
gates of the temple of Janus at Rome were closed in time of peace.
Julian edicts; laws promulgated by Augustus.
Getae: Thracian tribesmen.
Seres: Chinese.
Tanais: the river Don.

the progeny to Venus born: In the *Aeneid* Virgil traces the origin of
the house of Caesar from Venus, through her son, the Trojan Aeneas,
who journeyed to Italy after the fall of Troy.

WORDSWORTH CLASSICS
OF WORLD LITERATURE

The Koran

The Newgate Calendar

Njal's Saga

*Sir Gawain and the Green
Knight*

The Upanishads

APULEIUS
The Golden Ass

ARISTOTLE
The Nicomachean Ethics

MARCUS AURELIUS
Meditations

FRANCIS BACON
Essays

JAMES BOSWELL
The Life of Samuel Johnson
(ABRIDGED)

JOHN BUNYAN
The Pilgrim's Progress

CATULLUS
Poems

CERVANTES
Don Quixote

CARL VON CLAUSEWITZ
On War
(ABRIDGED)

CONFUCIUS
The Analects

DANTE
The Inferno

CHARLES DARWIN
The Origin of Species
The Voyage of the Beagle

RENÉ DESCARTES
Key Philosophical Writings

ERASMUS
Praise of Folly

SIGMUND FREUD
The Interpretation of Dreams

EDWARD GIBBON
*The Decline and Fall of the
Roman Empire*
(ABRIDGED)

KAHLIL GIBRAN
The Prophet

HERODOTUS
Histories

THOMAS HOBBES
Leviathan

HORACE
The Odes